KING OF THE QUEEN CITY

Music in American Life

+ + +

A list of books in the series appears at the end of this book.

King
of the
Queen City

THE STORY OF KING RECORDS

Jon Hartley Fox

Foreword by Dave Alvin

University of Illinois Press
Urbana and Chicago

Library of Congress Cataloging-in-Publication Data
Fox, Jon Hartley.
King of the Queen City : the story of King Records /
Jon Hartley Fox ; foreword by Dave Alvin.
    p. cm. — (Music in American life)
Includes bibliographical references and index.
ISBN 978-0-252-03468-8 (cloth : alk. paper)
    1. King Record Company—History.
    2. Sound recording industry—Ohio—
        Cincinnati—History. I. Title.
        ML3792.K56F69   2009
338.7'61781640973—dc22   2009015035

This is dedicated to my parents,
Lyle and Ellen Fox,
who taught me to love reading,
history, and music,
and to my wife and partner,
Kathryn Barwick,
without whose encouragement
and support this book
would not exist.

Truth is stranger than fiction,
but it is because fiction is obliged
to stick to possibilities; Truth isn't.

• MARK TWAIN •
"Pudd'nhead Wilson's New Calendar"
in *Following the Equator*, 1897

CONTENTS

•••

Illustrations follow page 116

FOREWORD

•••

Dave Alvin

I was a teenage record collector geek when I first discovered the magic, power, and importance of King Records.

It was in 1969 or so, and I was barely fourteen years old. A couple of years before then, my big brother Phil and I had fallen under the intoxicating spell of old music, especially blues. Back in those days there were only a few reissue albums of old and obscure recording artists available in regular record stores, so we were forced to start rummaging and searching through any location where we thought old 78s, 45s, and LPs could be found. We searched junk stores, thrift stores, antique stores, swap meets, garage sales, closets of old radio repair shops, old furniture warehouses, the backrooms of seemingly ancient record stores, the attics of our relatives and our friends' relatives, and even the attics of total strangers. We once even broke into an abandoned building based on a false rumor that it was filled with old records from an out-of-business jukebox record distributor.

In our constant searching, we came across many records on the King/Federal labels (one night my brother and I ran away from home right after he got his driver's license in order to drive 400 miles to Northern California where a record store was selling out of print King LPs for 99 cents each; we were that serious/ crazy about collecting). I was always thrilled to find amazing and rare King blues records by Lonnie Johnson, Ike Turner, Roy Brown, Freddie King, Eddie Vinson, and Johnny Watson, and I still consider them personal treasures. Soon, though, a strange thing happened. After collecting any record featuring the distinctive King label, hoping that it was a blues record, I quickly started to also dig (after overcoming my initial disappointment) the vast array of King's roots music: R&B, rockabilly, bluegrass, western swing, and country.

The heartbreaking voice of Little Willie John and Bill Doggett's pumping R&B instrumentals were extremely close to the hard blues I loved, as were "doo-wop" tracks by the 5 Royales, featuring the blistering guitar of songwriter Lowman Pauling, and Hank Ballard's downright nasty odes to teenage sensuality, but I found myself also starting to be moved by the deft finger-picking of Merle Travis with the Brown's Ferry Four as well as the tight, lonesome mountain harmonies of the Stanley Brothers and the Delmore Brothers. I found that Charlie Feathers' tough rockabilly sides on King could stand equal to (or often surpass) anything cut by any of the Memphis masters at Sun Records during the same time, and the hot western swing recordings of little-known performers such as Ocie Stockard and Jimmy Wyble could give Bob Wills a run for his money.

As I incessantly played each old King record I'd found, I started to realize that all the various strains of American folk music were connected. Certainly stylistic and cultural differences exist between the genres and the musicians, but the underlying structures of the music (whether based on blues and gospel progressions or other traditional folk forms) are pretty much the same.

As Jon Hartley Fox describes in this excellent book, the shrewd business strategy of King Records' colorful owner Syd Nathan and the talent of his visionary producer Henry Glover also enhanced this connection between the genres. Though having blues shouter Wynonie Harris record a jumping version of honky-tonk singer Hank Penny's (another King act) song "Bloodshot Eyes" had more to do with Nathan's efforts to double the financial values of a song he owned the publishing rights on than it did with bridging any racial or stylistic gaps, it did point out that a country song could be a blues song and vice-versa. In Glover's case, he was an African American who could comfortably produce a session by a bluegrass act in the morning and then switch to working with an electric blues guitar hotshot in the afternoon. This artistic and racial openness was in an era before the civil rights movement had made racial integration and equality a little less of a dream and somewhat closer to a reality.

A case could be made that if your record collection consisted only of King Records, you'd have a damn good overview of post–World War II American roots music. Although independent record labels of that era (such as Sun, Chess, Modern, Imperial, and Specialty) also recorded a variety of styles of urban and rural folk music, none of them recorded such a wide spectrum of styles as commercially and artistically successfully as King did. You could even make a decent argument that King was one of America's great folk music labels. The evolution of rural and urban working-class folk music documented over the history of King Records (whether intentional or not) captures the pivotal transition of the music from acoustic to electric, small town to big city, regional to national to international.

The perfect example is King's most successful act, James Brown. Starting out imitating other King artists such as Hank Ballard, the 5 Royales, and Little Willie John, over the course of Brown's tenure at the label, he revolutionized blues and R&B by creating funk and set the standard for almost all contemporary urban music on the radio today.

Okay, I'll leave the rest of the story in Jon Fox's more than capable hands. In his deeply researched yet highly readable book, Jon has done a great service for both the music historian and the music fan by telling the complete story of one of American music's greatest labels. Thanks, Jon; I've been waiting for this book since I was a teenage record-collecting geek.

PREFACE

...

King Records was all about "American music." King was the most important record company in the United States in the years between 1945 and 1960. Not the most successful or the most famous, necessarily, but definitely the most influential, innovative, and inspirational.

Founded by Cincinnati businessman Sydney Nathan in the mid-1940s, King Records led the way for the hundreds of independent record companies of the 1940s and 1950s. King changed not only the way American music was recorded and sold, it changed the music itself.

Whereas other record companies made their fortunes by concentrating on one style of music, as Chess did with the blues, King Records took the opposite approach. King was active in virtually all genres of vernacular American music, recording musicians and styles overlooked by the larger labels, making records for "the little man," as Syd Nathan often put it.

The King artist roster—unlikely to ever be equaled by another label—is astounding to contemplate. King didn't just dabble in these various styles; it attracted many of the top stars and released many of the biggest records of its time.

When it came to the music of "the little man," King had it covered: there was "jump blues" with Wynonie Harris, Roy Brown, and Bull Moose Jackson; country with Moon Mullican, the Delmore Brothers, and Grandpa Jones; blues with Freddie King, Lonnie Johnson, and Albert King; bluegrass with the Stanley Brothers and Reno & Smiley; black gospel music with the Swan Silvertones and the Spirit of Memphis Quartet; R&B with Billy Ward and the Dominoes, the 5 Royales, and Hank Ballard and the Midnighters; rockabilly with Charlie Feathers and Mac Curtis; and proto-soul music with Little Willie John and James Brown.

Born in Dayton, Ohio, in 1953, I claim King Records as a basic part of my cultural DNA. King's records were mainstays of the Dayton and Cincinnati radio stations we listened to; the records were prominently displayed for sale at groceries, drug stores, and barber shops; country singer Bonnie Lou was on *The Midwestern Hayride* TV show every Saturday night; and such King classics as "Honky Tonk," "Fever," and "Hide Away" just seemed to fill the air.

King Records helped shape the musical ethos that made the tri-state area of Ohio, Indiana, and Kentucky such a fertile field for musicians of all stripes. Many of these musicians (guitarist Lonnie Mack comes to mind as an example) seamlessly integrated ideas from blues, rock, country, bluegrass, and R&B into their playing. That in turn helped to develop a similar open-mindedness among listeners in this area. It's hard to say whether King Records created this situation or merely exploited it; I favor the former option.

King Records spoke to me at an early age. A fledgling record collector, I had noticed by my early teens that many of my favorite records were on the King label. What's more, these records resonated with me in a way that (say) Motown hits did not. King spoke my language.

It's probably because of Syd Nathan and King Records that I spent several years working in the record business. It's definitely because of King that I worked only at independent labels, including Vetco, Kanawha, Flying Fish, Sugar Hill, and IMG. I never had any desire to work at a "major" label. The music of "the little man" always won out.

The formal research and interviews that culminated in this book began in 1983, when I received a grant from the Ohio Humanities Council to produce a four-hour radio documentary on the history of King Records. The documentary consisted of four one-hour programs, also titled *King of the Queen City: The Story of King Records*, which mixed music, interviews, and commentary.

KOTQC first aired during the summer of 1986 on WYSO-FM in Yellow Springs, Ohio, where I had worked for most of the preceding decade. The series was nationally distributed by National Public Radio (NPR) the following spring, airing on something like 80 stations across the country. It was also broadcast in Canada, Australia, and England and on a short-wave outlet in Ghana. I've always wondered about that.

As soon as the radio series was finished, people began suggesting that I "turn it into" a book. I agreed that a good book about King Records was needed, but I didn't want to write it. Although I had learned a fair amount about King, the main things I learned were what a massive story it was and how little of it I knew. No, this was a job for an authority, maybe Peter Guralnick or Tony Russell, someone like that.

Fifteen years later, I was still waiting for that history of King. Michel Ruppli had published his indispensable two-volume discography of King Records in 1985, but while its 900 pages of raw data was stay-up-late-reading for me, it didn't tell the story of King in a way or format many people could appreciate.

At that point, Steve Tracy called to ask some bibliographic question about KOTQC, which he had cited in his book *Going to Cincinnati: A History of the Blues in the Queen City*. Steve and I had talked before and I'd learned much from his book, but we've never met. He's now at the University of Massachusetts, Amherst, a professor in the department of Afro-American Studies.

Steve suggested, not for the first time, that I write a book about King Records. I had just been downsized from a job, so lack of time was no longer a valid excuse. Steve encouraged me to at least start on a book, and clinched the deal when he said he would share interviews he had done with producer Henry Glover with me, as well as help in any way he could.

One thing led to another, very slowly it seems, and here we are. *King of the Queen City* owes much to Steve Tracy. He's been as good as his word about helping me, and he's aided me more than he probably knows. He has been there all along, encouraging when I was losing momentum, patiently answering my many questions, and offering valuable advice and insight whenever I asked, which was often. He has my eternal gratitude for his extraordinary generosity of spirit.

Working at International Marketing Group (IMG) in Nashville was a memorable experience, made even more so by a handful of coworkers, most notably Randy Merryman and Chuck Young. Randall Merryman, then IMG's mastering engineer, is a good engineer and a good friend who appreciated the music and history of King. Randy introduced me to some great King artists I had previously overlooked, and for that, and the good times, I owe him much.

Chuck Young was, and still is, IMG's art director. My office at IMG was next door to the art department, and I spent many hours talking with Chuck. We shared a lot of laughs during the time I was at IMG, and I would be grateful for that alone.

But Chuck has earned an extra helping of my eternal gratitude for serving in essence as this book's unpaid photo editor. After working with it for the last twenty-eight years, Chuck is intimately acquainted with the King Records photo archives and was the perfect person to help choose the photos for this book. He came up with some real beauties, including a few I had never seen before. I knew I could trust his artist's eye, and I wasn't disappointed. Thanks again, Chuck. Thanks also to his associate Matt Newberg, who helped prepare the photos for publication.

Special thanks to Moe Lytle, the owner of IMG, for his gracious permission to use those photos. Moe has now owned King Records for longer than Syd Nathan did and deserves his own book. He and Nathan are completely different in some respects, but in other ways, they are two peas in a pod. I'm sure Nathan would be very happy that Lytle has so much of the King catalog available for purchase online, at iTunes and other music-selling sites.

I take full responsibility for any and all mistakes or bonehead opinions found in this work. The conclusions and judgments are mine alone. That said, there are dozens of people I would like to acknowledge and thank for their contributions to this book. Some are close friends I've known since the 1970s, but most are writers I know (and respect) only through their work.

As is true of any writer of history, I owe a great debt to many scholars, writers, researchers, and historians. Their work has enriched and shaped my understanding of King Records and the world in which it existed. I've learned from many, but the following deserve special mention: Peter Guralnick, Tony Russell, Michel Ruppli, Neil Slaven, Charles K. Wolfe, Gary B. Reid, Bill Daniels, Rich Kienzle, Larry Nager, Randy McNutt, Jonas Bernholm, Bill Millar, Dave Penny, Cliff Radel, Marv Goldberg, J.C. Marion, Tony Watson, Dave Sax, Daniel Jacoubovitch, and Kevin Coffey.

I would also like to thank several people—especially Dave Barber, Randy Pitts, Steve Tracy, Jim Spangler, Kip Lornell, and Norm Cohen—who read all or part of the manuscript and offered countless suggestions and criticisms that improved this book.

For their help with photo identification and solving bibliographic mysteries, thanks to Ben Drees; John W. Rumble of the Country Music Hall of Fame and Museum in Nashville; Marianne Reynolds and Steve Headley of the Public Library of Cincinnati and Hamilton County; and Brian Powers, a music librarian at the Public Library of Cincinnati and Hamilton County and King Records scholar who is doing some great King-related programming at the library.

After I decided to write a history of King Records, there was no question in my mind where I wanted it published. I have been keen on the Music in American Life series since the University of Illinois Press launched it in 1972 with Archie Green's *Only a Miner*. As an undergraduate folklore student, I eagerly devoured that book and many that followed it in the series. There has never been a better collection of works about vernacular American music.

The Music in American Life series strikes me as the perfect home for *King of the Queen City*. To be in the company of such distinguished scholars and writers as Archie Green, Nolan Porterfield, Charles R. Townsend, Norm Cohen, Neil V. Rosenberg, Cary Ginell, Robert Pruter, Kip Lornell, Richard K. Spottswood, and Dena J. Epstein is an honor of which I am unworthy, but will nonetheless accept.

It was my good fortune to work with Judith McCulloh and Laurie Matheson as my editors at the University at Illinois Press. Both have been ardent supporters of this project and both went above and beyond the call of duty in shepherding this book to publication. Publishers make more money on shorter books, but Judith and Laurie both saw that sometimes a huge story requires a longer book. They fought hard for my vision and ultimately prevailed. I'm glad they were on my side.

Having Dave Alvin write a foreword for this book isn't really a dream come true, because I never would have dreamed of asking him to do such a thing until the moment I asked him. I've been a huge fan of Dave's music and writing since I first heard *American Music*, the debut album by the Blasters in 1980, and I'm honored, and humbled, more than I can say by his enthusiastic participation in this project.

As the lead guitarist and songwriter in the Blasters, Dave Alvin was the heart and soul of that outstanding band. In his subsequent solo career, Dave has continued to explore the nooks and crannies of musical Americana, producing a steady stream of brilliant rock-blues-country-R&B-folk albums. I think of Dave as kind of a one-man musical distillation of labels like King. He's the best songwriter in America. If you haven't heard him, you should.

Finally, though words truly are inadequate, I give all thanks to Kathy Barwick, my wife, partner, editor, and sounding board. Her patience and unwavering support made this book possible. She never doubted the idea of the book or the importance of telling the King Records story, even when I was tempted to give up at several points. Her good ideas made this book better, and her tough questions made me think and question my assumptions more than I might have otherwise. She made me do my best and, more to the point, helped show me how to get there.

KING OF THE QUEEN CITY

SYD STARTS A RECORD COMPANY

The Early Years, 1943–44

• • •

All you need to succeed in the record business
is a telephone, a desk, and an attorney.

—Sydney Nathan

The day had begun with such promise.

On this February Saturday in 1956, the twenty or so people crammed into the Cincinnati recording studio were ready to get down to business. The producer was enthusiastic, the featured artists—a young singing group out of Georgia called the Famous Flames—were excited, the studio musicians in place. Time to roll tape.

They hadn't even made it through the first song when the atmosphere was shattered by a loud voice shouting in the studio's control room. "Stop the tape. Stop the tape," yelled Syd Nathan, the founder and president of King Records. "This is the worst piece of shit I've ever heard in my life," spewed Nathan, turning on producer Ralph Bass. "Nobody wants to hear this crap. All he's doing is stuttering, just saying one damn word over and over."

The confrontation spilled out into the main studio. People watched in stunned silence. The out-of-towners had never seen Nathan and didn't know he was often like this in the studio, yelling and screaming, red in the face, seemingly out of control. The leader of the Famous Flames, a man named James Brown, was mortified. Though Nathan was blistering Bass, his problem was obviously with Brown's singing.

Brown was trying to keep his cool. His reign as "Soul Brother Number One" was still years in the future. In February 1956, Brown was a struggling, scuffling singer looking for a break. A chance to make records for King was an opportunity he couldn't afford to blow.

The song Nathan hated, "Please, Please, Please," had been written by Brown and fellow Flame Johnny Terry. The song seemed simple and pointless to Nathan, but Brown knew the song tore up audiences at the band's gigs and felt it could be a hit. So did Bass, who signed the group to the label. Nathan had given Bass hell for that decision, too.

This session was supposed to be the "big break" for James Brown and the Flames, but Brown couldn't help feeling that his recording career was over before it had even started. Nathan was not buying Bass's assurances that the song would be a hit, nor Brown's explanations that he was trying to do something new and that there was more to the song than Nathan was hearing. Nathan grew louder and more dismissive.

Nathan raged that he should fire Bass for starting this whole fiasco. That did it for Bass. "All right, old man," the producer fumed, "here's what you should do. Put the record out just in the Atlanta market. Test the water, you know. If it's not a hit, you won't have to fire me, because I quit." That wasn't enough for Nathan, who countered, "No, I'm going to put this out nationally to prove what a piece of shit it is. You'll be a laughingstock in the business."

With that, an uneasy calm settled over the studio. Brown, the Flames, and the King "house band" got back to their business. Four songs were recorded that day without further incident, including "Please, Please, Please." As they left the studio, Brown and the Flames were pretty low. Brown didn't know whether any of the songs would be released as records; after all, the owner of the company had called his best song "a piece of shit."

Despite Syd Nathan's disdain for the song, "Please, Please, Please" was released in March and gradually sold a million copies. The record wasn't really a national hit, but it made enough noise in enough places to crack the R&B chart in *Billboard* magazine, climbing to the number six position. It was a phenomenal debut for a new artist almost completely unknown outside Georgia.

"Please, Please, Please" launched the recording career of James Brown, an un-schooled visionary who would change the sound of music over the next fifteen years. Not just black music and not even just American music: the records James Brown recorded for King changed the world, as musicians in Africa, Europe, South America, and the West Indies avidly devoured and studied those records, incorporating Brown's polyrhythmic innovations into their own music.

In time, Brown would learn that Syd Nathan was an artist whose medium was bullshit. He was a master of the form. As did most of the artists who recorded for

King, Brown butted heads time and again with Nathan, sometimes quite violently. The two men also developed an improbably close personal relationship, almost a father-son bond. It was a deep friendship that ended only with Nathan's death.[1]

• • •

Cincinnati businessman Sydney Nathan launched King Records in 1943 and built the company into one of the most important, successful, and influential record companies in history. During the almost twenty-five years Nathan was at the helm, King recorded—and introduced to the American public—a stunning array of musical giants, from country stars Merle Travis and Grandpa Jones and bluegrass greats Don Reno and Red Smiley to blues guitarist Freddie King and R&B and soul stars Hank Ballard and James Brown.

Hundreds of independent record companies sprouted like mushrooms in the 1940s and 1950s, but King Records stands at the top. Sun, Chess, Atlantic, and Specialty, among other labels, made huge contributions to our shared musical culture, but none can match King for variety, innovation, depth of catalog, or sheer moxie.

Syd Nathan faced several major obstacles as he prepared to start his record company in 1943. The first was a world at war. By the fall of 1943, the United States had been at war with Germany, Japan, and Italy for almost two years. That created a serious problem for the recording industry: shellac, an essential ingredient in the manufacturing of the era's thick 78-rpm records, came primarily from southeast Asia, and the supply was largely cut off by the war in the Pacific.

Desperate record companies and pressing plants tried many substitutes for shellac, including such unlikely candidates as sawdust and ground-up asbestos. Some tried grinding up old records and reusing the powder. But nothing worked quite as well as shellac mixed with fine clay.

Some shellac *was* making it to this country, and although the War Production Board limited its nonmilitary use, a certain amount made its way to record companies. The three major labels of the day, RCA Victor, Decca, and Columbia, had first crack at the available shellac, but even so, the Big Three drastically reduced production, limiting releases to the most popular artists.

The second serious obstacle facing all record companies in 1943 was a ban on recording imposed by the American Federation of Musicians, the national musicians' union. Union boss James C. Petrillo had called for the recording ban, essentially a musicians' strike, because of his belief that radio stations that used records instead of live musicians (and, to a lesser degree, jukeboxes) were taking jobs away from the members of his union.

Those union members were used to the high-rolling days of the 1920s and 1930s when radio was king and every radio station in the land employed musicians to perform "live" all the music broadcast by the station. The bigger stations had staff orchestras and arrangers, vocal ensembles, solo singers, and a variety of musical groups.

That situation was threatened by the recording industry, in the union's view, in two different ways. The first was that records made jukeboxes possible, and the jukebox in the early 1940s was a growing cultural force that had begun to nibble away at radio's musical hegemony and taste-making monopoly. As widespread and relatively inexpensive as records, record players, and radios had become by this time, they were still beyond the means of millions of Americans. But now, thanks to the jukebox, anybody with a nickel could step into a restaurant, roadhouse, honky-tonk, or tumble-down joint and hear music from the world outside the local community, music by "real" musicians, often for the first time.

The recording industry also cut into the income of radio musicians in a more direct way. As records became increasingly widespread and popular in the 1930s and 1940s, cost-conscious radio executives realized they could fill radio airtime much cheaper by hiring someone to play records than by hiring an entire orchestra to perform. These new radio record-spinners came to be called "disc jockeys," and audiences seemed to like them just fine. That was the beginning of the end as far as live radio was concerned.

So Petrillo had legitimate reasons for his beef with the record companies. He demanded that they—again, essentially RCA Victor, Decca, and Columbia— establish a fund for unemployed musicians. The record companies refused, and the musicians stopped recording on August 1, 1942.[2] With the exception of a few records by a cappella vocal groups, there would be no recording until the companies settled with the union.

The big labels hung tough, as each had stockpiled a sizable backlog of material to release and felt confident they could wait out any kind of strike a bunch of musicians could put together. The major record companies were wrong, though, and their mistake opened a door through which dozens of entrepreneurs, hustlers, and visionary "record men" managed to squeeze. The recording industry would change immeasurably before the major labels realized their mistake and came to terms with the union.

Decca was the first, settling with the union in September 1943. Columbia and RCA Victor resisted until November 1944, but they finally capitulated, realizing that the public was demanding fresher music than the labels were able to deliver.

The musician's strike was not that much of a problem for a new label like the one Syd Nathan was planning. Fighting for the status quo simply wasn't an issue for a brash outsider like Nathan, or his numerous counterparts across the country planning their own record companies. If all you had to do to make records was to sign a piece of paper agreeing with the union, where's the pen? Let's get started.

The first of the great modern record companies, the Victor Talking Machine Company, was founded in 1901. The segment of the record industry that Nathan hoped to join had essentially begun in 1920. Prior to that year, most record company executives believed that black and rural white audiences simply had no interest in (or money to purchase) phonograph records. That changed in 1920 with "Crazy Blues," recorded by Mamie Smith, the first record made by a black performer and aimed at a black audience.[3] A vaudeville singer from Ohio, Smith was not really a blues singer, but "Crazy Blues" was a huge hit for the OKeh Record Company and helped prove the commercial viability of recorded black music. Its success prompted the recording of numerous other black artists and created the market for what were called "race records." Soon several labels were turning out records for this new market.

The birth of the country music recording industry came three years later, with the release of a record by Fiddlin' John Carson, an old-time fiddler and singer from Georgia. Carson's OKeh recording of "The Little Old Log Cabin in the Lane" and "The Old Hen Cackled and the Rooster's Going to Crow" is usually considered the first country record to be commercially distributed.

The recording of country music was actually an inadvertent result of the search for black talent. In the wake of Mamie Smith's hit, record company talent scouts went out looking for singers and musicians to record. Enterprising record men such as Ralph Peer fanned out across the south in an unprecedented search for native talent. It was on one such trip to Atlanta that Peer was persuaded to record Fiddlin' John Carson.

The success of Carson's record launched the "hillbilly" record industry just as Mamie Smith's hit had started the race record industry. By 1925, the game was fully afoot, and dozens of labels had entered the hunt, actively scouting the country, especially the southern states, looking for anybody—black, white, young, old, man, woman, or child—who might be able to sell records.

From its sales peak of $121 million in 1921, the recording industry spiraled downward throughout the 1920s and early 1930s. The bottom finally fell out, with sales plummeting to a low of $6 million in 1933.[4] Companies went out of business, careers ended, musicians faded into oblivion. Artists who had once sold thousands of each new release now sold hundreds. It was obvious that the recording industry would not survive the Depression without a massive shake-up.

Only Victor came through the Depression more or less unscathed, though even Victor started a low-priced subsidiary label, Bluebird Records, for jazz, blues, and country recordings. Numerous record companies had gone under, never to return. Several other companies changed ownership or otherwise restructured. The Columbia Broadcasting System (CBS) also entered the industry in 1938 with a label built from the remnants of Brunswick, American Record Corporation, Columbia, and OKeh. CBS gave its new label an old name—Columbia.

The most prominent newcomer was Decca Records, a subsidiary of a major British company of the same name. Established in America in 1934, Decca had a sure-fire gimmick: its records cost only thirty-five cents at a time when most other records sold for seventy-five cents. And because of Decca's aggressive pursuit of successful recording artists on other labels, Decca soon boasted a roster of top sellers headed by superstar Bing Crosby.

When the dust had settled, by around 1940, basically three major record companies were still standing in America: Victor, Columbia, and Decca. Not only were there fewer labels than just a few years before, but the three surviving companies had little interest in anything beyond the top-selling pop acts. Most country and blues artists were dropped from the companies' rosters or reassigned to cheaper and less prestigious subsidiary labels.

• • •

Sydney Nathan was born April 27, 1903,[5] in Cincinnati, Ohio, to Frieda and Nathaniel Nathan.[6] Sydney was never blessed with good health. In fact, he had a number of serious problems in his youth, from respiratory ailments to weak eyes. He had terrible vision—so bad that he dropped out of school after the ninth grade, explaining later with perfect logic, "I couldn't see, so why bother?"[7] As an adult, he wore the proverbial "pop-bottle glasses."

Nathan had asthma and, as an adult, spoke with a loud, raspy voice that carried remarkably well. Cincinnati writer Randy McNutt describes it nicely: "He always sounded as if he were on the verge of losing the last bit of his roar as he verbally battered some unlucky human obstacle who was standing between Syd Nathan and Success. He always found the breath to keep shouting."[8] By the early 1940s, Nathan also suffered from high blood pressure, obesity, cataracts, and respiratory problems no doubt worsened by his fondness for big, stinky cigars.

Nathan was quite a character. He could be obscene, loud, greedy, and crude—the very essence of a money-grubbing vulgarian. He often displayed an abrasive, obnoxious, confrontational, bullying, and coarse personality that drove more than a few King artists and staff members to the brink of serious mayhem.

On the other hand, Nathan was an expansive, fun-loving, joke-telling, charismatic guy usually found at the center of a laughing group of people. Jethro Burns called him "one of the most fun guys" he ever met.[9] Nathan loved holding court at some neighborhood bar or coffee shop when taking a break from the frenzy at King. It was almost impossible to stay mad at Syd Nathan, although quite a few people tried.

Nathan was an intelligent, complex, and unusual man, a guy who could get teary-eyed over a sappy old sentimental song and an hour later expound to his sales staff on the subtle differences between French and English hookers.[10] He was perhaps the perfect specimen of the cigar-chomping record man of the mid-twentieth century who changed American music and, in turn, changed the world.

• • •

One thing on Nathan's side as he prepared to launch King Records was that he had already tasted failure more than once and was not averse to taking risks. Since leaving school, he had spent a year in Arizona for his asthma and worked at a variety of off-beat occupations. He worked in a pawnshop, bussed tables in a men's club, ran a chain of shooting galleries, played drums in pick-up bands, operated an elevator, sold jewelry, and promoted professional wrestlers and their matches. His most successful wrestler was known as the Big Swede, who was billed by Nathan as the "Midwestern Champion."[11]

Nathan's lowest point as a businessman came in August 1938, when he was arrested in connection with operating a string of what were called jackpot shooting galleries, a popular Depression-era diversion. All a marksman had to do to win cash prizes in these games of chance was shoot out the outline of a heart (or spade or whatever) on a playing card mounted on a target several feet away.

Nathan's troubles began when a customer was given the runaround trying to collect his $5 prize.[12] Told he had a winning card at the gallery, the man was sent to a business office to collect his money. But when the man presented the winning card to Nathan, he placed the card under a handy microscope, examined it closely (remember his terrible vision), and told the man it was not a winner: he could still see a bit of the red outline. The man complained, and Nathan was arrested.

The same thing happened again less than a week later. This time, the disputed pay-off was $106.60.[13] Nathan was again arrested. The charges for both incidents—"obtaining money under false pretenses"—were dismissed in September. The judge, however, fined Nathan $50 and costs for "promoting a scheme of chance."[14]

Nathan's luck began to improve in the late 1930s. He acted on a long-time desire to enter the music business by opening, also in 1938, a retail store called Syd's Record Shop. Located on West Fifth Street in Cincinnati, the shop was moderately successful, selling primarily the mainstream pop hits of the day. Nathan was even feeling flush enough to loan $6 to a jukebox operator who often bought records at the shop. That loan would change Nathan's life.

The jukebox operator was slow in repaying the loan, which nettled Nathan a bit. "Six bucks meant more to me in 1938 than 1,600 dollars now," he told Jack Ramey of the *Cincinnati Enquirer* in 1949.[15] "One night I saw the fellow at Beverly Hills [a popular nightspot across the Ohio River in Kentucky] with a gorgeous babe. I figured he would be in the next day with my six bucks. He didn't show. For three weeks in a row I saw him at Beverly with the same babe. Finally, on the dance floor, I grabbed his shoulder, [and] told him that if he could afford Beverly, he certainly could repay me. He turned red, blue, and green, [and] told me he didn't have it.

"The next day he came in the shop and offered me 300 hillbilly, western, and race records, old ones from his jukeboxes, at two cents a platter. He figured that I could sell enough of them for ten cents each to get back my six bucks. I took him up. The first afternoon I made eighteen dollars. Naturally, I wondered how long this could go on. I bought more old records from jukebox operators. Some I sold for a dime, some for fifteen, twenty, and twenty-five cents."

Despite the success, Nathan decided to move to Florida in 1939 for a fresh start. His brother David was starting a medical practice in Miami, and Nathan told Jack Ramey ten years later that he had moved south because he "wanted to be certain his brother's offices were the best."[16] That statement doesn't really seem to explain why Nathan would quit the only successful business he had ever known, but who knows? Nathan sold the record shop to his brother-in-law Sol Halper and moved to Miami.

Nathan planned to open a photo-finishing business and make a killing on the tourists who were beginning to visit Florida again as the Depression slowly lifted. His hopes were dashed by some of the worst winter weather ever recorded in Florida. Snow and sleet hit hard that year, all but ruining the tourist season. Nathan's bad luck had returned.

Nathan hastily beat it back to Cincinnati with $900 to his name. He lived in the Hotel Gibson, where he woke up one morning and found himself down to his last three dollars. As he later recalled, "I decided it was time to go back into business or go to work for somebody. I decided for business."[17] It was time for the return of Syd's Record Shop.

Nathan found a spot for his new store at 1351 Central Avenue, next to a joint called The Cat and Fiddle. The place was decrepit, but the price was right—only $30 a month. He told the landlord he'd take the place but wanted two weeks to clean it up. That was fine with the landlord until he found out that Nathan didn't have *any* money, let alone $30 a month. At the landlord's statement of outrage, Nathan shot back, "You don't think I'm going to waste two weeks cleaning it if I'm not going to make it go, do you?"[18] The deal held.

Nathan reestablished contact with the jukebox operators he had dealt with earlier and stocked his shop with new and used records he got from them. The store was in an area of Cincinnati that was heavily populated by black people from the south, so Nathan stocked mostly black music—blues, gospel, some swing and jazz—with a smattering of current pop. He was back in business.

One day in 1940 or 1941, Nathan happened to enter the Vine Street radio store of Max Frank, a store where Nathan had once worked. In fact, Nathan had convinced Frank to add records to the store's inventory. Frank now wanted out of the record business and had a proposition. If Nathan would pay him fifteen cents a record, Frank would throw in the sales racks and listening booths for free. Nathan accepted the deal, gaining several thousand records in the process. As he began examining his new purchases, he was shocked at what he discovered.

"I found that 85 per-cent of the records was hillbilly stuff I had never heard of," Nathan told writer Richard L. Gordon for a 1951 article for *Saga* magazine.[19] "Gently I mentioned it to Max. I told him I didn't know what I was getting, all that hillbilly stuff. So Max says, 'That isn't all you get. You get the customers, too.'"

Frank was right about that. As Nathan got to know his new customers, "those tall, gaunt-faced folks with the lonesome sound of the mountains in their talk,"[20] he found that most of them listened to Cincinnati radio station WLW, especially the station's early-morning country programming and its star-studded variety show, *The Boone County Jamboree*. Nathan started listening to WLW and became familiar with the station's stars, enjoying the music of such established recording artists as the Delmore Brothers as well as talented newcomers Merle Travis and Grandpa Jones.

• • •

"Me and Grandpa Jones and Alton and Rabon Delmore, we'd sing a lot of spiritual songs there on the radio, and we'd run out of material," Merle Travis told folklorist William Lightfoot in 1979.[21] "Me and Grandpa found a source for songs. Down on Central Avenue, there in the black section of Cincinnati, was a little, used record shop run by a little, short Jewish man with real thick glasses. He had asthma and a scratchy voice and his name was Syd Nathan. We got acquainted with him and we'd go down to Syd's used record shop and find all these great records by the black spiritual quartets. We'd learn the songs and sing them on the air as the Brown's Ferry Four."

Travis, Jones, the Delmores and other WLW entertainers were frequent visitors to Syd's Record Shop, one of the few places in Cincinnati that sold country, blues, and gospel records. Nathan spoke and dealt straight with these folks and never treated them like "hillbillies," which was appreciated, because that wasn't always the case in Cincinnati. Nathan had a genuine respect and affection for the musicians. In time, he began also to see them as his ticket to success.

"Syd got all het up wanting to start a label, a country label," remembered Grandpa Jones.[22] "He came over to WLW where we were doing *The Boone County Jamboree* and wanted to sign some of us up and make records."

Merle Travis picks up the tale: "One day Syd said, 'Why don't you boys make a record of your own?' And I said, 'Ain't nobody asked us.' He said, 'Well, I'm gonna start me a company. Why don't you record with me?' We said, 'Well, we can't. We're under contract to WLW and they won't allow us to work anywhere else.' Syd said, 'We'll slip out of town to make a record. We'll go up to Dayton.' So me and Syd and Grandpa went to Dayton and cut a couple of sides."[23]

The fifty-mile drive to Dayton took place in September 1943.[24] The recordings were made in a makeshift studio in a room above a Wurlitzer Piano Company store.[25] The plan was to record two songs by Jones and Travis as a duet and two solo songs by Travis. None of the three participants had ever been in a recording studio before, even one as primitive as this, but they plunged in.

"We had to change our names on the records [because of the situation with WLW] and we were stuck for a name," explains Travis.[26] "Now Grandpa had a habit, he'd get his pen out and as he talked, he'd draw this little cartoon character—a little old fellow with long underwear and glasses on, with a kerosene lamp in his hand and a pipe in his mouth.

"The first time I saw it, I asked who it was. And Grandpa said, 'That's Mr. Sheppard. That's Jim Sheppard.' Grandpa drew this Jim Sheppard character all the time and it got to be kind of a joke at the station. So when we were stuck for a name for our duet, I said to Grandpa, 'Why don't we call ourselves the Sheppard Brothers?' He just laughed and said, 'I reckon that's as good a name as any.'"

The duo went first, recording "You'll Be Lonesome, Too" and "The Steppin' Out Kind." Travis decided to use the name Bob McCarthy for his solo efforts, "Two Time Annie" and a wartime novelty, "When Mussolini Laid His Pistol Down." Satisfied with their work, the three men drove home to Cincinnati. Grandpa Jones still chuckled forty-one years later when he thought about the trip: "Coming back, Syd said, 'What are we gonna call the company?' So we thought about it some and came up with 'King.' 'Yeah, that's good. The King of them all,' said Syd, laughing that big laugh of his."[27]

• • •

The label wouldn't get there with its first two releases, though. The four songs were officially released on November 15, 1943.[28] The two by the Sheppard Brothers bore label number King 500; Bob McCarthy's debut was King 501.[29] The release was more official than actual. Very few records were manufactured, probably because of problems with the original acetate recordings made at the Dayton session. Travis said in 1979 that he once had one copy of each record and had never seen another.[30] Jones believed into the 1970s that the Sheppard Brothers record had never been released. He was stunned when a fan sent him a copy as a gift.

Exact production numbers are unavailable for King 500 and 501, but the numbers could not have been high. Based on the records' scarcity today, it seems safe to assume that as few as one hundred copies of each title were manufactured and released. If the memories of Jones and Travis were accurate as to how the records sounded, that rarity might be a good thing, at least in artistic terms.

According to Jones, "Some of those early King records came out warped so badly you could use them for bowls or ashtrays; as Merle said, watching a needle go around one was like watching a stock car on a banked race track."[31] "When I got the record," Travis remembered, "I took it home and put it on my player. It went round and round and round and I sat there and waited and thought, 'Well, there ain't nothing on this record.' It got way over to the end of the record and then directly you could hear me and Grandpa. It sounded like we were recording in Dayton but the microphone was in Cincinnati, way off in the distance. It wasn't much of a record."[32]

It certainly wasn't the kick-off Nathan had wanted, but it was a start. However feeble, it was a tentative first step on a long, strange journey that would bring many a change to the musical landscape over the next quarter century.

THE HILLBILLY BOOGIE

Country Music on King Records, Part 1

• • •

Syd didn't care about prestige.
He just wanted to make money.
—Grandpa Jones

The Bob McCarthy/Sheppard Brothers debacle of 1943 was a keen disappointment to Syd Nathan, Grandpa Jones, and Merle Travis. It's one thing to have an unsuccessful record, but to be part of such a complete and utter flop—a total fiasco—was another thing altogether. All three were anxious to redeem themselves in the studio, so Nathan arranged another recording session for early January. They all hoped for a fresh start in 1944.

Grandpa Jones had enlisted in the Army and was due to leave for basic training at the end of January. Nathan had no idea when he might get Grandpa back into a studio, so he wanted to record as many songs as possible. Jones cut eight songs, of which six were released as singles. He played acoustic guitar and sang on all songs and was accompanied by Merle Travis on electric guitar.

It was a strong session, animated by Grandpa's spirited singing and Travis' distinctive finger-style guitar brilliance. Nathan released two Jones originals, "It's Raining Here This Morning" and "I'll Be Around If You Need Me," as King 502, usually considered the first "real" King release.

Before releasing Jones's record, Nathan sought a second opinion from Jim Stanton, a young man from Tennessee who was in Cincinnati working for the jukebox division of the Wurlitzer Company. "Syd didn't know anything about country music," said Stanton.[1] "When he cut that 'Raining Here This Morning' acetate, he brought it to me over at the Wurlitzer Company.

"He said, 'You're a hillbilly, and since you are a hillbilly, I want your opinion of this.' I listened to it and I said, 'Hey, man, that is good.' And he said, 'You wouldn't kid me? You wouldn't tell me wrong?'" Reassured by a genuine hillbilly, Nathan rushed the record out. (Stanton, by the way, soon returned to Tennessee and started his own record company, Rich-R-Tone, an important early outlet for regional bluegrass bands.)

Louis Marshall "Grandpa" Jones (1913–98), a native of Niagara, Kentucky, was raised in Akron, Ohio. Jones apprenticed early in his career with country radio pioneer Bradley Kincaid but had worked mostly as a solo act since 1937. In addition to singing and playing guitar, Jones played the banjo, frailing it in the old-time way he had learned from banjo picker and singer Cousin Emmy in the late 1930s. By the time he landed at WLW in Cincinnati in 1942, Jones was already a ten-year veteran of radio broadcasting in Akron, Boston, and Wheeling, West Virginia.

Jones made it back to Cincinnati on furlough in late summer 1944, and Nathan promptly hustled him into the studio. Working with a steel guitarist, Jones recorded another eight songs, including the two done earlier by the Sheppard Brothers. Jones wrote the majority of the songs, including the session's most successful record, "East Bound Freight Train."

Grandpa Jones's third King session came in March 1946 after he had been mustered out of the Army. The session was held in Hollywood, which perhaps explains the high drama at the session. Jones was no longer a callow rookie who was thrilled just to be making records. He already had two hits to his credit, as well as two years as a military cop in a war zone.

Jones was unhappy with the relatively low per-record royalty rate he had accepted early in his career. Although he was glad to be reunited at the session with Travis, Jones found that his appetite for Nathan's abrasive personality had diminished significantly during his time away. A clash in the studio was inevitable.

"Syd was wanting another hit record from me," Jones wrote in his autobiography,[2] "something that would go as well as 'It's Raining Here This Morning.' He thought 'Eight More Miles [to Louisville,' a song Jones had just written] was it . . . We had quite a time making that recording . . . I would do a clean take of the song, but Syd wasn't happy, and he'd shout from the control booth, 'Pa, put some life into it!' And I'd do another one and he'd say, 'We need more life!' I finally got mad and stormed out of the studio.

"Pretty soon Merle came after me. 'That Syd makes me so mad,' I said. 'Yeah, he does kind of get you, doesn't he?' said Merle . . . 'Come on back in and take a drink of this stuff.' He had asked one of the studio men to go across the street for a bottle of whiskey. 'I'm not much of a drinkin' man,' I said. 'How much should I drink?' Merle got a paper cup and filled it half full of whiskey. I drank it all down at once . . . Pretty soon I was feeling more ambitious. 'All right, Syd,' I shouted, 'see if this has enough life,' and Merle and I ripped into 'Eight More Miles.'"

"Eight More Miles to Louisville" was a big hit, and not the last hit Nathan would bully out of one of his artists. Although Jones stayed with King until he left for RCA Victor in 1951, the clashes with Nathan lost their charm pretty fast. "We were arguing one time," said Jones, "and Syd hollered, 'What do you want, my blood?'"[3] Jones would nonetheless produce the best music of his career on King.

Jones's next two hits after "Eight More Miles" were the first to feature his banjo playing and quickly became his trademark songs. "Mountain Dew" and "Old Rattler" were recorded in 1947, the year after Jones joined the *Grand Ole Opry*. "Mountain Dew" was recorded in Nashville, with backing by Ramona Jones on mandolin and Cowboy Copas on guitar. It was released in May.

"Right away it started selling," recalled Jones.[4] "My quarterly royalty statement in June showed that it had already sold 20,000 copies—not bad for those days. The next quarter showed another 20,000. All of a sudden I had a hit that was a lot bigger than anything I'd had before.

"Naturally, Syd was anxious to get out a follow-up to 'Mountain Dew,' and he got after me to find another 'banjo song.' 'Old Rattler' was just an old song I grabbed for when Syd was looking for another song. Syd had 'Old Rattler' out in a couple of months, and it took off like a one-eyed cat in a dog pound. It was the fastest selling record I ever had."[5]

Grandpa Jones had a long and fruitful career after leaving King in 1951 and is today recognized as one of the most popular comedians in country music history. Many people today remember Grandpa best for his years on the cornpone TV comedy show *Hee Haw*, a sort of cross between *The Beverly Hillbillies* and *Laugh-In*. Jones was elected to the Country Music Hall of Fame in 1978.

• • •

As did Grandpa Jones and Merle Travis, many of the country musicians who recorded for King in the early years worked on Cincinnati radio station WLW. Started by inventor/entrepreneur Powel Crosley, Jr., in 1922,[6] WLW by the mid-1940s was a powerhouse station, one of the most respected in the country. WLW reached a national audience, thanks to its powerful 50,000–watt clear-channel signal, and received mail from listeners as far away as California, Maine, and Florida. And that was *before* it increased its broadcasting power tenfold.

Crosley was bitten by the radio bug in the early 1920s and began selling a low-cost radio receiver called "The Harko." The next step was logical, at least to Crosley: He started WLW so that people who bought "The Harko" would have something to hear. Within five years, WLW was a powerful member of the National Broadcasting Company (NBC) network. The station employed some of the biggest pop stars of the time.

WLW also featured lots of country music. Beginning with an early morning show starring Ma and Pa McCormick, the station's country offerings included such programs as *Top o' the Morning, Renfro Valley Barn Dance, Rural Roundup, Boone County Caravan, The Lucky Penny Club*, and, beginning in 1938, *The Boone County Jamboree* (known after 1945 as *Midwestern Hayride*).

The Boone County Jamboree, a "barn dance" country music variety show, was launched in 1938 by George Biggar,[7] hired away from WLS in Chicago and its popular *National Barn Dance*. Biggar brought with him such established radio stars as Lulubelle & Scotty and the Girls of the Golden West; they were soon joined on the show by such acts as the Delmore Brothers, Grandpa Jones, Homer & Jethro, the Drifting Pioneers (with young guitarist Merle Travis), and Bradley Kincaid.

Four years before *The Boone County Jamboree* debuted, WLW had increased its broadcasting power from the legal maximum of 50,000 watts, which already allowed the station to reach most of the country, to 500,000 watts, giving WLW a truly global audience. The station would broadcast at 500,000 watts off and on into the 1940s, part of a government experiment to determine the limits of radio broadcasting.[8] This tremendous power built a huge audience for many of WLW's stars. Jethro Burns remembered one time asking for letters on-air and receiving fan mail from Australia, Hong Kong, and China.[9]

• • •

The Delmore Brothers, Alton and Rabon, were seasoned professionals when they connected with Nathan in the mid-1940s. The brothers, who were from Sand Mountain, Alabama, had been recording since 1931 and had enjoyed several big hits on Victor's budget label, Bluebird. Alton (1908–64) and Rabon (1916–52) had also been stars on the *Grand Ole Opry* for five years in the mid-1930s.

Alton and Rabon Delmore recorded some of the most beautiful and moving country music of the 1930s, including "Blue Railroad Train," "Gonna Lay Down My Old Guitar," "The Nashville Blues," and their theme song, "Brown's Ferry Blues." They tended to wear out their welcome at radio stations fairly quickly, however. Both brothers had tempers and alcohol problems. The Delmores lasted five years at the *Opry*, but after leaving that high-profile show in 1938, their career went into decline. Not even a move to Decca in 1940 could entirely right the ship.

Getting a job at WLW in the early 1940s, however, rejuvenated the careers of Alton and Rabon Delmore. Recording for King Records completed the process and took the brothers back to the top. But the Delmore Brothers who recorded for King were not the same two men who recorded for Bluebird in the early 1930s. Gone was the duo's air of wistful innocence. In its place was a world-weary case of the blues. By their first King session in 1944, the Delmore Brothers had fully matured as artists and were ready to make some noise during what they probably knew was their last chance at the big time.

The Delmore Brothers, or perhaps Nathan, played it safe it at the start, emulating the brothers' previous hits. The songs Alton and Rabon recorded through 1945 were similar to their earlier records (many were remakes of songs recorded for Bluebird), combining close duet harmonies, traditional sensibilities grounded in southern blues, and nimble guitar picking by both brothers. Two such numbers, "Prisoner's Farewell" and "Sweet Sweet Thing," both written by Alton, were released as King 503; these cuts were also recorded in Dayton.

The bulk of the material the Delmores recorded in 1944 and 1945 was in this general vein, but only "Midnight Special" attracted much attention. At this point, Nathan apparently suggested that Alton and Rabon make an attempt to update their sound by trying some "boogie" material.

The next session, in January 1946, produced Rabon's original "Hillbilly Boogie," a big hit with a scorching guitar solo by Merle Travis. The Delmore Brothers' new record adroitly caught the rising tide of boogie-woogie music that had recently come to country music in the form of "guitar boogie" records by Arthur Smith and Porky Freeman.[10]

Both Alton and Rabon were skilled lead guitarists—Alton on a standard acoustic guitar and Rabon on a smaller-bodied four-string tenor guitar. Virtually all of their records from this time contain hot picking from both brothers. "Mobile Boogie" from 1947 was an especially good showcase for their instrumental skills.

The Delmore Brothers' boogie records owe much of their excitement to the electric guitarists who worked with the brothers. The duo's records included some dazzling and highly influential work by such early electric guitarists as Roy Lanham, Zeke Turner, and, perhaps most surprisingly, Jethro Burns, who tears it up on "Freight Train Boogie" and "Boogie Woogie Baby," both from 1946.[11] (These same electric guitar licks would show up five to ten years later in the playing of such Memphis guitar hotshots as Scotty Moore, Paul Burlison, and Carl Perkins and be hailed as a fresh new thing called rock and roll.)

The Delmore Brothers were not limited to boogie material. Often recording with harmonica players Wayne Raney and Lonnie Glosson, the Delmore Brothers in the late 1940s had the best groove in country music. The duo flirted with laid-back greatness on "Trouble Ain't Nothin' but the Blues," "Field Hand Man," and "Blues You Never Lose" but hit it dead-center with "Blues Stay Away From Me," one of the biggest-selling records of 1949.

Graced by an unforgettable opening electric guitar lick played by Zeke Turner and haunting, echoey harmonica work by Raney and Glosson, the song came together in the studio as the result of a collaboration among Alton and Rabon Delmore, Wayne Raney, and Henry Glover, a black musician, songwriter, arranger, and producer at King. A couple of stories circulate as to how the song was created.

According to Alton Delmore's autobiography, *Truth Is Stranger Than Publicity*, Nathan asked Delmore to write "a hillbilly version" of "The Hucklebuck," a huge rhythm-and-blues hit for sax player Paul Williams. Delmore listened to Williams' record a few times, got some ideas together, and began working out some riffs with Glover and Zeke Turner, eventually finishing the song in the studio.[12]

The story told by Henry Glover is equally plausible. In his staff role at King, Glover had worked out an arrangement for R&B bandleader Lucky Millinder in 1948. Before Millinder got around to recording the song in April 1949, "The Hucklebuck," which appeared to have been poached from Glover's charts, became a big hit.

"I felt out in the cold," Glover recalled later.[13] "So I went to Cincinnati, got the Delmores together, and came up with 'Blues Stay Away From Me,' based on the same melodic structure and the [electric guitar] doing the same moving at the bottom.'"

"Blues Stay Away From Me" was a huge hit, the biggest of the Delmore Brothers' career. The record was on *Billboard*'s country charts for almost six months, eventually making it to the top spot. It is now an oft-recorded country classic. The record's massive success put the Delmore Brothers back into the national spotlight and greatly increased the demand for the duo's personal appearances.

• • •

George Biggar, the program director at WLW, was in a jam. He badly needed a new gospel quartet to fill a daily half-hour program that had just been vacated by the Drifting Pioneers, who had in fact drifted away, leaving behind only their guitarist Merle Travis. Little did Biggar know that his problem was being solved for him just down the hall.

Alton Delmore had it all figured out. "Alton got me, Travis, and Rabon together for this group," remembered Grandpa Jones.[14] "We marched up to the studio and told Mr. Biggar he had his gospel group. We sang a couple of songs and it sounded pretty good to us. Mr. Biggar said, 'Good. Start in the morning.'

"Alton had learned to read shape notes and do real gospel singing as a boy in Alabama, and he taught us; he called them 'the rudiments of music.' He taught us how to sing the old shape notes, so we could just open up a book and start singing. A lot of good gospel songs were printed in these little paperback books using the shape notes—where the shape of the note tells you its pitch rather than its place on the lines. So we got up some numbers, me and Merle and Alton and Rabon, and started out."

The group needed a name. After many possibilities had been proposed and rejected, one of the four jokingly suggested the Brown's Ferry Four, after the Delmore Brothers' bawdy hit of the 1930s. The guys cracked up, hooting about a gospel group named after such a risqué song. After the laughter died down, somebody said, "You know, it's really not such a bad name when you think about it." With that, they were ready for the next morning.

The Brown's Ferry Four was an instant hit on WLW. The group sang such gospel songs as "Will the Circle Be Unbroken," "I'll Fly Away," "Just a Little Talk with Jesus," and "Rockin' on the Waves" in straightforward, four-part harmony— Alton sang the lead vocals, Rabon the tenor harmonies, Grandpa the baritone, and Merle the bass—backed only by Travis's tasteful guitar playing. It was a gentle, old-fashioned sound, almost delicate, yet it possessed an undeniable strength and power. Nathan definitely wanted the group for King.

The quartet started working on WLW in 1944, but because of the wartime service of Jones, Travis, and Alton Delmore, it was March 1946 before the group got the chance to record. Nathan, Jones, and the Delmore Brothers flew to California and reunited with Travis, who was living in the Los Angeles area after getting out of the Marines. The quartet entered Radio Recorders studio in Hollywood for a session that proved to be very profitable for King Records.

The session produced not only the first hit by the Brown's Ferry Four, a coupling of "Will the Circle Be Unbroken" and "Just a Little Talk with Jesus," but also Grandpa Jones's big hit "Eight More Miles to Louisville" and five more songs by Jones with Travis on electric guitar. The Brown's Ferry Four recording was released in May and was a big hit. Nathan quickly booked another session.

On a return visit to Hollywood in September, the quartet recorded twelve songs in a marathon session. Most of the songs were from shape-note hymnals published in the 1920s and 1930s, including such radio favorites as "I'll Fly Away," "If We Never Meet Again," and "On the Jericho Road." These were the last recordings by the quartet to feature all four original members. For the remainder of the group's recordings, the bass vocals were provided by Red Foley, Clyde Moody, or Ulys "Red" Turner. Alton Delmore played the guitar on those records.

Except for one session in August 1952, Grandpa Jones was present on all of the Brown's Ferry Four's recordings. The Delmore brothers took part in all seven of the group's sessions. The quartet's final session occurred just three and one-half months before Rabon Delmore's death, which brought an end to the Brown's Ferry Four as well. The popular quartet recorded forty-five songs for King, but its musical legacy is greater than that number might suggest.

The enduring popularity of the Brown's Ferry Four has been confirmed many times during the ensuing decades. In the 1980s, *Hee Haw* had a surprise hit on its hands with the Hee Haw Gospel Quartet, a virtual clone of the Brown's Ferry Four. The new quartet, which included Grandpa Jones, had two top-selling albums despite industry skeptics who said that such "dated" material would never sell. The original recordings of the Brown's Ferry Four have never stopped selling, either, and in 1997, *Rockin' on the Waves*, a two-CD collection of their entire King output, brought the group into the digital domain.

• • •

One day in 1945, not long after the Delmore Brothers had moved from WLW to WMC in Memphis, someone knocked on the door of Alton Delmore's West Memphis house. When Alton opened the door, he saw a young man standing there—a tall, slim man with a gaunt face and hungry eyes. The stranger said he was a harmonica player and singer from Arkansas and he wanted to "meet the famous Delmore Brothers."[15] His name was Wayne Raney. He had some ideas about how his harmonica might fit in with the brothers' distinctive two-guitar sound. Country music's greatest duo was about to become a trio.[16]

Harmonica ace Wayne Raney (ca. 1920–93) was born and raised in Wolf Bayou, Arkansas, where he learned to play the harp from a street musician. Wolf Bayou offered little in the way of opportunities, so Raney took to the road at a young age, hoboing around the country and living by his wits. In 1934, while rambling through Texas, Raney was hired to perform on XEPN, one of the so-called "border radio" stations that flourished in Mexico at the time.

A few years later, Raney met Lonnie "Buck" Glosson, a harmonica player twelve years his senior who would be Raney's mentor and musical partner off and on into the 1980s. The two began working on radio as a twin-harmonica act in Arkansas in 1938, and later spent many years at WCKY in Cincinnati.

Raney had a successful and enduring (if intermittent) relationship with WCKY from 1941 until 1960, gaining fame as an influential DJ and on-air salesman of considerable repute; he sold several million "talking harmonicas" over the air in the late 1940s. Raney's first stay at WCKY was relatively brief, though. He was living in Arkansas again when he met the Delmore Brothers in 1945.

Raney and the Delmores started tinkering with their music, fine-tuning the instrumental interplay and joining their country and blues-based sound to the nascent boogie trend that was beginning to be felt in country music. The trio developed a winning formula—often including Glosson on second harmonica—that led to chart-topping hits for both Raney and the Delmore Brothers and some of the best proto-rockabilly records of the late 1940s and early 1950s.

Raney's first trip into the King studio came as a sideman with the Delmore Brothers in February 1946. He helped record sixteen songs, including the hits "Freight Train Boogie" and "Boogie Woogie Baby." Some time remained at the end of the session, so Raney got the chance to record three songs of his own. "Fox Chase," a staple of the folk harmonica repertoire, was released as his first single.

Raney had his first hits in the fall of 1948, when "Lost John Boogie" and "Jack and Jill Boogie" cracked the Top 15 of the *Billboard* country chart. A session in May 1949, featuring backing by the Delmore Brothers and Lonnie Glosson, produced four excellent records: "Del Rio Boogie," "Red Ball to Natchez," "Don't Know Why," and "Why Don't You Haul Off and Love Me." The last record, a catchy original song graced by Raney's laconic vocals, climbed to the top of the country charts. It held the top position for three weeks and crossed over to the pop charts, breaking the Top 25.

Although Raney is primarily known for his harmonica skills, his King releases also showcased his singing. Raney had a pleasant voice with a soft Arkansas twang that translated well to records. He was most effective on novelties such as "Why Don't You Haul Off and Love Me" and "Pardon My Whiskers," up-tempo boogie numbers, and country trios such as "Lonesome Wind Blues" and "Don't Know Why."

The success of "Why Don't You Haul Off and Love Me" brought an invitation to join the cast of the *Grand Ole Opry,* which Raney did for approximately a year. He also spent several months touring and recording with Lefty Frizzell in 1953. Raney stuck with King until 1955, but he never had another hit after "Why Don't You Haul Off and Love Me."

He recorded some great stuff, though, from tough, proto-rockabilly and boogie songs, such as "We Love to Live," "Gone With the Wind This Morning," and "Catfish Baby," to country novelties ("Adam" and "The Roosters Are Crowing") and traditional-sounding Raney originals. After leaving King, Raney recorded for Decca and Starday without much success, although one of his Starday albums contained his should-be-classic original song "We Need a Whole Lot More of Jesus (and a Lot Less Rock and Roll)."

Raney's work on King deserves more attention than it has received. One could say Raney was a missing link between country and rock and roll, but it's hard to call someone "missing" who recorded nearly sixty songs and had three hits, including one of the biggest records of 1949. Still, when the founders of rock and roll are discussed, Raney is rarely mentioned. Between his own records and those by the Delmore Brothers, Raney was an important influence upon early rock and roll and should be better known for it.

Raney returned to Arkansas in the late 1950s to raise chickens. He also started two record labels, Poor Boy and Rimrock, which released his own albums (containing most of the material he recorded for King in the 1940s and 1950s) and records by bluegrass stars the Stanley Brothers, Carl Story, and Red Smiley. He had a cassette-duplicating plant for a while, as well. Raney's health had deteriorated badly by the late 1980s, but he rallied enough to issue the autobiographical booklet *Life Has Not Been a Bed of Roses* in 1990. He died three years later.

• • •

Despite the musical conservatism of some of the Delmore Brothers' earliest King records, most of the music the Delmores recorded for the label was "remarkably contemporary," said British writer Tony Russell.[17] "Few country artists with their depth of experience . . . had both the skill and the temperament to take on, and enjoy, the challenges of playing country music in the postwar South."

The commercial success of "Blues Stay Away from Me" should have set the Delmore Brothers up for life, but it was not to be. The brothers "chased their dream from [radio] station to station"[18] but never quite caught it. After leaving WLW in 1945, the two worked in Memphis, Indianapolis, Chattanooga, Houston, and border radio station XERF in Del Rio, Texas.

Though their records continued to sell well, the radio jobs did not work out for one reason or another, with the exception of the stay at WMC in Memphis. The duo split up in 1951. Rabon died the following year from lung cancer.

Alton was rocked by his brother's death and, though he returned to the recording studio a few more times before his death in 1964, his career as a professional musician was essentially over. The Delmore Brothers were inducted into the Songwriter's Hall of Fame in 1971 and the Country Music Hall of Fame in 2001.

THE KING GETS A QUEEN
The Short but Important Life of Queen Records
•••

I'm a plain person and I like plain music.
—Sydney Nathan

Syd Nathan often said he made "records for the little man." By August 1945, buoyed by the end of the war and the moderate success of his initial country releases, Syd had decided to more fully embrace his vision of music for "the little man." King Records was a country music label, but the time had come to expand. The King needed a Queen.

Nathan launched Queen Records in August with the express purpose of recording black musicians. The new label had its first release within a few weeks—a cover of Joe Liggins's big hit "The Honeydripper" by singer/saxophonist Bull Moose Jackson. Thirteen more Queen releases followed in the next six months, including sides by singer Walter Brown, jazz hepcat Slim Gaillard, and the Chubby Jackson Sextet.

Nathan met Bull Moose Jackson at a gig by the Lucky Millinder Orchestra in the Cincinnati area. Nathan went there to ask Millinder to record for him. Nathan also approached Henry Glover, trumpet player and arranger for the band. "I came through Cincinnati with the Lucky Millinder Orchestra," Glover told writer Steve Tracy,[1] "and Syd came to see Millinder and me about making some records.

"Millinder couldn't do anything himself [because he was under contract to Decca] but he let the band's vocalist Bull Moose Jackson, Panama Francis, Sam 'The Man' Taylor, and me record. I scratched out some songs and arrangements, like overnight. Out of all of us in the band, Bull Moose Jackson happened to be the one to come up with the hits. His first very big hit for King was a thing called 'I Love You, Yes I Do,' which I wrote."

Benjamin "Bull Moose" Jackson (1919–89) was a singing saxophone player from Cleveland. Jackson had been a child prodigy on the violin, and his parents wanted him to become a concert violinist.[2] He switched to saxophone while in high school, though, and formed a jazz band called the Harlem Hotshots. By the time he joined Millinder's band in 1943, Jackson was a tenor saxophonist with a sound similar to Coleman Hawkins.

He was also an effective singer. "One night in Lubbock, Texas," Jackson told writer Peter Grendysa,[3] "Wynonie Harris got his 'habits' on. He was the type of guy that would say, 'Well, I'm not going to sing tonight. I'm going home.' They [the rest of the Millinder band] had to do a little coaxing to get me up there to sing . . . After I got out there, I loved it."

Jackson was a skilled saxophonist, but most of his success on records came as a singer. He cut twelve songs for Queen, recording as Bull Moose Jackson and His Band, which was actually a pared-down version of Millinder's band. "The Honeydripper" was a strong regional hit, but Jackson's biggest record from the period was "I Know Who Threw the Whiskey (in the Well)" in 1946. That was also his last record for Queen. His biggest hits would come on King.

• • •

It remains unclear why Syd Nathan started a new label for these records instead of releasing them on King. He clearly saw the two labels as separate and distinct from each other, because the initial records on King had red labels and were numbered sequentially beginning with 500, whereas the Queen records had black labels and began a new numerical series starting with 4100.

Perhaps Nathan felt the wholesalers and retailers who handled the records would prefer two labels. It was certainly nothing new for labels to establish subsidiary labels to release different kinds of music. Maybe Nathan thought record-buying fans would be confused if the two styles of music were on the same label.

At any rate, two labels existed: King and Queen. The new label grew quickly, as Nathan augmented his own recording efforts by purchasing material from other labels. His first purchase was the acquisition of nearly twenty masters from Southern Records, a New York company headed by pioneering black executive J. Mayo Williams.[4]

Nathan bought master recordings from Williams again in 1947, from his Southern and Harlem labels, and from the 20th Century and Gotham labels.[5] The

Gotham deal was notable in that it began a long and fruitful relationship between Nathan and saxophonist Earl Bostic, who would sell millions of records for King in coming years with such smash hits as "Flamingo" and "Sleep."

The most significant music recorded on Queen was the forty-some sides of black religious music recorded in June and July of 1946. These records featured the Wings Over Jordan Choir and three gospel quartets, the Gospel Trumpeters, the Harmoneers, and Swan's Silvertone Singers, led by the magnificent singer Claude Jeter.

The rest of the Queen catalog was filled out by such journeymen recording artists as Annisteen Allen, Tab Smith, Johnny Temple, Harold Tinsley, and the Jubalaires. The final Queen release, Earl Bostic's "That's the Groovy Thing," was issued on August 21, 1947.

Nathan had seen enough. The sales of the records on Queen convinced Nathan that "black" music could be profitably recorded and marketed by an independent outfit such as King. He retired Queen Records and henceforth issued all styles of music on King. All seventy-five Queen singles were reissued with King labels and catalog numbers. In the final analysis, he figured it was all music for "the little man."

Maybe Queen Records was nothing more than an experiment for Nathan, a trial balloon. His decision to meld the R&B and black gospel records into the general King catalog, and treat all releases the same, signaled a major commitment to the thriving postwar scene in black music.

• • •

Those of us who wonder about such things have long wondered about four unissued Queen recordings from 1946 by Jimmy Wyble, a hot electric guitarist who was playing at that time in Spade Cooley's western swing band. Not to put too fine a point on it, but Wyble was white, as was the band on his session. Given that the whole point of Queen was to record black musicians, what were Wyble and his bunch of western swingers doing on Queen?

The group's four-song recording session was held in Los Angeles, at the end of a month-long recording frenzy during which Nathan cut tracks on dozens of California-based acts. Recorded under the name of Jimmy Wyble and His Rifftette—an instant inductee into the Band Name Hall of Fame—the four songs represent what seems to be "a deliberate attempt by Nathan to cut a 'Race' session . . . using white western swing players for the date."[6]

In addition to electric guitarist Jimmy Wyble, who went on to fame playing with jazz bandleaders Bennie Goodman and Red Norvo, the session included fiddler and vocalist Buddy Ray, tenor sax player Calvin Martin, pianist Freddy Haynes, drummer Johnny DeMaris, and an unknown bassist.

Although Ray's singing doesn't sound especially "black," it's not hard country, either. The playing by the musicians falls much closer to the jazz end than the country end of the western swing continuum. Wyble's bop-influenced guitar work is superb, and hot solos by Martin on "No More Blues" and Haynes on "Goodbye My Heart" and bluesy fiddle-sax ensemble playing add up to some outstanding small-band western swing. Not the most obvious music for a crossover attempt at the R&B market, to be sure, but the idea might have worked if given a chance.

Nathan never released the four songs—on Queen or King. It's hard to guess why he didn't use them, because he certainly released lesser music from other artists. The four cuts finally saw the light of day in 2000 on an English CD, *Shuffle Town: Western Swing on King, 1946–50.*

Aside from the recordings' musical and entertainment value, the session is most important, in retrospect, as an example of Nathan's willingness to blur the racial lines that were all too present in American music in the aftermath of World War II. He would do this more successfully on King Records by having his country artists cover rhythm and blues hits, and his R&B artists cover country hits.

Nathan also supervised racially mixed recording sessions and had Henry Glover, a black producer, working with such country acts as Grandpa Jones and Moon Mullican. So the idea of trying a "race session with white players" was not out of character for Nathan. In fact, it fit perfectly with the rest of his philosophy.

So why were the records never released? We'll probably never know. Singer Buddy Ray felt that Nathan wanted "something a little more 'raunchy' and loud" but also thought Nathan "seemed pleased with the final results."[7] Perhaps Nathan had already decided to fold Queen into King, so the songs' release on Queen became moot. Perhaps he lost interest in the experiment and moved on to something else.

Too bad. These records by Jimmy Wyble and His Rifftette might have changed musical history as we know it. It wasn't like Syd Nathan to back off a project once interested, but he did in this instance. It would be interesting to know why.

HENRY GLOVER

An Unsung Hero of American Music

•••

Henry Glover wrote so many killer tunes
it makes your mind bend.

—Mac Rebennack, aka Dr. John, pianist

Henry Glover was the living embodiment of the color-blindness and open-minded spirit that Syd Nathan espoused and attempted to live by at King Records. Glover was a black man from the south, but he was as comfortable in the studio producing white country acts as he was producing rhythm and blues acts. Glover knew the barriers erected between white and black music were artificial and not reflective of the way life was actually lived in America. Music was music, and a good song was a good song. It really was as simple as that.

Henry Bernard Glover was born May 21, 1921, in the resort town of Hot Springs, Arkansas. A natural musician, Glover played the piano and cornet by his teenage years, despite his parents' objections. "They looked down on the entertainment field," Glover told writer John W. Rumble; musicians, to them, were a subject of contempt, "people off the levee camp."[1] Still, Glover played on, absorbing the country music he heard on local radio stations, the jazz and blues he heard on records, and the formal music instruction he received in high school.

After graduation, Glover attended Alabama Agricultural and Mechanical College in Huntsville. He quickly earned a musical scholarship and began playing in several of A&M's student ensembles. In addition to the formidable technical knowledge he gained in Huntsville, Glover developed a philosophy that would help guide him as he made his way through the world.

One day in 1940 Glover was telling his A&M mentor, bandmaster James Wilson, about a concert he had played with white musicians the preceding summer back in Hot Springs. Wilson kidded him about playing with "Ofay," a phrase for white people that Wilson explained was the "pig latin" word for *foe*. He also had some advice for Glover. "He said, 'You can't be afraid of the foe. You can't fear the foe. You gotta go with it.' And that's what I did my whole career. I was not afraid of the Ofay, or anybody else, really, when I had prepared myself not to be."[2]

Glover received his degree in education in 1943 and enrolled in a master's program at Wayne State University in Detroit. He still had the music in his blood, though, and when bandleader Buddy Johnson offered the young musician a job, Glover jumped at the chance. He lasted only a few months playing trumpet and arranging for the Johnson band, but subsequent gigs with the bands of Willie Bryant, Tiny Bradshaw, and Lucky Millinder further honed his skills.

"Syd Nathan gave me a job back in the 1940s as his Artists & Repertoire (A&R) Director, and I was perhaps the second black man to ever have an executive position with a record company in the United States. The first was a gentleman called by the name of Mayo Williams, who was connected with Decca Records.[3]

"I can recall the first date that I did for Syd, for the company as an employee, as the recording director," Glover said. "It was with Todd Rhodes, a piano player from Detroit. I came in and we did a couple of instrumentals, 'Teardrops' and 'Pot Likker.' I was impressed with Todd's band because he had a couple of very fine musicians in it."

Nathan put together an attractive deal for Glover that included a regular salary as well as a weekly advance against songwriting royalties and an expense account. He persuaded Glover to move to Cincinnati to more fully learn the mechanics of running a record company. "I moved to Cincinnati in 1949 and stayed until 1950 in order to learn the basics of the recording setup—a rare opportunity not only for a black man but also for a white,[4] said Glover.

"I worked with Syd on many projects in the early days of the record company. Naturally, with him putting together a pressing, printing, studio, and distribution complex, there were many things that you could do, and at the same time learn. I was taught the basic fundamentals of the business of music and the studio mechanics and such. I received a great knowledge of the business end as well as the complicated copyright situation, licensing and publishing."

Glover enjoyed his first success as a producer with Bull Moose Jackson. Glover not only produced Jackson's recording sessions but also wrote (or co-wrote) many of Bull Moose's early hits, including "I Love You, Yes I Do," "All My Love Belongs to You," "I Want a Bow Legged Woman," and "Love Me Tonight." It was not long before Nathan asked Glover to work in the studio with King's country artists. "My duties were not limited only to the blues and R&B," Glover said. "I did many of the country-western artists like Moon Mullican. I did all of Moon's early recordings. I recorded Grandpa Jones, Cowboy Copas, and the York Brothers."[5] Glover also collaborated in the studio writing songs with Mullican, the Delmore Brothers, Grandpa Jones, and a host of others.

"Moon and I wrote [a song] together called 'I'll Sail My Ship Alone,'" said Glover.[6] "We stood there over the piano and took the remnants of a thing that he halfway remembered that he had gotten from a buddy of his, and we made a song out of it. You know, the structure was there, because he had the title and a couple of lines. Way back in the 1930s, Jimmie Lunceford had a record called 'I'm Like a Ship at Sea' and I borrowed some ideas from that." The new song shot straight to the top of the *Billboard* country charts and was one of the biggest hits of 1950.

The record's flip side, the rollicking "Moon's Tune," was an upbeat boogie number and a revelation to Glover. "I hadn't seen anything like that. I know there must have been some [pianists like Mullican] playing in those western bands. But I hadn't seen a white man play the boogie-woogie piano. Moon had such a great soul. He was just like a black man to me, the way he thought, felt, and expressed himself."[7]

Glover and Mullican enjoyed a particularly close personal relationship. Mullican was an avid devotee of black nightclubs around the country, both the bigger venues where the national bands would appear and the smaller clubs that featured local talent. "We would go to a club together during the time we were rehearsing for a session," Glover recalled.[8] "They'd call him up on stage in a black club and he'd get up there and play. They loved him."

On the road, a different dynamic was sometimes in order. Of one trip to Texas with Mullican, Glover said, "Moon sort of realized that maybe there was no hotel that would make an accommodation for me. With great diplomacy, he came right to the rescue. And he carried me over to a black family's house, friends of his, that put me up and fed me good."[9] On rare occasions in the south, Glover would slip on a driver's cap and pretend to be the chauffeur for Nathan or Mullican or whatever other white person might be along for the ride.

Glover's thorough knowledge of music was very helpful in the studio, but it was his demeanor as much as anything that made him invaluable during the sessions. Nathan's gruff, abrasive manner alienated many musicians in the high-pressure studio environment, but Glover's style was just the opposite.

"There were not many unusual things that happened at [my] recording sessions," Glover stated, "because I had a manner about me that it was business and

I conducted it as a business. There were musicians in those days that gave me more respect than they did other recording people because I had a good musical knowledge that they respected. I didn't allow drinking in the studio—we tried to run a pretty tight ship to keep people as straight as possible at the studio."[10]

"At King," Glover told writer Arnold Shaw,[11] "we worked with white country artists as well as black R&B performers, [so] we constantly crossed boundary lines. Syd Nathan had me record blues with C&W singers like Cowboy Copas and Moon Mullican. And I did country songs with Wynonie Harris. In fact, 'Mr. Blues,' as he was called, had one of his biggest sellers covering a Hank Penny song, 'Bloodshot Eyes.' And Bull Moose Jackson had a big disc on a country song called 'Why Don't You Haul Off and Love Me,' cut originally by Wayne Raney.

"Sam Phillips has received great recognition because he did the novel thing of recording R&B with white country boys. He deserves credit, considering that Elvis Presley, Jerry Lee Lewis, Roy Orbison, Carl Perkins, and Johnny Cash all emerged from the Sun label. But the fact is that King Records was covering R&B with country singers almost from the beginning of my work with Syd. We had a duo called the York Brothers who recorded many of the day's R&B hits back in 1947–48.

"We were more successful in doing the reverse—covering C&W hits with R&B singers. I'll confess that we didn't think we were doing anything remarkable. It's just that we had both types of artists, and when a song happened in one field, Syd Nathan wanted it moved into the other. Since Syd published most of the songs we recorded, he was also augmenting his publishing income and building important copyrights. He was a smart businessman and didn't miss a trick."

In time, the business relationship between Nathan and Glover became strained. Glover had decided to leave King Records by the late 1950s. The catalyst for the split came during the congressional investigations of payola in the recording and radio industries. Although Nathan never denied paying radio DJs to play records, he attempted to shift at least some of the blame to Glover.

"Syd said, 'Whatever was done in connection with payola was done out of the New York office [of King Records],'" remembered Glover.[12] "That'd mean me, you know." That was the final straw for Henry Glover. An era had ended at King Records.

After leaving King, Glover briefly worked for Old Town Records and released some sides on his own Glover Records. His next stop was Roulette Records, where he worked through the early 1960s, producing such artists as Ronnie Hawkins, Sam & Dave, Dinah Washington, Sarah Vaughan, and Tommy James & The Shondells.

Glover returned to King Records for a brief period in the late 1960s, but after about 1971, he primarily concentrated on production. Financially comfortable from his lucrative publishing copyrights, he had the luxury of producing only those acts that really excited him. His production credits from this period include *The Muddy Waters Woodstock Album,* which won Waters his first Grammy Award in 1975, *Put It In Your Ear* by Paul Butterfield, and a solo album by Levon Helm, the drummer from the Band.

• • •

Despite their disagreements over the years, the friendship between Henry Glover and Syd Nathan survived the rifts and tensions and lasted until Nathan's death in 1968. Glover was certainly aware of Nathan's personality quirks, but he always spoke with respect and affection for his mentor in the recording industry.

"He thought he knew more than anyone would ever know about the business," Glover recalled.[13] "And he perhaps did." But Glover took credit for improving Nathan's fashion sense. "I taught him how to dress. He was so corny in his dress until I carried him downtown to my tailors, and they dressed him up pretty good."[14]

The National Academy of Recording Arts and Sciences (NARAS) honored Henry Glover in 1986 for almost forty-five years of work as a musician, arranger, songwriter, producer, and record company executive by adding him to its Honor Roll of A&R Producers. Glover also deserves enshrinement in the Country Music Hall of Fame and the Rock & Roll Hall of Fame for his unique contributions to American music. Those honors will be, unfortunately, posthumous—Glover died in 1991 after a massive heart attack—but they would help tell the story of an American original.

In an interview with writer Steve Tracy in the early 1970s, Glover remembered an earlier time and a simpler way of doing business: "I had a batch of contracts in my briefcase at all times. In those days, you would just get a contract out and get it signed. If you got an artist, you recorded the next day ... Every artist that I ever recorded had to be a favorite. Otherwise, I didn't record them. All of them were my favorites. We didn't care what label it carried. In those days, all it had to do was just be a hit."[15]

Henry Glover was involved with a lot of hits. He was a Grammy-winning producer, a prolific writer of great songs, a sophisticated arranger and musician, a diplomat in the recording studio, and, certainly not least, a bridge between the races. Glover always downplayed that aspect of his career, said it was nothing special, just business as usual.

Nor did he think that what he was doing—a black man producing white country artists—was that unusual or noteworthy. "Even when I traveled in the south recording country people, [there was] never a big deal about it. They took it as something altogether different, not me trying to integrate or anything like that. They saw that I had something to offer. I knew what I was doing, and people had me there because I could be of benefit to the artist."[16] Business as usual.

With all due respect, Glover was wrong on that count. It was not business as usual, not in the recording industry, not in the United States, not in the 1940s and 1950s. Glover made history while he made hits. By capturing on record the music that existed *between* the categories of black and white—indeed *beyond* black and white—Henry Glover was an American synthesist of the highest order. He helped make King Records matter.

GOOD ROCKIN' TONIGHT

Rhythm & Blues on King Records, 1947–54

•••

The crooners get swamped with bobby-soxers.
I like to sing to women with meat on their bones
and that long green stuff in their pockets.

—Wynonie Harris

King's new "Rhythm and Blues" series picked up where Queen left off without missing a beat. The first release in the new series was "Cuttin' Out" by Earl Bostic, one of the masters Nathan purchased from Gotham. The immediate fireworks, however, were supplied by Bull Moose Jackson.

Jackson made the most of his "promotion" from Queen and scored big with his first King recording, Henry Glover's "I Love You, Yes I Do." A fine example of Jackson's crooning, "I Love You" was a huge hit, by far the biggest in King's short history. Released late in 1947, the record was one of the biggest hits of 1948, selling more than a million copies and earning the first gold record ever awarded to an R&B song.[1]

The hit didn't make Jackson rich, but as he later noted, "We toured for three straight years after that one song."[2] The massive success of "I Love You, Yes I Do" allowed Jackson to leave Lucky Millinder's band and hit the road with his own septet, the Buffalo Bearcats, which over the years attracted such top musicians as pianist Randy Weston, drummer Philly Jo Jones, and legendary sax player John Coltrane.

Jackson was a versatile performer for King. He scored Top Ten R&B hits with the ballads "All My Love Belongs to You," "I Can't Go On without You," and "Little Girl Don't Cry." He was also one of the first to benefit from Nathan's strategy of having King R&B acts record country hits, with successful covers of Wayne Raney's "Why Don't You Haul Off and Love Me" and Moon Mullican's "Cherokee Boogie."

From his earliest days on Queen, Jackson proved himself a master of up-tempo tributes to good times, good whiskey and, particularly, the pleasures of the flesh. These songs usually didn't make the charts or get much radio airplay, but they burned it up on the jukeboxes. He had many of these records: "I Want a Bow Legged Woman," "Big Fat Mamas Are Back in Style," "Sneaky Pete," "Nosey Joe," and so on. The unquestioned champion of the bunch is "Big Ten-Inch Record," a lusty and memorable paean to the singer's big ten-inch . . . 78-rpm record.

Jackson recorded for King through 1954, but the hits stopped after "Why Don't You Haul Off and Love Me" in 1949. He was out of the music business by the 1960s, and later managed food service at Howard University in Washington, D.C. Jackson returned to performing and recording in the last few years of his life, becoming something of a cult figure around Pittsburgh. He died in 1989.

• • •

The January 1950 issue of *Ebony* included a profile of Bull Moose Jackson with the rather unflattering title, "Without Usual Glamour of Most Crooners, He Warbles Romantic Songs and Draws Record Crowds." The magazine calls Jackson "the most unusual new singing talent to rise into the big-money class since the war ended," but the writer notes that "in the midst of a lean [year] for entertainment in general and dance bands in particular . . . Bull Moose had outstripped both Ella Fitzgerald and Sarah Vaughan in terms of gross income.[3]

"Fitzgerald and Vaughan may get the kudos from sophisticated big-city jaz-zophiles and win critics [sic] awards for their musicianship, but it is Bull Moose whose unpolished vocal performances get thousands at whistle-stop dance halls sighing and crying, teen-agers and middle-aged spinsters alike . . . Bull Moose is a rarity in these days of glamorous, velvet-voiced crooners . . . He is far from handsome. His rugged countenance and ungainly gait are hardly calculated to stimulate female passion. He wears spectacles at all times with the dignity of a high school mathematics teacher."[4]

• • •

The next big R&B star for King was Wynonie Harris, a flamboyant soul who went by the handle of "Mr. Blues." A native of Omaha, Nebraska, Harris (1915–69) had it figured from the start: "I knew I had to be different if I was going to make my bread singing the blues. The woods are full of blues singers—some good, some

great, and some who stink. I wanted to be the greatest of them all. Since I don't
play piano or guitar, I had to work out a new approach."[5]

That he did. Despite accounts that Harris spent two years as a premed student
at Creighton University, he was actually a high-school dropout who broke into
show biz as a dancer and club emcee. He sang some in Omaha nightclubs and
was a bit of a local celebrity, but it wasn't until he moved to Los Angeles in 1940
that his career began to gain some momentum amid the music scene developing
on Central Avenue.

After his "discovery" in 1944, Harris joined the Lucky Millinder Orchestra. A
blues shouter in the Kansas City style of Joe Turner and Jimmy Rushing, Harris
sang on Millinder's Decca hits "Hurry, Hurry" and "Who Threw the Whiskey in
the Well," a smash in 1945. Harris soon began recording on his own but experienced only modest success on such labels as Philo, Aladdin, and Apollo. He was
desperate for a hit when he arrived at King at the end of 1947.

Nathan was desperate, too—to record as much material as possible before
another American Federation of Musicians recording ban took effect on January
1, 1948. Harris had four recording sessions during December. The first session
yielded four songs. The second session was more productive, with eight songs
recorded, though none generated much of a buzz. The third session, however,
caught Mr. Blues in especially fine form.

"I heard the news/There's good rockin' tonight." Thus begins "Good Rockin'
Tonight," Wynonie Harris's first big hit on King. Written by fellow blues shouter
Roy Brown, the song topped the R&B charts in 1948. Harris had turned the song
down when Brown first offered it to him. Brown had then recorded the song
himself on DeLuxe, only to have Harris steal the hit with a hastily recorded cover
on King.

Harris had to wait for the recording ban's end on December 14, 1948, to follow
up his mammoth hit. He did so in 1949 with "All She Wants to Do Is Rock," his
second number-one R&B hit. That record started a hot streak of Top Ten R&B
hits for Harris that included "Sittin' on It All the Time," "I Like My Baby's Pud-
ding," "Bloodshot Eyes," "Oh Babe," and "Lovin' Machine." Those titles indicate
Harris's penchant for double-entendre songs, a fondness that increased after the
success of "Good Rockin' Tonight." Harris was a master of the form; in addition
to the songs already mentioned, his canon also includes "Quiet Whiskey," "I Want
My Fanny Brown," "Luscious Woman," and "Keep on Churnin' (Til The Butter
Come)," which Billboard called "a slick double-entendre blues which should draw
lots of coin from his fans."[6]

Harris also covered several King country hits. He had big hits with "Bloodshot
Eyes" (originally done by Hank Penny) and "Good Morning Judge" (Louis Innis),

as well as more moderate success with "I Feel That Old Age Coming On" (Homer & Jethro), "Adam Come and Get Your Rib" (Wayne Raney), and "Triflin" Woman" (Moon Mullican).

Wynonie Harris was arguably the best of the postwar blues shouters, a supremely manly singer and entertainer. He was also realistic (some would say cynical) about his niche in the music business: "The crooners star on the Great White Way and get swamped with Coca-Cola-drinking bobby-soxers ... I star in Georgia, Texas, Alabama, Tennessee, and Missouri, and get those who have money to buy stronger stuff and my records to play while they drink it."[7]

Harris was still brash enough in 1954 to boast, in an article in *Tan* magazine, "I'm the highest-paid blues singer in the business. I'm a $1,500–a-week man."[8] In fact, his star had significantly dimmed with the advent of rock and roll. He helped create the new music, but, try as he might, Harris couldn't sustain a career in rock and roll.

His last hit was "Lovin' Machine" in 1952. The times were passing him by. At thirty-nine, Harris was just too old to be a rock and roll star. At a time when teen-aged audiences wanted teen-aged singers to moon over, Harris came across as a dirty old man singing dirty old songs.

Harris made a few more records over the years, with a brief return to King in 1957, before hanging it up with a last session for Chess in 1964. He worked as a bartender after his retirement from the music business. He died in 1969 in Los Angeles. Harris has yet to be inducted into the Rock and Roll Hall of Fame despite being a huge influence on everybody from Elvis Presley to Michael Jackson.

• • •

Did Wynonie Harris record the first rock and roll record in 1948 with "Good Rockin' Tonight"? That is, of course, a highly subjective question and impossible to answer, but, yes, he did. There are those who contend that "the first rock and roll record" was "Rocket 88," a hit in 1951 by singer Jackie Brenston (fronting Ike Turner's Kings of Rhythm) on Chess. But why that record and not "Good Rockin' Tonight"? What does "Rocket 88" have that "Good Rockin' Tonight" lacks? Listen to the two records side by side. "Good Rockin' Tonight" is a blueprint for dozens of rock hits to come: screaming tenor sax solo, handclaps beefing up the backbeat, drummer riding the cymbals like a jockey, a walking bass line, restrained piano boogie in the background, and Harris modestly proclaiming that he's "a mighty, mighty man."

"Rocket 88" is a great record with a lot going for it. It's about a car, it has a nasty groove framed by Ike Turner's piano playing, and the sax work is better than on "Good Rockin' Tonight." Plus "Rocket 88" gets bonus points for its impeccable pedigree—recorded in Memphis by Sam Phillips of Sun Records fame and released on Chess Records, the premier label for modern American blues.

But those bonus points are offset by the cooler title of the Harris hit (a valid factor in rock and roll), the historic primacy of "Good Rockin' Tonight," and the fact that "Good Rockin' Tonight" was a much bigger hit and presumably more influential than "Rocket 88." The tie-breaker in this momentous debate is that Elvis Presley recorded "Good Rockin' Tonight" in 1954 for Sun and created a teen anthem, one of the first in rock and roll. (Curiously, Elvis rephrased the song's opening assertion as a question: "Have you heard the news?") That makes "Good Rockin'" Tonight" our winner.

• • •

If Roy Brown had done nothing more than write "Good Rockin' Tonight," the New Orleans singer would have earned a reserved spot in rock and roll paradise. But Brown (1925–81) had far more in his bag of tricks than just one hit song. He should be much better known for his accomplishments.

A prolific songwriter who wrote most of what he recorded, Brown was a best-selling recording artist who twice topped the R&B charts, with "Along about Midnight" and "Hard Luck Blues." He was a powerful, emotional blues singer and a major influence on countless vocalists including Elvis Presley, B. B. King, Little Richard, James Brown, Bobby "Blue" Bland, Johnny Ace, and, perhaps most obviously, Jackie Wilson. Roy Brown was one of King's premier hit makers and a trailblazing pioneer of rock and roll.

Brown was born in New Orleans, raised in Eunice, Louisiana, and schooled in religious music by his church-organist mother, True Love Brown. Roy was singing in a gospel quartet called the Rookie Four by the time he was thirteen. His life was uprooted the following year with the death of his mother and subsequent moves to Houston and Los Angeles, but his brief training in gospel music would benefit Brown later in life.

Brown became a huge star with a powerful, cleanly enunciated "shouting" style of blues singing that developed completely by accident, according to Brown. Until around 1947, Brown was a Bing Crosby man, plain and simple. He even won first prize (and $60) at a 1943 talent contest in Los Angeles singing two of Crosby's hits, "San Antonio Rose" and "(I've Got Spurs That) Jingle, Jangle, Jingle." By 1946, Brown was in Galveston, Texas, leading a band called the Melodeers. Brown sang the pop songs of the day in his best Crosby baritone, while trumpeter-vocalist Wilbert Brown (no relation) handled the blues and jump blues numbers in the group's repertoire. One day, during the band's radio program, Wilbert Brown was taken by a sudden illness just as the announcer introduced a jumping new song written by Roy Brown, "Good Rockin' Tonight." As Wilbert made a hasty exit, Roy stepped to the microphone and began singing.

"Not singing; I was shouting," he said later.[9] With no experience as a blues singer to draw upon, Brown reverted to his gospel roots, wailing like a church singer seized by the Holy Ghost spirit. Those who heard the performance were stunned. Things were never the same after that for Roy Brown.

Back home in New Orleans the following year, Brown approached Wynonie Harris at one of Harris's gigs and tried to sell him "Good Rockin' Tonight" for fifty dollars. Harris blew him off, so Brown then pitched the song to singer Cecil Gant, known for his 1945 hit "I Wonder." Gant was so impressed, he called the president of his record company—collect and extremely late at night—and had Brown sing the song to him over the phone.

Jules Braun, the head of DeLuxe Records, wasted no time in getting to New Orleans, signing Brown to a recording contract, and getting him into the studio. "Good Rockin' Tonight" was a smash hit, peaking at number thirteen on the national R&B chart, an unusually strong showing by an unknown artist. The record would have been even bigger had Wynonie Harris not realized the magnitude of his mistake and cut a cover version for King, one of the Top Five R&B records of 1948.

DeLuxe Records had been launched in 1944 in Linden, New Jersey, by brothers Jules and Dave Braun. The label in its early years was home to a curious mix of artists ranging from jazz modernists to black gospel quartets to old-time country duets—sort of like King, though less successful. Nathan purchased 51 percent of DeLuxe Records in 1947. The partnership was never a smooth one, and Nathan acquired the remainder of the company a year later amid a flurry of suits, counter-suits, and assorted other legal wrangling.[10]

Roy Brown recorded frequently for DeLuxe beginning in 1947 and was one of the best-selling black artists in the country between 1948 and 1951. Brown had more than a dozen Top Ten R&B hits during the period, including "Long About Midnight," "Hard Luck Blues," "Boogie at Midnight," "Love Don't Love Nobody," "Cadillac Baby," "Long about Sundown," "Big Town," and "Rockin' at Midnight." Brown was not the first to apply the techniques and fervent singing style associated with Pentecostal and Holiness gospel music to secular music, but his synthesis of the sacred and profane was audacious, even if it was, at first, more a matter of instinct than intent. Brown said in 1970 that the way he sang as an adult had changed little from his singing in the Rookie Four: "The same style I'm using singing the blues, I did when I was singing spirituals."[11]

The key element Brown brought from gospel to blues was an intense delivery, a sense of abandon that came from profound involvement with the material. "You tell the story and you have to feel it," he once explained. "This is why I wail and cry when I'm singing slow tunes and get happy when I'm shouting."[12]

The mixing of gospel and blues was nothing new for Brown: "I had about six or eight ounces of blackberry wine, and my boys and I [the Rookie Four], we got in the church and we started to sing. And we started doing things we'd never done before. The sisters started clapping their hands and patting their feet. They were shouting 'Amen! Amen!' and we had them rolling. And I was so very proud because my mother was there.

"My mother didn't say anything on the way home. When I got home, she said, 'Take off your clothes.' I knew what that meant—a whipping. I said, 'Mama, what did I do?' She said, 'I'm gonna teach you to jazz up spirituals.' I said, 'What do you mean, jazz?' I didn't know what she was talking about. She said, 'That wasn't a spiritual you were singing. I don't know what it was, but it wasn't a spiritual!' And she just ripped me apart."[13]

Brown's mature vocal style contained several elements of sanctified gospel singing—the soaring falsetto, the extensive use of the word or note-stretching technique known as melisma (what W.C. Handy called "worrying the note"), the effective use of repetition, and a fevered presentation that might have shocked his early idol, Bing Crosby. Brown's use of the techniques and tricks of gospel singing was quite influential upon such followers as Jackie Wilson, James Brown, and Clyde McPhatter.

Brown is often called a blues shouter, but he also *cried* the blues. He put so much raw emotion into a song (check out the autobiographical "Hard Luck Blues") that it can make for almost painful listening. Brown's vulnerability and emotional openness was in marked contrast to the stoicism and control of most blues singers of the time. It was this emotionalism, or more accurately the "permission" to draw upon the full range of human emotions, that was Roy Brown's greatest gift to subsequent soul singers.

After his remarkable four-year run of hits beginning in 1948, Brown cooled off completely. There wasn't any decline in the quality of Brown's recordings. In fact, many of his later efforts (including "Old Age Boogie," "Trouble at Midnight," "Queen of Diamonds," "Shake 'Em Up Baby," and "Black Diamond") rank among his best. It was simply a matter of changing times.

Caught between a waning interest in blues shouters and the sudden dominance of R&B by vocal groups, Roy Brown and many of his peers found themselves on the sidelines watching. Though Brown by rights should have been a big part of the rock and roll explosion of the 1950s, he was unable to ride the wave he helped create.

Brown explained his lack of hits after 1951 with a bluesman's directness: "Nobody can last forever. I had reached the stage where some of my ideas were becoming what I'd call obsolete."[14] Henry Glover always felt that Brown had the talent and the songs to maintain a hot career, but suggested one reason why that didn't happen: "If Roy had been a guitarist, he would be as popular today as B. B. King."[15]

The fates were kind to Roy Brown and allowed him a victory lap in the last years of his life. After years of recording for obscure record companies in the 1960s, Brown was "rediscovered" after a sterling performance at the 1970 Monterey Jazz Festival as part of bandleader Johnny Otis's show. Encouraged by the audience response, Brown began performing and recording again.

He made a triumphant return to his hometown in 1981, for a highly acclaimed appearance at the New Orleans Jazz and Heritage Festival. A few days later, Roy Brown was dead, the victim of a heart attack. Though it seemed he had been around forever, he was only fifty-six. The last song he performed on stage was "Good Rockin' Tonight." He has not yet been inducted into the Rock & Roll Hall of Fame.

As to whether Roy Brown was the first soul singer, as some have maintained, that's an ear-of-the-beholder kind of thing. Brown was at his peak about a decade before soul music is generally thought to have begun, but it's next to impossible to hear James Brown sing "Love Don't Love Nobody," or Jackie Wilson sing anything, and not hear Roy Brown loud and clear.

James Brown once said of his influence, "No one inspired me more than Roy Brown. Brown had the dynamics. That's the main reason I was able to sing hard, because I emulated him when I first started. I got the power and the drive from him and combined it with my gospel background. *That's* where the soul comes from."[16]

• • •

One of the more successful recording artists of the 1950s, Ivory Joe Hunter (1914–74) was just beginning his career when he recorded for King. His two biggest records, "I Almost Lost My Mind" and "Since I Met You Baby," would come for other labels, but the pianist and singer from Texas attained his hit-making stride with three big records on King in 1948. Hunter was gone by 1950, but he scored eight hit singles during his brief tenure on King.

Part of Hunter's success on King is due to the excellent musicians backing him on the thirty-plus songs he cut. "We had a special sound coming from Ivory Joe Hunter," explains Henry Glover, "and I would always make arrangements to catch the Duke Ellington band and use the men from that band to play behind Ivory

Joe. Russell Procope, who's a very fine alto saxophonist, played some of the leads. We had Ray Nance on some and had Sonny Greer on some, also Oscar Pettiford, Tyree Glenn, and Johnny Hodges. We used many of the Ellington musicians."[17]

Hunter's hot streak on King began with "What Did You Do to Me," "Don't Fall in Love with Me," and "I Like It." He cracked the R&B Top Ten in 1949 with "Guess Who" and "Landlord Blues," and had smaller hits with "Waitin' in Vain" and "Jealous Heart." In 1950, Hunter had hits with "I Quit My Pretty Mama," "Changing Blues," and "Please Don't Cry Anymore." And then he was gone to the greener pastures of MGM.

Myron "Tiny" Bradshaw, a native of Youngstown, Ohio, was a piano player, singer, songwriter, and bandleader who led one of the hottest R&B bands in an era of hard-stomping outfits. Bradshaw (1907–58) started his career as a drummer and then sang with a few groups before forming his own band in the mid-1930s. Bradshaw's band could excite any audience with its bluesy, Ellington-based sound. Over the years, the band produced such highly regarded tenor sax stars as Sonny Stitt, Red Prysock, and Sil Austin. Drummer Phillip Paul remembers those days well: "We knew we had to work hard . . . Oh God, we wore out tenor players."[18]

In many respects, Bradshaw's band illustrates the changes taking place in black popular music as it evolved from big-band swing in the 1930s to jump blues in the 1940s to rhythm and blues in the 1950s. Bradshaw's 1930s group was a typical big band, more hard-driving than some, but staffed by schooled, sophisticated players who had played with Duke Ellington and other prominent bandleaders.

By the time Bradshaw started recording for King in 1949, his band had been pared to a septet of trumpet, tenor sax, alto/baritone sax, piano, bass, drums, and guitar, plus Bradshaw on vocals. Bradshaw would occasionally augment the band with another piece or two, but the small band is heard on most of his King recordings. The band's stripped-down but powerful sound was immensely popular with R&B fans.

"Gravy Train," an instrumental from the band's first session, was a minor hit, but "Well, Oh Well," a Bradshaw vocal from the second session, raced up the chart, peaking at number two on *Billboard*. "Well, Oh Well" was King's biggest-selling R&B record of 1950.

Bradshaw's follow-up, "Boodie Green," was only a regional hit, but *its* follow-up, "I'm Going to Have Myself a Ball," was another smash, reaching number seven on the charts. He had three more hits the following year: "Breakin' Up the House," "Walk That Mess," and "Walkin' the Chalk Line."

The Tiny Bradshaw band was an especially popular live attraction, traveling the country on a regular basis in the early 1950s. The hits slowed down, with only

"The Train Kept A-Rollin'" and "Mailman's Sack" scoring in 1952. Bradshaw's original "The Train Kept A-Rollin'," however, would go on to become one of the archetypal songs of rock and roll, thanks to recordings by the Rock & Roll Trio (Johnny and Dorsey Burnette and Paul Burlison) in the 1950s, the Yardbirds in the 1960s, and Aerosmith in the 1970s.

Bradshaw bounced back in 1953, with the instrumental hits "Soft," "Heavy Juice," "Later," and "South of the Orient." Most of Bradshaw's big records from this point on were instrumentals, perhaps because of his worsening health, perhaps because of changing tastes in music, perhaps both.

Bradshaw had his last hits in 1954—"Ping Pong" (with a fine tenor sax solo by Sylvester "Sil" Austin), "Overflow," "Don't Worry 'bout Me," and "Spider Web." He had a stroke that same year and was left partially paralyzed. Bradshaw died four years later, not long after he cut a final record for King, a cover of the Royal Teens' hit "Short Shorts." It didn't make the charts.

• • •

King Records had a remarkable run of success during its first five years of recording and selling what was then called "race music." The first "race" record on King was released in the fall of 1947. By the end of 1948, King Records was the top-selling "race" label of the year, the first time an independent record company (that is, not Decca, Columbia, or RCA Victor) had achieved that feat.[19] This unprecedented coup was largely the result of three huge records: "Tomorrow Night" by Lonnie Johnson, "I Love You, Yes I Do" by Bull Moose Jackson, and "Good Rockin' To-night" by Wynonie Harris.

King Records dominated the year-end chart figures. Not only was King the top label, but Bull Moose Jackson was the year's top-selling "race" artist and "Tomorrow Night" was the year's top-selling "race" record.[20] Other King artists ranked in the "race" top ten for 1948 were Lonnie Johnson, Ivory Joe Hunter, The Ravens, and Wynonie Harris. Of the top eight "race" records of the year, five were on King.[21]

The pace waned only slightly in 1949, the year *Billboard* replaced the term "race" with "rhythm and blues." King slipped to third place among labels, but Bull Moose Jackson and Wynonie Harris kept their places in the artists' top ten.[22] King roared back into the top spot for 1950. Tiny Bradshaw's "Well, Oh Well" was the label's top R&B record for the year and Wynonie Harris its most successful artist. Over the next four years, King would never rank lower than third in the annual listing of R&B labels.[23]

By 1951, the sound of R&B was changing from jump blues bands fronted by a solo singer to close-harmony vocal groups. In true pop music fashion, it was out with the old and in with the new. The vocal groups were what the kids wanted.

WHERE THE HELL'S THE MELODY?

Country Music on King Records, Part 2

•••

People use that term "hillbilly music" wrongly.
Actually, this music is the music of the masses.

—Sydney Nathan

According to mandolinist/funnyman Jethro Burns, a banner hung across the entrance to the King recording studio that asked the pointed question, "Where the hell's the melody?" Even if that's not literally true, and with Jethro one never knew, it *should* be true, because it was one of Syd Nathan's favorite questions in the studio—usually delivered in a hoarse, raspy, high-volume roar, sarcasm dripping from every word.

When Nathan asked Burns a similar question before hiring him to play on King recording sessions, Burns thought Nathan was pulling his leg. "Syd heard us [Burns and his partner, guitarist Homer Haynes] on an early-morning radio program one time playing an instrumental, just mandolin and guitar," said Burns.[1] "Right after the show he called and I talked to him. And he says, 'Can you play melody?' I said, 'Well, certainly I can play melody.' Then he said, 'Let's put it this way: *Will* you play melody?' I said, 'I'll do whatever the job calls for.'

"What he wanted was just a plain, simple melody that people would recognize, but he said everybody was so intent on being a hot-shot musician, nobody would do that. So, that's how Homer and I got the job in the so-called house band at King."

At various times and in varying combinations, that King "house band" would include Burns, Haynes, steel guitar master Jerry Byrd, fiddlers Tommy Jackson

and Red Herron, pianist Shorty Long, bass player/rhythm guitarist Louis Innis, and electric lead guitarists Zeke Turner, Al Myers, Roy Lanham, and Jackie
Phelps. Sometimes artists would bring one or two members of their bands into
the studio, and the house band would fill in as needed. For other sessions, the
house band was the only backing.

Nathan loved having this talented bunch of seasoned professionals available to
him, not only because they were great musicians but also because of the comfort
that came from working with the same people on a regular basis. Nathan didn't
much care for chaos in the recording studio unless he was the one creating it. As
Grandpa Jones laughingly recounted, "One time he had a bunch of musicians in
there in the studio and they couldn't get it together. Syd hollered through the
mike, 'Boys, shake hands and get acquainted.'"[2]

Unlike many who worked with Nathan in the studio, Jethro Burns appreciated
Nathan's contributions. "Sydney could spot a good take," said Burns.[3] "A lot of
guys, a lot of A&R men, can't do that. He had a feeling for it. Sydney could always
pick out the one that had the fire, the one that was exciting. What I liked about
Syd was that he wouldn't throw away a great take—say the vocalist had a great
take—because of a slight clinker in the instrumental track. He'd say, 'Nobody's
gonna notice that on a jukebox or when they hear it on the radio. Nobody will
notice one bad note if it's a great song.'"

The country releases on King possessed a distinctive feel, characterized by "a
mixture of acoustic and electric instruments," according to country music historian
Charles Wolfe. "Usually a rather delicate mixture—the electric instruments were
not overdone. Most of the King sessions would have maybe one electric guitar
and maybe a steel guitar, but the rest of it would be acoustic [instruments]. The
'King sound' still had a down-home sound to it.

"Syd Nathan let the musicians do what they wanted to do. So you had people
up there like Merle Travis experimenting with the sounds of the new electric guitar. You had Zeke Turner virtually inventing what later became [the foundation
of] rockabilly guitar licks. These people were allowed to get in the studio and do
pretty much what they wanted to with their music. That was one of the things
that made King great."[4]

• • •

One of the biggest records in King's first couple of years was a song dating to the
Spanish-American war, performed by a singing "cowboy" from Ohio. Lloyd Estel
Copas (1913–63) might not have been much of a hand at ropin' steers or bustin'
broncs, but as Cowboy Copas, he helped keep King Records afloat in the early

years. His string of successes began with his first release, "Filipino Baby," a Top Five *Billboard* country hit and among the top records of 1946.

Copas was born in rural Adams County, Ohio, and was still a teenager when he teamed up with Lester Storer, a fiddler whose stage name was Natchee the Indian (the likely origin of the "Cowboy" nickname). Natchee and Copas played at fiddler's contests and exhibitions throughout the area, often in staged "competitions" with famed fiddler Clayton McMichen. Copas eventually went out on his own, and by the early 1940s, he was in Cincinnati working on *The Boone County Jamboree*.

Copas first recorded for King in 1944, backed by a small group that included fiddler Red Herron and electric guitarist Roy Lanham. That initial session produced "Filipino Baby," "I Don't Blame You," "There Ain't Nobody Gonna Miss Me," and the hit "Tragic Romance."

The popularity of those singles earned Copas an invitation in 1945 to join Pee Wee King & The Golden West Cowboys, a popular act on the *Grand Ole Opry*. That group accompanied Copas on his next recording session, held during the summer of 1946. Highlights of the session include a beautiful version of Buddy Starcher's ballad "Sweet Thing," as well as a romping "Sundown and Sorrow" and the charged playing of fiddler Shorty Boyd and electric guitarist Jimmie Wilson.

Copas really hit his stride in 1947, when he formed his own group, the Oklahoma Cowboys. He had four big hits the next year, "Signed, Sealed and Delivered," "Breeze," "Tennessee Moon," and "The Tennessee Waltz" (recorded roughly three years before Patti Page's huge pop hit with the song).

The hits continued into the early 1950s: "I'm Waltzing with Tears in My Eyes," "Candy Kisses," the sardonic "Hangman's Boogie" (with a great guitar solo by Merle Travis), "The Strange Little Girl," and "'Tis Sweet to Be Remembered." And then in 1952, the hits dried up for the "Waltz King of the *Grand Ole Opry*."

Despite his stage name and the fact that he often claimed to be from Oklahoma (his publicity materials worked this angle shamelessly), Cowboy Copas was not a singing cowboy. Nor was he a honky-tonk singer, as were most of the country singers who rose to popularity in the post-war years. Copas had a lilting yet powerful tenor voice that was well suited to the waltzes and love songs that made up most of his repertoire.

The records Copas made for King display the delicate balance between tradition and modernism that Charles Wolfe felt was so distinctive to King. Copas was among the most traditionally oriented country stars of the post-war years, firmly rooted in an earlier era and seemingly unfazed by the changes of the honky-tonk movement within country music. The instrumentation for most of his records was relatively spare, usually just Copas' acoustic guitar and an electric guitar and fiddle, with bass or steel guitar added occasionally.

But then right in the middle of one of those records, the electric guitarist—it might be Roy Lanham, Jethro Burns, or Zeke Turner—rips off some totally unexpected bebop-tinged solo that is both astounding and completely appropriate to the song. These moments just kind of pop up in the records.

After Copas's string of hits ended for King in the mid-1950s, he, as did many other country artists upended by the rock and roll juggernaut, drifted through the end of the decade. But lightning struck twice for Copas. After being signed to Starday in 1960, Copas enjoyed the first number one hit of his career, "Alabam."

He followed that with a few smaller hits for Starday over the next three years. Copas is best remembered today, unfortunately, for being killed in the same 1963 plane crash that took the lives of fellow country stars Patsy Cline and Hawkshaw Hawkins. Copas's final hit, co-written with Lefty Frizzell, was "Goodbye Kisses."

Bandleader, guitarist, and singer Hank Penny was among the artists who helped launch King in 1944. Herbert Clayton "Hank" Penny (1918–92), a native of Birmingham, Alabama, placed three records in the country Top Five during his tenure with King in the late 1940s. An early and ardent proponent of the hot jazz sounds of western swing, he was one of the few bandleaders of that style based in the southeast.

Penny formed his first band, the Radio Cowboys, in 1936 after spending three years in a group led by "Happy" Hal Burns. He worked on powerful radio station WSB in Atlanta for four years and then moved to WLW in Cincinnati in 1942 to join *The Boone Country Jamboree.* Once there, Penny began working with the Plantation Boys, an outfit of WLW regulars that included the great Roy Lanham on electric guitar.

A popular singer and comedian on WLW, Penny first recorded for King late in 1944. His debut release coupled "Tear Stains on Your Pillow" and "Last Night." Two more songs were recorded at the session, and although none of the four made much of an impact, "Last Night" is a satisfying slice of pounding swing with a hot solo by Lanham.

Penny was a realist. He knew early on that he wasn't a great singer. "I [didn't] have an identifiable Ernest Tubb-Roy Acuff-Al Dexter sound," Penny said.[5] "And that's good, fine for them. But for me it poses a problem . . . Let me do something I know I can entertain them with, and that's comedy."

Modern listeners might think Penny was a bit hard on himself as a singer. He wasn't the best in the business, but Penny was far more than adequate as a vocalist. He had an accessible and pleasant sound, and was quite effective on such songs as "My Little Red Wagon," "Bloodshot Eyes," "Locked Out," and "The Solitary Blues."

Clever novelty songs such as "Bloodshot Eyes," his original and mordant classic from 1950, accounted for part of Penny's appeal, but another factor was the extremely high level of musicianship in his band. Among the superb players who recorded in Penny's band are steel guitarists Noel Boggs, Speedy West, and Herb Remington; fiddlers Buddy Ray, Harold Hensley, and Zed Tennis; electric guitarists Roy Lanham and Jimmy Wyble; and pianist Jo Ella Wright.

That firepower is best heard on such instrumentals as "Steel Guitar Stomp," "Steel Guitar Polka," "Jersey Bounce," "Hillbilly Bebop," and "Remington Ride," the steel guitar standard that's been recorded by musicians ranging from bluegrass banjo picker Don Reno to blues guitarist Freddie King. "Hillbilly Bebop" is likely the first country music tune to acknowledge (and embrace) the style that revolutionized jazz in the late 1940s.

Penny was a funny and fun-loving kind of guy, but Nathan badly misjudged Penny's sense of humor in 1947 and inflicted a mortal blow to their relationship. Penny showed up for a recording session in Cincinnati and found that Syd wanted him to record a pair of double-entendre numbers, "The Freckle Song" and "Let Me Play with Your Poodle," a blues hit for Tampa Red earlier in the decade.

Penny was appalled. "I did not want to record these [songs]. Nathan insisted that I record them. I felt they were too risqué and recorded them under the condition that [King] would release them under the name of the Freckle Faced Boys. I turned around and he'd released them under *my* name. It got some dates canceled for me and caused extreme difficulty. I feel that was the thing that caused Syd and me to eventually split up."[6]

After making nearly seventy records for the label, Hank Penny left King in 1950 for RCA Victor. He had no more hits after that but had a full and varied career nonetheless, doing extensive TV work as a comedian, recording for RCA and Decca, helping to establish country music as a viable attraction in Las Vegas, appearing in several films, and owning and operating one of the west coast's premier country music nightspots, the Palomino Club in North Hollywood. He died in 1992.

The musical comedy duo of Homer & Jethro recorded around thirty songs for King (and had just one hit, "I Feel That Old Age Creeping On" in 1949), but the importance of the two men to the label was much greater than those numbers suggest. Henry "Homer" Haynes (1920–71) and Kenneth "Jethro" Burns (1920–89) were key members of King's house band and played on dozens of the label's early country records. And after they convinced Nathan to let them try, the two men launched a recording career that would eventually earn them a Grammy Award and induction into the Country Music Hall of Fame.

Nathan had first contacted Haynes and Burns after hearing them play "Swanee River" with just mandolin and guitar on an early-morning program on WLW. Nathan loved their direct approach to the tune and hired them to "play the melody."

"We did two years of just sideman stuff, studio stuff," said Burns.[7] "Meanwhile, we were just pestering Sydney to death to let us do our own record. He said, 'Aw, that crazy stuff ain't gonna sell.' And we said, 'How do you know? You've got to let us try it.'

"Finally, we had gotten to be such good friends with Syd from working together so much, he said, 'Okay, I'll let you make a record. But I'm not gonna put out any money for a band, so you can have a bass player.' So we cut our first tune with just mandolin, guitar, and bass, and, of course, the vocal. It was a tune called 'Five Minutes More,' a take-off on a Frank Sinatra hit, and it was an instant hit."

Doing "take-offs" on pop songs was nothing new for the duo. Though Homer and Jethro claimed to hail from Hoot 'n' Holler, Tennessee, the two were actually from the Knoxville area. Twelve years old when they met, Homer, then known as Junior, and Jethro, then known as Dude, hit it off right away. Placed together in a band called the String Dusters by the program director of Knoxville radio station WNOX, Junior and Dude played a bit of everything with the band—country, pop, jazz, blues, show tunes—whatever was currently popular.

Mandolinist Burns and guitarist Haynes continued on the station as a duo after the band broke up. The two had started to specialize in versions of current pop hits delivered in the style of a country music "brother duet." At the beginning of one of their programs, the announcer went completely blank on their names, finally stammering out "Homer and Jethro." The highly amused teenagers would use those names for the next four decades.

Homer and Jethro came to Cincinnati in 1945 to work at WLW, appearing both on country programs and on the station's pop and variety programs. They were soon playing on sessions for King.

Over the course of the next five years, Burns and Haynes played on a staggering number of King sessions. Together and separately, they provided instrumental support for Grandpa Jones, Moon Mullican, the Delmore Brothers, Cowboy Co-pas, Hank Penny, Hawkshaw Hawkins, Wayne Raney, Clyde Moody, and many more. As gifted musically as they were funny, they made major contributions to King's distinctive "modern traditional" sound.

Playing on sessions at King was never dull. "Grandpa Jones in the studio was like a wild man," Burns laughingly recalled.[8] "We were in the studio one time working on the song 'Mountain Dew.' He must have done twenty-five or thirty takes on the thing. And that's when they used the discs to record on [magnetic recording tape was still a few years in the future], and every time you goofed, they had to take the disc off, throw it away, put on a new one, and start all over.

"This went on and on and on, and finally Grandpa got it so it was just perfect. He was so happy. 'We got her,' he said. 'We got her.'

"About that time, Syd walks into the studio with a group of maybe twenty people. Tourists, you know, just some people who wanted to see a recording studio. Grandpa says, 'That was pretty good wasn't it, Sydney, that last take? That was pretty good, wasn't it?'

"And Syd says, 'I don't know, Grandpa, I didn't have the machine on.' With that, Grandpa let some obscenities go that would have shocked even Lenny Bruce and fired his banjo into the nearest wall. It took us a couple of hours until we could get Grandpa settled down enough to continue."

Although their records for King were not as successful (or as sophisticated) as their later RCA hits such as "(How Much Is) That Hound Dog in the Window" and "Baby, It's Cold Outside," the King releases by Homer & Jethro are entertaining. "Over the Rainbow," "It Bruised Her Somewhat," "Night and Day," and "Glow Worm" are among the high points in their catalog, but worthwhile moments are scattered throughout the duo's recorded blend of lunacy and instrumental virtuosity.

According to Burns, "The reason we left King was that Syd and I got into it over a song. Homer and I wrote a song called 'I Feel That Old Age Creeping On,' and we recorded it and had a nice little record on it. Well, then, Syd took the song, changed one word in it—from creeping to coming—and had Wynonie Harris record it.

"Of course, it was a big hit and made a lot of money, but Syd took half of the song. It was out and out thievery. He just took the song. I had him over a barrel and he knew it. I said, 'Okay, you've got my song but instead of going to court over it, just give me Homer & Jethro's contract.' So he gave us the contract, gave us our release, and we immediately signed with RCA."[9]

Homer & Jethro had a number of hits for RCA, won a Grammy Award in 1959, worked extensively with comedians Bob & Ray, appeared on the major television variety shows, and did a series of funny radio and TV commercials for Kellogg's Corn Flakes. The two also recorded a pair of outstanding instrumental albums for RCA that showcased their musical prowess, *It Ain't Necessarily Square* and *Playing It Straight*.

After Homer Haynes died in 1971, Jethro Burns worked for a few years with Chicago singer/songwriter Steve Goodman, recorded with Chet Atkins, and toured and recorded as a solo act. Burns was also something of a guru for young, progressive-minded mandolinists such as David Grisman and Sam Bush. Jethro Burns died in 1989. The duo of Homer & Jethro was inducted into the Country Music Hall of Fame in 2001.

BUSINESS AS USUAL
WAS PRETTY UNUSUAL

Behind the Scenes at King Records

• • •

I sold records in a location nobody could sell a
record in. It was like trying to sell grand pianos
out in the desert. But we done business because
we knew how to do business.

—Sydney Nathan

Syd Nathan *was* King Records. The company was shaped in his image and mir-
rored his eccentricities. By turns progressive and conservative (sometimes both
at one time), King Records was an unusual company, to say the least. The label
was every bit as innovative and influential in its business practices as it was on
the creative side of the company.

King Records changed the way vernacular American music was recorded and
marketed, and King was the model for more than one record company. After a
couple of stumbles at the beginning, King prospered and grew, eventually becoming
one of the country's most successful record companies. Nathan's bravado helped
to mask his doubts and inexperience, but he was often making it up as he went
along, following his instincts and hoping for the best.

By the time he was through, Nathan had assembled a business empire that
included a record company (actually several labels), a recording studio, a pressing plant to manufacture records, a printing plant to print the record covers and
promotional materials, a national sales and distribution network with thirty-three
regional branch offices, a trucking company to deliver the records to the branches,
and even a line of record players—achieving as close to complete vertical integration as any record company has ever come.

Nathan marched to his own drummer when it came to running a record company. King was never a democracy. Nathan was the absolute monarch of this King-

dom. He was open to innovation and new ideas, but he could also be an autocratic ruler, sometimes crude and bullying. James Brown called him "Little Caesar."

Nathan was matter-of-fact about his management style: "You may disagree with me one hundred percent, but somebody has to be the chief, and I am elected. I am spending my money, not yours, so it will have to be as I say . . . The Big Chief is the one who tells you what to do."[1]

On the other hand, Nathan addressed King employees at an open meeting of the Artists and Repertoire (A&R) department in 1954 and said, "We have told other people throughout the organization that they are welcome to attend, welcome to talk, welcome to voice themselves in any way that they want to. Because only by voicing yourself are we able to get to the basis of what we might call company policy. Somebody has to set the company policy. I try to. And I'm pretty damn stubborn. But I'll tell you this: You show me something better than what I'm doing, you convince me in my mind, I'll do it."[2]

Nathan had a gruff manner, but he was also a charming and funny man. Most of his former associates and employees remember Nathan fondly. King Records in its heyday was an exciting place to be, its atmosphere charged with possibility. A big part of that came from Nathan's vision for King: "The impossible we can do right now. The absolutely impossible takes a day longer."[3]

Though he released records in late 1943 and early 1944, Nathan had neglected a few technicalities, including actually "forming" King Records in any legal sense. Perhaps Nathan wanted to make sure the company was a go before he did anything that cost money. By August 1944, he felt secure enough to make it official. King Records was legally incorporated in the state of Ohio.

Besides Nathan, the original partners in the corporation were Nathan's sister Dorothy Halper; Doris Nathan, the wife of Nathan's brother David; Bernice Steinberg, a cousin; Howard Kessel, another cousin; and family friend Lawrence Sick. The corporation was started with around $25,000 in capital.[4]

King Records needed a home, which was found on Brewster Avenue in the Evanston section of Cincinnati, in a neighborhood of residential, commercial, and industrial buildings. Nathan signed a five-year lease for a building at 1540 Brewster that had most recently housed a chemical extract manufacturing company. Next door, at 1538 Brewster, was the Avondale Ice Company.[5] Because of that building, which King eventually occupied, the King complex would forever after be known as "the icehouse."

The place must have come cheap, because little else would seem to recommend it. The building was a dump and required extensive work before the company could move in. Nathan and his fellow owners plunged in, doing much of the manual labor themselves. As Nathan told a reporter in 1951, "I dug holes and put in pipes.

I tore down stuff and put stuff up. And this building we had found, it used to be some sort of chemical plant and they had made a kind of syrup. There was sticky stuff all over everything."[6]

In the midst of this construction work, Nathan made several trips to New York for cataract surgery. His vision, which had always been poor, was now just about gone. Nathan was practically blind. Surgery offered hope of restored vision, but also the risk of total blindness. Nathan took the gamble. It required four operations, but the procedure was successful. Outfitted with new, ultra-thick, "triple-lensed" glasses, Nathan could see again.

Between operations, Nathan returned to Cincinnati to work on his new building. He usually had a patch over one eye and minimal vision in the other. He had to be led around the site, but Nathan worked anyway, though he really couldn't see what he was doing. He hammered his thumbs, sawed his fingers, banged his head on dimly seen obstacles. Finally, by the end of October, Nathan and his crew had made enough progress to let the world in on their secret. The time had come for King Records to be formally introduced.

The world was not exactly overwhelmed. *The Cincinnati Times Star* ran a small article on November 1, 1944, under the bare-bones headline "Phonograph Records to Be Made Here."

"A new industry for Cincinnati," announced the article, "was revealed in the formation of the King Record Company to manufacture phonograph records. Sidney [sic] Nathan . . . senior partner and majority owner of the new enterprise here, stated that a factory site already has been leased . . . Machinery and equipment is being installed in the area of 9,000 square feet and production is expected to be underway in about 30 days.

"'At the outset,' Nathan said, 'we will use only hillbilly music and vocal numbers. We intend to later produce records of "hot jazz" and sepia music. All recordings will be original numbers and made by our company.' A staff of writers has been secured and such stars of the hill-billy field as the Delmore Brothers [and] Grandpa Jones . . . have been signed, according to Nathan . . . About 70 persons will be employed when the plant begins operations and an initial output of 10,000 records a day is expected by Nathan."[7]

Years later, Nathan's sister Dorothy Halper said even that interest was more than King usually received: "The newspapers weren't interested. Nobody cared about King Records. The city wasn't proud of its association. I think people in other cities were more interested and impressed with the company."[8]

• • •

Nathan learned an expensive but valuable lesson from the Bob McCarthy and Sheppard Brothers records in 1943. To oversimplify a complicated process, there are basically five areas in which a record can go bad: (1) the artist; (2) the material; (3) the performance; (4) the recording of the performance; and (5) the manufacturing of the actual record. King's first releases were disasters in the latter two areas.

Many people would have quit then and moved on, but that wasn't Nathan's way. What he learned from the fiasco was that the more parts of the process he could control, and the less he left to other people, the greater his odds for success. Nathan was a firm believer in the old adage "If you want something done right, do it yourself." He took that idea about as far as a person could over the next two decades.

Before Nathan built his own recording studio, he worked with Earl Herzog, a WLW engineer who was doing freelance recording at his house. Herzog had been engineering remote broadcasts for WLW for several years and was, like many early studio operators, an ardent tinkerer and electronics hobbyist. Forty years later, he still got excited as he described his first studio.

"Out of a lot of junk material, I built a recording table—all out of scrap, junk," Herzog said.[9] "I had it set up at home. I was doing things thing like 'air checks' for the artists at WLW, various radio programs, and making very good quality records. Somehow or other, Syd Nathan heard about this recording equipment I had and he called me up.

"He insisted that I try to make some master recordings for him. These were some of the very first that he ever put out. So I reluctantly gave in, and we had the group right there in my living room at home. We cut right on to the acetates then, and if they flubbed it, you put a new disc on and cut another one."

It got pretty hectic at Herzog's home studio, and Herzog soon realized he would have to move the studio out of his house if he wanted to have any family life or sanity left. His new operation, E.T. Herzog Recording Studio, opened in 1945. It was one of the first commercial studios to record country music, and Herzog was kept busy. He modestly downplayed his technical expertise and gave the credit for the studio's success to the availability of the outstanding musicians working at WLW, several of whom also played in the King "house band."

"There was available in Cincinnati at that time the best back-up men of any place in the country," asserted Herzog.[10] "They were here before Nashville ever knew what it was all about. Over at our studio there, we had Capitol, Columbia, [and] RCA bring talent to Cincinnati for the sidemen." "I'm So Lonesome I Could Cry" and "Lovesick Blues" by Hank Williams and "Foggy Mountain Breakdown" by Flatt & Scruggs are just three of the many hits recorded at Herzog's studio.

"They came in there for Jerry Byrd on that steel guitar—he was one of the greatest in the country. And Homer [Haynes] and Jethro [Burns] were two of the greatest sidemen you ever saw. Those guys were just tremendous, one with guitar and one with his little old mandolin. We worked with all the big names in the business at one time or another over there because of the sidemen.

"I built a recording studio down at 811 Race Street. We had pretty good equipment then, commercial equipment, and a nice size studio. [Nathan] started bringing talent in there, both country-western and some of the black groups. He was doing stuff there, he was doing stuff in New York, and various places wherever he could get talent signed up.

"Syd was rather difficult to work with, to put it mildly. He seemed to have a difficult time trying to get across what he had in his mind to the musicians. He would go into tantrums when something went wrong and just cuss out everybody in the place. If he would have been calm, and stopped and thought and listened, but he didn't do it that way. He'd get up and blow his top first and get everybody upset. The sessions would get worse, and the worse they got, the worse he got.

"It made it very difficult to record with him. We finally couldn't take it anymore and had to ask him to take his business elsewhere. Well, there was no place else in Cincinnati he could take his business. That's when he started building his own studio."[11]

Nathan had painted himself into a corner and had no choice, really, but to build his own studio. It would take a couple of years, but a fully functional recording studio was up and running in the Brewster Avenue complex by the late 1940s, a first for an independent label.

Until that studio was finished, recordings were done at Brewster Avenue, in the office of King's accounting department—but only at night. When the whistle blew and the staff went home for the day, Nathan and anybody else who might be around for the session pushed the desks and filing cabinets to one side of the room and set up microphones in the cleared space. A small control booth sat at the end of the room, separated from the room by a glass window. It wasn't elegant, but it worked.

Nathan found that building a record manufacturing facility (or "pressing plant") was much more difficult. Pressing records was a complex industrial process, involving several intermediate manufacturing steps and a variety of specialized machinery. It required extensive capital and technical knowledge that Nathan lacked, so he first tried finding established pressing plants he could use as an independent client.

The search didn't go well. Plant after plant shipped Nathan defective records. Some were warped, some were pressed off-center, some were mislabeled. "Nobody did it right," Nathan complained. "They kept bouncing me around."[12]

Remembering those first records at a King sales meeting in the early 1950s, Nathan deadpanned, "I don't know if they used them for soup bowls or records. They would have made beautiful soup bowls. Oh, they were dished beautifully. You could have run a little mouse race around there—it was perfectly banked."[13]

In desperation, Nathan decided that King Records would have to build and operate its own pressing plant. There was simply no other way. Nathan knew nothing about building a pressing plant, not even where or how to get started. So he went to the public library. He found only one book on the subject, a work about "gramophone records written by an Englishman" that was of little help. "I couldn't catch on," Nathan confessed to a reporter a few years later. "I didn't know what he was talking about."[14]

Nathan asked around at a few pressing plants, but found there was little interest in sharing technical information with a would-be competitor. He was at wit's end when he heard of a pressing plant just a couple of hours away in Louisville, Kentucky, that was, by its very nature, accessible to the public. This facility had been established by the American Printing House for the Blind, under the aegis of the Library of Congress, to make "talking books" for the visually impaired.

As a tax-funded public institution, the pressing plant was more or less open to visitors, and Nathan took full advantage of this policy. He found an invaluable adviser at the plant in George W. Weitlauf, a recording engineer who had worked with Decca and Victor.

Nathan visited Weitlauf frequently in Louisville, absorbing all he could from the engineer and then returning to Cincinnati to try to put the knowledge into practice. When technical problems arose, Nathan phoned Weitlauf and picked his brain about possible solutions. Finally, in 1945, Nathan persuaded Weitlauf to move to Cincinnati to become King's general superintendent of operations, a post he held for several years.

Even with Weitlauf on board, there were problems with the equipment. One early machine exploded on being started and others refused to work properly. A 1951 magazine article captured those early days of setting up King's pressing plant:

"Back in 1945 a half-dozen men stood around a phonograph record press in a Cincinnati building which had been a chemical plant not long before. Inside the press was a record on which a gentleman named Cowboy Copas sang. And outside the press was that expectant air which comes at great moments, for this was the first record to be pressed in the King record plant. 'Okay, open it,' said one of the men.

"It was then that they discovered there [was no way to open] the press. An oversight. They got it open with a six-foot crowbar. Then they couldn't get the record loose. After a half-hour of prying with pocket knives, it came clean. At this point, a short, round man with heavy-lensed glasses [Nathan] held the record aloft and said in a tone of solemn pronouncement, 'This ——— record cost sixty-five thousand dollars.'"[15]

Despite the problems, King's pressing plant was soon operational, turning out two hundred records per day in 1945. By 1951, the company had almost forty record presses online, capable of producing approximately one million records per month.[16] At that time, the company made only 78-rpm records; it would later make both 45-rpm singles and 33⅓-rpm albums.

Technically, the pressing plant was a separate company, the Royal Plastics Company, headed by Howard Kessel.[17] This in-house capability to manufacture records, again a first for an independent label, gave King a tremendous advantage over its competitors.

For one thing, it allowed King a high degree of flexibility. "If one of King's 33 branches suddenly calls long-distance for, say, 300 copies of a record which can't be supplied from inventory," explained an early 1950s account, "a number less urgent will be jerked off a press to make way for the order. Syd rides herd on this production problem like a bellowing cow-hand directing the doggies into the right corrals."[18]

"King was successful for several reasons," says historian Charles Wolfe.[19] "One of the main ones was because they had their own pressing plant and could therefore control the product that came out. They didn't have to depend on the big companies to do it. I think people underestimate the importance of that pressing plant there in Cincinnati. You talk to other independent record labels, and that's always a problem for them—getting those records pressed up and sent out."

The other big advantage the pressing plant gave King was speed. "King was a completely self-contained unit," says Jim Wilson, a long-time record man who started with King in 1949 as a branch manager in Detroit. You could literally go in and cut the record in the morning and walk out with the finished product in your hand that evening.

"We were able to move very quickly on a record. We could cover a record on a smaller label that did not have [national] distribution. Say a record was breaking out in California. If it was something we felt had national possibilities, we could get a copy of the record in, bring in the artist we thought would fit to the [song], cut it, and have it out on the street and selling before the other record ever got out of California."[20]

• • •

For all its musical, business, and technical innovations, what *really* set King Records apart from other record companies of the time was what we now call a company's "culture." King was dominated by the larger-than-life presence of Syd Nathan, whose management style could perhaps best be described as "autocratic anarchy." King, however, ran along remarkably progressive lines in many respects. One theme in particular pops up time and again in talking with veterans of King. Jim Wilson expressed it simply: "There was no color line at King."[21]

That was because of Nathan. "We give everybody an even break," he said in 1950. "This is because I'm a Jew and I know what obstacles are. A Jew may have it rough but a Negro has it a lot rougher. A good man is a good man; his religion or his race isn't going to make any difference. At King we pay for ability and that's what we get. Our people get along fine together, and we aren't fooling when we say we don't discriminate."[22]

Nathan's personal feelings laid the philosophical groundwork for the label, but the 1947 hiring of Ben Siegel as King's personnel manager established a progressive racial approach as formal company policy. Siegel took the position with the understanding that he could shape and implement King's human resources policies "as he saw fit."

Siegel's vision was a color-blind company in which everyone got an equal chance to succeed and talent and ability were what mattered, not race or gender. This is not to suggest that King was a utopia of perfect harmony and peace—this *was* King Records, after all—but Siegel's policies were innovative enough to attract outside attention.

A 1949 article in the *Cincinnati Post* noted Siegel's achievements. "Two years ago," wrote Jerry Ransohoff, "they told Ben Siegel, of the King Record Co., that it couldn't be done. 'Cincinnati is a border town,' said the skeptics. 'You can't get Negroes and white people to work together. It's too close to the south.'

"But Mr. Siegel didn't believe them. He told Sidney [*sic*] Nathan and Howard Kassel [*sic*], officers of the company, that he'd be King's personnel manager only if they'd let him run his department as he saw fit. They backed his policies.

"The skeptics were wrong. King [now has] 400 employees and the non-discrimination policies have needed no 'backing.' Here's the way things stand today: The musical director, assistant office manager, foreman of the mill room, set-up man on the production line, assistant promotion director, legal secretary, a dozen stenographers and 20 percent of the factory workers are Negroes. There is a Chinese bookkeeping machine operator and a Japanese comptometer operator.

"All groups have joined on summer picnics, Christmas parties and baseball games. 'We pay for ability,' says Mr. Siegel, 'and ability has no color, no race and no religion. Our hiring policy and our promotion system are based only on the question of the individual's capacity to fill a given job.'"[23]

The application form for employment at King Records asked if applicants would have any problems working with, or for, a person of another race, religion, or nationality. An affirmative answer to that question did not necessarily disqualify an applicant, however, because Siegel believed that people could change and that prejudice is most often rooted in the fear of the unknown.

Siegel felt that the personal relationships forged by working together—by simply getting to know people as individuals—could overcome all but the most stubborn bigotry. It seems he was right more often than not when it came to King Records.

The "skeptics" who tried to discourage Siegel had it backwards when they said that King Records couldn't succeed in a "border town" like Cincinnati. In fact, King Records could have flourished *only* in a border town like Cincinnati. "What happened at King," says Robert Santelli, historian at the Rock & Roll Hall of Fame, "couldn't have happened in New York or Los Angeles. Cincinnati always had one foot in the North, and one in the South, with access to blacks of the industrial cities as well as the Appalachians."[24]

Or, as Nathan so diplomatically put it: "We're in the mid-West, and we are not contaminated by New York, Los Angeles, or Chicago."[25]

• • •

As difficult as it was for a small record company to get a song recorded and pressed, that turned out to be the easy part. The hard part for an independent record company was—and is today—getting records into retail stores and then getting paid for those records. The major labels solved the first part of the problem by handling distribution in-house. Columbia, RCA, and Decca had sales and promotion people in key cities around the country to get their records to retail and jukebox accounts and played on the radio.

The newer independent companies did not have the money for that approach and had to rely instead on a new player in the record business, the independent distributor. These distributors popped up across the country in the 1940s and 1950s and played a vital role in marketing and promoting the music of hundreds of record labels.

In theory, the distributors—which were often small, undercapitalized companies—would provide the local sales and promotional muscle for each of the labels the distributor represented. Sometimes the process worked great, but even in the best of times, any label was still just one of many the distributor was selling.

"My problem with Starday Records," said label president Don Pierce, "was always to get an adequate effort from a distributor who was representing thirty or forty different small labels. Really, they can't go out and work on each of those lines. They largely become simply an order-taker [from retail accounts]. RCA Victor had strictly RCA distributors, and Decca had its own branch distributors, as did Capitol and Columbia. I had to share my distributors with fifty competitors."[26]

Another problem with independent distributors was that they were usually regional in scope rather than national. A label wanting a national presence had to put together a network of distributors, each of which represented the label in its own region. To achieve national distribution, a label might have to work with ten or fifteen different regional distributors, each with its own sales and promotion staff.

Nathan didn't think much of that system. He realized early that without good distribution, the rest of what you did as a record company didn't really matter. As he often pointed out, when it comes to records, "There's only one guaranteed sale: the guy's mother."[27]

To solve King's distribution problems, Nathan emulated the major labels and set up his own system of regional branch sales offices. These offices handled only King products, representing the label to retail accounts, jukebox operators, and radio stations. At its peak, the network included thirty-three branch offices in such major cities as New York, Los Angeles, and Chicago, as well as in such regional music centers as Cincinnati, Detroit, Memphis, Philadelphia, Dallas, Nashville, and Charlotte. As the sales reps at these offices made contacts within the industry and learned the ropes of local promotion, the branch offices grew into an invaluable resource for King Records.

Jim Wilson remembers the early days of the branch offices as hectic, but also satisfying: "At the beginning, we didn't have a promotion person, per se, at the Detroit branch office. Every King branch was the same way. I covered the radio stations, the retail accounts, packed records, whatever. We all really worked at it, and developed the Detroit branch from nothing into King's number one branch. Detroit was a very good market, both for country product and black product."[28]

King's salesmen spent countless hours on the road, but their work paid off, sometimes in ways that weren't fully reflected on the industry charts. In many small communities, King records were sold in unconventional locations—general stores, barber shops, restaurants, juke joints, and furniture stores—places that were not tracked by the trade magazines that published the weekly record sales charts.

Veteran musician Rusty York noticed something on his travels through backwater America: "In the little hollows down in Kentucky, and in the coal mining towns, you could always buy a King record. You couldn't find too many RCA Victors or Columbias down there in those days, but you could find the Kings. That's why Nathan was so successful."[29]

The time spent on the road by King's salesmen paid another dividend, as their travel expenses were at least partly responsible for Nathan's decision to start recording black musicians on Queen. Nathan realized travel was a necessary evil for his salesmen, but the fact that they made no money while driving from town to town irked him so much that he took steps to maximize their sales opportunities.

"We started as hillbilly," Nathan explained. "Then, we saw the need to go into other categories in the record business. Why should we go into these towns and only sell to hillbilly accounts? Why can't we sell a few more while we're there? You don't make any money when your car's rolling. So we branched into the race business and started the Queen label."[30]

King's distribution network was effective, but also quite expensive to maintain. The expense was bearable as long as King was cranking out hit records on a regular basis and making lots of money. But that was no longer the case by the early 1960s, and Nathan was forced to close the branch offices in 1964. While it lasted, though, King's distribution system worked very well and was a significant factor in the growth and profitability of the label. It's a big reason why King enjoyed national success for almost twenty-five years while so many other independent labels failed.

Other pieces of infrastructure would be added at Brewster Avenue as Nathan had the money or felt a need. A printing shop was set up to produce advertising and promotional materials, record labels, and album covers. A shipping department was added to service the branch offices. There was even a fleet of delivery trucks for a couple of years.

"One of Syd's early innovations," remembers Jim Wilson, "was taking a panel truck, stocking it up with records, and going out on the road. We tried this first in West Virginia, in the area where West Virginia, Kentucky, and Ohio all come together. We'd call on the dealer, go back out to the truck and pull his order, go back inside and hand it to him. I think this may have been the first use of the mobile branch office. It ran into some problems, though, and was eventually shelved. It may have been ahead of its time."[31]

Even without the trucks, Nathan had it pretty well covered by the early 1950s. It's often said that King was "self-contained," which meant that every step of making a record, from recording to pressing to printing, was done in-house under one roof. What *that* meant is that an artist could walk into 1540 Brewster in the morning with the idea for a song and walk out that afternoon, literally, with a finished record.

Such speed in production turnaround was virtually impossible then and would be today, as well, but King accomplished it on a routine basis. And in the entire process, from start to finish, the only pieces not made in-house were the cardboard cartons the records were shipped in and the records' paper sleeves.

• • •

King Records was a good training ground where one could get a thorough, hands-on education in all facets of the recording industry. One of the label's enduring legacies is the large number of producers, A&R men, and sales or marketing executives who "trained" under Nathan. Among the King alumni who enjoyed successful careers at other labels are Seymour Stein (Sire, Sire-London, and Elektra), Hal Neely (Starday and King-Starday), Henry Glover (Old Town, Roulette, and King-Starday), Ralph Bass (Chess), Jim Wilson (Starday and Sun), Alan Leeds (Paisley Park), Ray Pennington (Step One), and nearly a dozen others.

These men tended to be well-rounded and multiskilled executives, thanks to their experiences at King. "One week I'd be doing country, then bluegrass, then R&B," remembered musician and producer Ray Pennington (aka King recording artist Ray Starr). "It was an exciting time to work at King. In my four years there, I got a college degree in the record business.

"[Syd] was a pioneer. He was smart, too. Some people said he was gruff and mean, and he smoked those foul-smelling cigars. But, I tell you this: if Syd Nathan were alive today, I'd probably still be working for him. He had insight, a special way of seeing talent in people."[32]

Talking with those who worked at King Records, one is struck by two things. The first is the sheer abundance of "Syd stories." Everybody has them, and most tell the tales in their best imitations of Nathan's distinctive rasp. The second is the respect in which Nathan is held, decades after his death.

Jim Wilson and Seymour Stein worked at King in different eras, but both have vivid memories of their boss. "Syd was one of the most unforgettable characters you could ever meet," recalled Wilson with a chuckle. "He was quite a brilliant person, quite innovative. Every day was a new day with Syd. You never knew. He was a bit eccentric. Syd could be very gruff and demanding. He could also be quite pleasant, and I always enjoyed my time together with him. He was a pretty down-to-earth guy."[33] To Stein, "Syd Nathan was an original, a one-of-a-kind. He was the greatest influence in my life."[34]

• • •

No detail was too small to escape Nathan's notice. As he sat at his massive desk, usually described as looking like a 45-rpm record cut in half, with Nathan sitting in the hole of the record, Nathan kept an ear tuned to the roar around him, pulling bits of intelligence from the air to help him rule his kingdom.

The King complex was wired with an intercom system, a necessity given the plant's size and sprawl. The receptionist used it to page people for phone calls, and others used it to communicate within the facility as needed. As the Big Chief, Nathan had the engineers rig up a special override feature he could activate from his desk. With this device, he could interrupt anyone and talk over any announcement.

One of Nathan's employees at the time was a young man named Seymour Steinbigle. Nathan had befriended the Brooklyn teenager a few years earlier, and Steinbigle even spent a summer vacation with Nathan in Cincinnati. Steinbigle, who began working at King full time in 1961, called Nathan "a second father."[35]

"When I first started working at the company full-time," he recalled, "I got a phone call, and they started paging me. "Seymour Steinbigle, Seymour Steinbigle." All of a sudden, over her voice, [Nathan] comes in, "Okay, it's either Stein or Bigle or back to New York."[36] It's been Seymour Stein ever since.

Stein put his King education to good use and started his own record company, Sire Records, in 1966. Thanks to important records by the Ramones, Madonna, the Talking Heads, and others, Sire has been a major force in the music business since the 1970s. Stein recently reactivated Sire, after spending two years as president of Elektra. Described by Hank Ballard as "a clone of Syd Nathan," Stein served as the first president of the Rock & Roll Hall of Fame and was inducted into the Hall in 2005.

MASTERS OF THE GROOVE

Earl Bostic, Bill Doggett, and The Honkin' Tenors

• • •

The recording artists are all hoping and praying
they catch the public fancy. It is a senseless
proposition in a crazy business.

—Todd Rhodes, King recording artist

Virtually all styles of American music underwent drastic transformations in the decade following World War II. Black popular music in the immediate post-war years had been ruled by blues singers like Wynonie Harris, Roy Brown, and Bull Moose Jackson, men who sang the praises of wine, women, and high-rolling good times. By the early 1950s, however, the emphasis within commercial R&B had shifted almost entirely to vocal harmony groups.

These groups tended to be young, male, and urban, and their vocal styles were deeply rooted in the gospel quartet sound, as secularized by such popular vocal groups as the Ink Spots, Orioles, and Ravens. In keeping with the singers' youth, much of the groups' repertoire dealt with teenage concerns—young love, sharp clothes, cool cars, and being misunderstood by the world.

One strand of old-style R&B stood the test of time, though, maintaining an unbroken line from the 1940s into the early 1960s—the dance record. These records, usually instrumentals, ranged somewhere between jazz and R&B stylistically, usually featured the tenor saxophone and, later, the Hammond B-3 organ as lead instruments, and were intended primarily to get people out on the dance floor.

The genesis of the era's honking tenor sax sound, in fact the very idea of the tenor as heroic honker, can be traced to one song: "Flying Home," a major Decca hit in 1942 for Lionel Hampton's band, featuring the peerless Illinois Jacquet on tenor sax. Jacquet's hard-blowing solo inspired a generation of horn players, including many of the sax men discussed in this chapter. "Flying Home" became the template for an entire sound.

• • •

Alto saxophonist Earl Bostic (1913–65) was among the most popular and successful saxophonist/bandleaders of the 1950s. He recorded numerous hits for King and was a consistent seller from the late 1940s to the late 1950s. He should be much more famous.

Bostic was born in Tulsa, Oklahoma, prime breeding ground for the important musical outfits of the 1920s and 1930s known as "territory bands." These regional swing bands operated far from the lights of New York, playing for dances in the midwestern and southwestern states, and most of these bands never made a national impact. Bostic apprenticed in several territory bands, including ones led by Bennie Moten, Ernie Fields, and Marion Sears.

The hot young alto player made it to New York by 1938, where he quickly found work playing in the bands of Don Redman, Cab Calloway, Hot Lips Page, and Lionel Hampton and arranging for such white bandleaders as Gene Krupa and Paul Whiteman.

Bostic first recorded as a leader in 1945. The following year he signed with Gotham Records, where he cut such fare as "8:45 Stomp," "Earl's Rhumboogie," "Bostic's Jump," and "That's the Groovy Thing." These were among the twenty-two sides by Bostic leased from Gotham and reissued on Queen and King.

At his first proper King session, in January 1949, Bostic cut eight sides, including "Earl Blows a Fuse," one of his hottest performances. Bostic had four more sessions over the next two years, scoring R&B hits with "Choppin' It Down," "Seven Steps," and "Serenade." Vibraphonist Gene Redd joined the band in 1950, completing the format for most of the subsequent recordings: Bostic's alto sax, tenor sax, trumpet, vibes, piano, guitar, bass, and drums.

Bostic's commercial breakthrough came in 1951 and 1952 with the R&B hits "Always," "Lover Come Back to Me," "Moonglow," "Smoke Gets In Your Eyes," "Linger Awhile," and "Velvet Sunset." He had two of the biggest records of 1952 in "Flamingo" and "Sleep." Bostic's version of Duke Ellington's "Flamingo" topped the R&B chart and was King's second-best-selling record of the year, behind only "Have Mercy Baby," by Billy Ward and the Dominoes.

"Flamingo" was the biggest hit of Bostic's career and it changed his music in a variety of ways. Some critics maintain that the record's success had a detrimental effect on Bostic's music—that in his pursuit of subsequent hits, he softened the raspy, honking edge that made his records so exciting, and that he was "no longer the aggressive young virtuoso who had given [Charlie Parker] a run for his money."[1]

A closer listen to those records shows that this criticism is not really valid. Although a few of Bostic's hits from 1953 and 1954 (including "The Very Thought of You" and "These Foolish Things") approach the schlock threshold, others ("Cherokee," "Mambostic," "Mambolino") show absolutely no signs of weakness compared to the pre-"Flamingo" recordings.

The *real* decline in Bostic's records came when King began issuing LPs in the late 1950s, but the decline was the fault of King's marketing policies rather than anything Bostic did or didn't do. Beginning in 1958, King worked him at an insane pace. Bostic had been recording about twelve songs a year, but that changed.

In 1958, Bostic and his band recorded 73 songs, enough material for six twelve-song albums. It got worse. The next year, during marathon three- and four-day recording sessions between January and June, Bostic recorded 154 songs, enough for almost thirteen albums. That's eighteen-plus albums in less than eighteen months. What on earth could the folks at King have been thinking?

Bostic was game—after all, it had been five years since his last hit, and he had seen many of his jazz and R&B contemporaries fall by the wayside—but nobody could maintain quality at that pace. To make it worse, Bostic was often given mediocre material to record, much of it no better than easy-listening dross.

For reasons that defy logic, King had Bostic re-record many of his earlier hits in the new stereo format, sometimes with major changes in the arrangement or instrumentation ("Don't You Do It," for example). The new records were given the same catalog numbers as the older recordings they had "replaced," but often both versions of a tune remained in use, showing up on albums seemingly at random.

Those King albums, reissued endlessly over the years, have not helped Bostic's reputation. Perhaps more than any other jazz or R&B performer from his era, Bostic has been unfairly criticized and dismissed, not only by the jazz elite but also by the R&B community. The problem seems to be that he was musically neither fish nor fowl.

To the R&B fan, Bostic was too much of a jazzman to be a "real" R&B star. The condescension from the jazz establishment is more complex. Critics have long assailed Bostic for catering to dancers in his music, for being willing to "entertain" his audiences, a criticism that says more about jazz in the 1950s than it does about Bostic. As a graduate of the territory bands, Bostic saw jazz as dance music *and* entertainment. It never would have occurred to him to perform with his back to the audience, as 1950s icon of cool Miles Davis sometimes did.

After jazz lost its mainstream audience with the waning of swing, artists such as Bostic who enjoyed commercial acceptance were always somewhat suspect in purist quarters. Critics sniffed that Bostic played "jazz for strippers." But Bostic was a serious jazz musician in his heart, and it is within the context of jazz that his music can best be appreciated.

Bostic had fierce jazz chops on the alto sax and his playing influenced a number of younger musicians, including John Coltrane and some of the "free" jazz players of the 1960s. Coltrane called Bostic "a very gifted musician with fabulous technical facilities . . . who showed me a lot of things on my horn."[2] Legendary hard bop drummer Art Blakey was speaking from vast experience when he said, "Nobody knew more about the saxophone than Bostic, I mean technically, and that includes Bird [Charlie Parker]."[3]

Many of Bostic's recorded performances on King hold up remarkably well as hard-blowing jazz from a transitional period in the music's history. This list of should-be classics includes such cuts as "8:45 Stomp," "Cherokee," "Earl Blows a Fuse," "Don't You Do It" (a breathtaking back-and-forth between Bostic and tenor sax player Lowell "Count" Hastings), "Filibuster," "Mambostic," and "Harlem Nocturne."

Bostic was held in high esteem by his peers, and many outstanding jazz musicians played in his band over the years, including tenor saxophonists John Coltrane and Stanley Turrentine; pianists Jaki Byard and Sir Charles Thompson; trumpeter Blue Mitchell; guitarists Jimmy Shirley and Rene Hall; alto saxophonist Benny Carter; and drummer Jimmy Cobb.

Writing in the November 1984 issue of *Jazz Journal*, Victor Schonfield argues for Bostic's rehabilitation: "Bostic not only did all the things 'pure' jazz musicians try to do, but by and large he did them better, whether we focus on swing, soul, presence, technique (though not its display) [or] individuality. But his greatest gift was the way he communicated through his horn a triumphant joy in playing and being, much as Louis Armstrong and only a few others have ever done . . . The bottom line when it comes to music must be its power to move people, and this Earl Bostic had to the highest degree."[4]

After his herculean recording efforts of 1959, Bostic returned to the studio only four more times for King, in 1963 and 1964. His health was failing by that point and he toured infrequently. Earl Bostic died of a heart attack in 1965 at the age of fifty-two.

Born in Kentucky and raised in Springfield, Ohio, Todd Rhodes (1900–1965) was a talented pianist, bandleader, and arranger and a mainstay of the Detroit jazz and R&B scenes beginning in the late 1940s. Rhodes got his start as a charter member of the early jazz band McKinney's Cotton Pickers, described in *The Encyclopedia of Jazz* as "possibly the No. 1 Negro orchestra of the mid-1920s in terms of general popularity."[5]

When the Cotton Pickers, famous for 1928 recordings of "Four or Five Times" and "Milenberg Joys," broke up in the mid-1930s, Rhodes settled in Detroit, eventually resurfacing as an R&B pianist with his own small group, the Toddlers. He recorded in the late 1940s for Sensation Records, scoring such hits as "Teardrops," "Pot Likker," and "Red Boy at the Mardi Gras" (all of which were reissued by King).

After Sensation fizzled out, Rhodes signed with King, where he did session work behind Hank Ballard & the Midnighters, Wynonie Harris, and Lonnie Johnson, as well as worked with his own band. Rhodes had several hits for King—"The Red Boy Is Back," "Rocket 69," and the Ellingtonian "Blues for the Red Boy," DJ Alan Freed's theme song, as well as hits with band singers Li'l Miss Sharecropper (a pre-stardom LaVern Baker) and Pinnochio James, whose big song was "Your Mouth's Got a Hole In It."

Alphonso "Sonny" Thompson (1916–89) was a Mississippi-born pianist/band-leader who played a huge role at King as a musician, producer, and A&R man. He is perhaps best known for his session work backing such vocalists as Bull Moose Jackson, Wynonie Harris, Freddie King, Little Willie John, and Lula Reed.

Thompson was also active as a recording artist in his own right. He recorded nearly one hundred sides for King beginning in 1950. His band had less of a jazz feel than the Todd Rhodes outfit, but it was a tight, versatile group that had a way with a groove. Thompson's King hits included "Blues for the Night Owls," "Mellow Blues," "Let's Call It a Day," and his biggest record, "I'll Drown in My Tears," with vocals by Lula Reed.

When Ralph Bass left King in the late 1950s, Thompson succeeded him as King's A&R director in Chicago. After the Chicago branch office closed in 1964, Thompson did session work and occasional touring. He died in 1989.

Renowned for his blistering work on countless Bill Doggett records, tenor and alto saxophonist Clifford Scott (1928–93) had a varied career as a session musician and also recorded for King as a leader in 1958 and 1960. A native of San Antonio, Texas, Scott worked in the early 1950s with R&B singers Roy Brown and Roy Milton before joining organist Bill Doggett's band in 1955.

Scott's buzzy, big-toned tenor sax was a key element of the Doggett sound, never more so than on the band's biggest hit, "Honky Tonk," which has sold an estimated five million records since 1956. Scott played on several other hits with Doggett, such as "Slow Walk," "Soft," and "Ram-Bunk-Shush." His session work included records with James Brown ("Please, Please, Please" and "Try Me") and Freddie King.

On his own, Scott recorded almost twenty songs for King. Though they featured such esteemed musicians as Malachi Favors, Charles Brown, Hank Marr, and Earl Palmer, none of the singles made much of a splash, perhaps because they were competing against Scott's records with the Doggett band, which were generally better promoted and received far more radio airplay.

Big Jay McNeely (born 1927) may well be the ultimate "honking" tenor saxophonist of the 1950s. A *Billboard* review of McNeely's 1952 single "The Goof" pretty much defines the ideal R&B instrumental of the era: "This should wake up the crowd. It's a frantic, uninhibited performance of a driving, pounding jump effort, featuring a lot of honking on tenor, and some wild clapping and shouting by the band and the audience."[6]

A native of Los Angeles, Cecil James McNeely was already leading his own dance band in high school. He signed with Exclusive in 1946 and recorded some bebop for the label, but it was not until he moved to Savoy in 1948 that he attracted national attention with such records as "Deacon's Hop." McNeely has said that "Deacon's Hop" freed him from a perfectionist mindset—that he "just abandoned all that and let myself go."[7]

That's an understatement. McNeely was among the first R&B saxophonists to employ such crowd-pleasing stagecraft as playing on his knees; flopping onto his back while blasting out a cascade of notes; strolling out into the audience honking and screeching at attractive women; or playing outside on the sidewalk.

He was doing that last bit one night in San Diego when the police arrested him for disturbing the peace, leaving a baffled audience and band inside the club wondering if this was a new part of the show. On other nights, McNeely honked up a storm while lying flat on his back, pulled along on the sidewalk on an auto mechanic's "creeper."

McNeely first tasted real success after he was signed by Ralph Bass to record for the King subsidiary label Federal in 1952. McNeely had kept his wildness somewhat under wraps previously (hoping for pop stardom that didn't come) but he let it all hang out at Federal. He recorded only seventeen songs between 1952 and 1954, but these performances are among the best of his career. The cuts were released on a number of singles and an album, *Big Jay in 3-D.*

On raucous tunes such as "Earthquake," "Mule Milk," "Just Crazy," "The Goof," and "Nervous Man, Nervous," Big Jay anticipated rock and roll and notched a high-water mark for honkin' sax. For an amazing, mind-opening sample of Big Jay at full roar, listen to the tune "3-D," in which Big Jay and his older brother Bob (a seriously underrated talent on the baritone sax) blow incredibly complex lines in perfect harmony, all of it at a supercharged tempo that would make dancers explode.

It's an almost unbelievable performance. As Big Jay put it, "When Bob and me would get going real good, some kind of ESP would kick in. You'd hear notes that weren't being played."[8]

These frantic tunes went over well on stage, too, at least with the audiences. Other performers were often less amused by the mayhem. "When I opened for Johnny Ray, I blew that poor cat off the stage," Big Jay told biographer Jim Dawson. "The audience got so rowdy he didn't even want to go on. There was no way he could follow me. So his manager knocked me off the tour. Same with Nat King Cole. After I opened for him in San Francisco, he said, 'You'll never work for me again.'"[9]

McNeely left Federal for Vee-Jay Records in 1955, but his career was already in decline. The reason was obvious to McNeely. He and his contemporaries had made tenor saxophone *the* cool instrument in the early days of rock, but their time was passing. "The guitar took over, it became the engine, and the sax sorta got shoved over to the side. It was a little too black for most white kids coming on."[10]

But Big Jay, an acknowledged influence upon jazz greats Ornette Coleman and Pharaoh Sanders, kept on. He had the biggest hit of his career in 1957 with "There Is Something on Your Mind" and recorded a live album in 1963. McNeely made a comeback in the 1980s and was active into the late 1990s, one of the last of the original honkers.

If contemporary accounts can be believed, tenor man Lynn Hope (born 1926) could inspire almost as much pandemonium as Big Jay McNeely. The bar-walking tenor players of the 1950s were like gunslingers coming to town, each hoping to establish a reputation as the baddest, wildest cat of all. Hope was a solid contender for the crown; with his jeweled turban and custom-made suits, he cut as fine a figure as any in R&B.

Hope was a native of Cincinnati who had a Top Ten R&B hit in 1950 with "Tenderly" on Premium. When Premium folded, Hope signed with Chess and later moved to Aladdin. Sometimes known as "The Amazing Man with the Turban," the well-traveled Hope landed at King in 1960. He cut thirteen songs in March, twelve of which were issued on the LP *The Maharajah of the Saxophone*.

It was fine, jumping R&B sax combo music, with a groove not unlike that of Earl Bostic, an early influence on Hope. The album never really connected with an audience, though, and Hope drifted into obscurity—except in Jamaica, where his records were extremely popular. A major influence on Jamaican players, Hope is recognized today as one of the fathers of *ska* music, a precursor to reggae.

Among the other saxophonists who recorded on King were alto sax player Frank "Floor Show" Culley; tenor player Al Sears, who cut eight songs in 1951 (with Johnny Hodges on alto); Hal "Cornbread" Singer, who backed up Wynonie Harris, Lonnie Johnson, Little Willie John, and Bill Doggett and also recorded a few titles as a leader; Joe Thomas (who had an early hit with "Page Boy Shuffle"); Eddie "Lockjaw" Davis; Red Prysock; and Willis "Gator Tail" Jackson.

• • •

Of all the instrumentalists on King, nobody sold as many records as organist Bill Doggett. Born in Philadelphia, William Ballard Doggett (1916–96) had a background similar to most of the musicians in this chapter, though Doggett had less of a jazz pedigree. Perhaps that explains the lack of ambiguity in Doggett's King recordings. He made music for dancers, plain and simple.

Doggett became famous as an organist, but he started on the piano. He was leading his own band by age fifteen, but his first significant exposure came when he joined Lucky Millinder's band in 1940. In 1942, Doggett joined the popular vocal group the Ink Spots as pianist and arranger. He was also an active session musician, working with Helen Humes, Jimmy Rushing, Wynonie Harris, and Jimmy Witherspoon, among others.

In 1949, Doggett joined Louis Jordan's Tympany Five, the most popular act in black music. "Nobody showed me more about show business than Louis did," said Doggett. "He taught me how to gauge a crowd's response and how to react to it. And believe me, I had plenty of opportunities to learn. We worked as many as eighty one-nighters in a row."[11]

After leaving Jordan's band in 1951, Doggett worked sessions and began experimenting with the Hammond organ, inspired by Wild Bill Davis's attempts to make the organ a legitimate jazz instrument. Doggett was soon leading an organ-guitar-drums trio in New York clubs.

Henry Glover signed Doggett to King, and the organist first recorded for the label in January 1952. Doggett had not yet found the sound that would make him famous, but the trio funk of "Big Dog (Parts 1 and 2)" from that session is enjoyable. Doggett had other solid early releases, including "Moondust," "Early Bird," and the Mildred Anderson vocal showcases "You Ain't No Good" and "Your Kind of Woman," but the sales weren't what Doggett wanted. He decided to change his basic trio format.

"Bill Davis and I played a lot alike because we both played in an organ trio," explained Doggett. "So I called up Henry Glover and told him I was going to add a saxophone to the group to get a different sound."[12] His first tenor player was Percy France, who was replaced by Clifford Scott by 1955.

The other key move Doggett made as bandleader was hiring the great guitarist Billy Butler. The gritty blues playing of Butler, a Philadelphia session musician, meshed perfectly with that of Doggett and Scott on such scorchers as "Ding Dong," "Hot Ginger," "Hammer Head," "Ram-Bunk-Shush," "Shindig," and their pinnacle, "Honky Tonk (Parts 1 and 2)."

Technically, Doggett was not a great organist, but when it came to setting a danceable groove, he was superb. He soloed on occasion, but mainly concentrated on the rhythm and the groove and left the heavy lifting for Clifford Scott and Billy Butler. Doggett, Scott, and Butler made a formidable trio. Add drummer Beresford "Shep" Shepherd and bass player Carl Pruitt or Edwyn Conley, and it was among the best R&B bands of the decade.

"Honky Tonk" is one of the all-time great R&B and rock instrumentals. It was the top R&B record of 1956, spending seven months on the charts, and it reached the number two spot on the *Billboard* pop chart. The record won numerous industry awards and sold a staggering 1.5 million copies by the end of 1956.

The song was little more than a goof, the result of Billy Butler messing around on-stage at a Sunday-night dance in Lima, Ohio. As Doggett remembered, "We got there early and set up, shot some pool, went to the restaurant, the guys had a few tastes, and then we went to play the dance. We did a few of our numbers and everybody at the dance was enjoying themselves.

"All of a sudden Billy starts playing the front part [of the tune] on the bass strings of his guitar. We didn't know what to do but we didn't want to stop because the people had already started to dance. So Billy finished his twelve bars and then I fell in with the shuffle beat on the organ and everybody else fell in.

"After Billy plays his three choruses, Scotty falls in and plays his three choruses and looks at me as if to say, 'Hey, Bill, you want some of this?' I shook my head and said, 'No. Sounds goods enough just like it is. Let's take it out.' So, spontaneously, we all did that bridge and took it out. We laughed about it at the end of the tune."[13]

After the band played a few more tunes, a dancer approached the stage and asked the musicians to play that hot new song again, not realizing it was just a spur-of-the-moment jam. Amused, the band played it again and the crowd went wild. So they played it again and the crowd went wild again. By the time the night ended, the band had played the new song at least ten times. Doggett knew he had a smash on his hands.

He called Nathan. The good news was that Doggett had a monster hit. The bad news, he told Nathan, was that the song was a long one and would need to be on both sides of a single, as that was the only way a song longer than about three minutes could be presented in those days.

Nathan threw a fit about that, protesting somewhat illogically that jukebox operators hated two-sided hits because they occupied two slots on the jukebox. Doggett stuck to his guns, though, and "Honky Tonk" (parts 1 and 2, thank you very much) was recorded in New York in June 1956. According to Doggett, the session was a snap: "We did it in one take. Everything worked. It was just one of those things that was impossible to duplicate consciously. It was in the pocket right away.

"The first week they pressed 5,000 records and they sold out. The second week they pressed 12,500. After that they started pressing 100,000 a week. Syd had to keep the pressing plant open day and night to keep up with the demand. Syd was so happy, he never had a record like 'Honky Tonk' before. It took off so fast."[14]

Nathan thoroughly exploited "Honky Tonk." It appeared on countless Doggett LPs as well as numerous multi-artist compilations on King. In addition to tunes that more subtly attempted to cash in on the hit, Nathan also had Doggett record such blatant fare as "Honky Tonk, part three," "Honky Tonk Bossa Nova," "Honky Tonk Popcorn," and even a vocal "Honky Tonk," featuring Atlanta singer Tommy Brown.

The Doggett band was soon touring nationally, playing more than two hundred gigs a year. They recorded when they could and produced a pair of Top Five R&B hits, "Slow Walk" and "Hold It," as well as several lesser hits through the late 1950s: "Ram-Bunk-Shush," "Soft," "After Hours," "Rainbow Riot," and "Monster Party." Doggett also teamed with Earl Bostic for two hits, "Bo-Do Rock" and "Bubbins Rock."

When it came time to negotiate a new recording contract in 1960, Doggett asked for a modest increase in his royalty rate, mindful of the millions of dollars he had made for King over the past four years. Nathan turned him down flat. Angry and hurt, Doggett left for Warner Bros. Things didn't really work out for him there, but it's hard to blame Doggett for leaving King.

"Syd was pretty tight with money and gruff to most of his artists," Doggett ruefully recalled. "Syd would always say that the record business was a penny business, and you know, he was right. I'd say he was the smartest record man in the business of his era. He had absolute control of everything that had to do with King Records."[15]

Bill Doggett never had another record as big as "Honky Tonk," but he did all right. After leaving Warner Bros., he recorded for Columbia, ABC, Sue, and Roulette. And there was always the road, always a crowd of people somewhere who wanted to dance the night away to the familiar sound of "Honky Tonk."

The eternal road warrior, Bill Doggett worked steadily until shortly before his death in 1996. He graciously accepted his status as an "oldies" artist, because it didn't really matter to him. A gig was a gig and he gave his best at each one. And, no, he never got tired of playing his big hit: "I just wouldn't be Bill Doggett if I didn't play 'Honky Tonk.' That's what the people pay to hear, so that's what they get."[16]

Nine

I'LL SAIL MY SHIP ALONE

Country Music on King Records, Part 3

• • •

I play piano because the beer
kept sliding off my fiddle.
—Moon Mullican

Moon Mullican is a key figure for anyone trying to understand American music, yet he remains vastly underappreciated. The 1930s was a time of superb piano players, from boogie-woogie greats Albert Ammons, Meade "Lux" Lewis, and Pete Johnson to western swing masters Fred "Papa" Calhoun and Al Stricklin. The 1950s belonged to such rock and roll piano players as Jerry Lee Lewis, Little Richard, and Fats Domino. The connection—both cultural and musical—was Moon Mullican.

A piano-pounding wild man from the piney woods of east Texas, Aubrey "Moon" Mullican (1909–67) liked to say he played music that "made the bottles bounce." Mullican was a true hard-rocking daddy who lived up to his billing as the "King of the Hillbilly Piano Players."

Mullican grew up playing piano in the brothels and saloons around his hometown of Corrigan, Texas, and had a solid grounding in the western swing scene of 1930s Texas. His first significant experience was with the Texas Wanderers, led by fiddler Cliff Bruner. Mullican recorded extensively with Bruner, as well as with Buddy Jones, the Blue Ridge Playboys, and others. By the time Moon formed his own band in 1945, he had already played on more than one hundred records.

Mullican signed with King in 1946 and recorded eighteen songs in September or October in Houston. Moon's band, the Showboys, was a fire-breathing outfit rarely equaled in country music history for sheer instrumental power and drive.

Mullican's barrelhouse piano was at the center of the band's attack. Moon was a piano pounder rather than a virtuoso pianist, but he could play some decent jazz, as he showed in the introduction to "What Have I Done to Make You Leave" (which contains perhaps the ultimate country music lyric: "True love's not like lard").

Moon and the Showboys rocked like rolling thunder. A souvenir photo album sold by the band in 1946 offers this explanation: "The smilin' Showboys are sometimes called the 'Band With a Beat' . . . This particular kind of rhythm is referred to as 'Texas Socko' or 'East Texas Sock.' Technically, it is two-four rhythm with the accent on the second beat. And when we say accent—we mean accent . . . The Showboys offer this walloping up-beat as their main stock in trade. Sparked by the piston-like pianistics of 'King' Moon, these boys give out with it in a most solid way."[1] Indeed.

Already known for his blues-drenched playing on Johnnie Lee Wills's 1941 hit "Milk Cow Blues," fiddler Cotton Thompson gave the Showboys a distinctive sound. Thompson's fusion of traditional Texas country fiddling with the sophisticated blues and jazz playing of such fiddlers as Stuff Smith and Joe Venuti was both ahead of its time and perfectly suited to Mullican's music.

And then there was young Mutt Collins, perhaps the hottest unknown electric guitar player of the 1940s. Collins was a fiery lead player with the same savage grace as Lester "Junior" Barnard in Bob Wills's band. Collins's work on "What Have I Done to Make You Leave," "Shoot the Moon," and "Don't Ever Take My Picture Down" blends barely controlled aggression and killer chops. He's scarcely known today, but in 1946, for this one session, Collins sounds like the hardest-rocking guitarist in the world.

The most successful record from Mullican's first session was "New Pretty Blonde (New Jole Blon)." One of the dumbest songs in country music history—and that's saying something—"New Pretty Blonde (New Jole Blon)" was "inspired" by a hit recording of an old Cajun song by Harry Choates. Mullican wanted to cover the song at the session, but he had a problem: Choates sang in French and Moon had no idea what the lyrics were.

At what sounds to be a pretty well-lubricated point in the session, Mullican begins singing nonsense verses, combining quasi-Cajunisms such as "filé gumbo" with old country phrases like "possum up a gum stump." In some places, Moon is kind of scat singing; in others, he sounds as though he's speaking in tongues. There was probably some cringing the next morning listening to it, but the record was released and became a huge hit, one of the biggest of 1947.

"Jole Blon's Sister" was the follow-up single (imagine that), and the song starts off as if it were actually written ahead of time. That illusion crumbles about the time Moon sings "pass me the black-eyed peas and a cup of cocoa." Roughly ninety seconds into the record, Moon sounds like a man who has just realized he's made a bad, bad mistake.

The song runs out of steam shortly after that, literally, stumbling to an end as Moon's muse wafts away. The last thing on the record is Moon's voice saying, "Ah, excuse me, please." "Jole Blon's Sister" was a pretty big hit, though not nearly as successful as Moon's first stab at the idea.

The saga concluded, mercifully, with "Jole Blon Is Gone, Amen." The most coherent and witty of the three songs, Moon explains in this self-referential song how he happened into a Louisiana honky-tonk and heard a Cajun fiddler singing "Jole Blon." Mullican couldn't understand the lyrics and found them "peculiar," but recorded the song anyway.

A year or two later (in the song), Moon wanders back into the same honky-tonk and hears the same fiddler singing a different song, a sad song about how his pretty blonde has gone away. The fiddler recognizes Mullican and cries out to him, "What have you hillbillies done to my song?" The record ends with a chorus solemnly intoning the familiar two-note benediction, "A-men."

This is a universe of truly infinite possibility: A reasonable person could listen to "New Pretty Blonde (New Jole Blon)" and think the record is as bad as it could be. How could it *be* any worse? One way is shown on *Moon Mullican Sings His All-Time Hits*. At the time this album was released, around 1958, someone at King had the bright idea that the hit would be improved by adding a snare drum drilling out a martial rat-a-tat-tat rhythm and a cooing, wordless vocal chorus of the kind that almost killed country music. It's a grotesque and utterly tasteless pastiche of sounds and styles, but always good for a laugh.

Mullican next hit the charts with an atypical recording, the sentimental ballad "Sweeter Than the Flowers," reportedly recorded as a tribute to his recently deceased mother. Moon's broken-hearted vocal is one of the best performances of his career. Though firmly rooted in the country music of an earlier era, "Sweeter Than the Flowers" was one of the biggest hits of 1948.

For many modern listeners, Mullican's proto-rockabilly records overshadow his more straightforward country efforts, but he was a superb country singer in the postwar honky-tonk mold. This side of Mullican was more obvious when he recorded with King's house band instead of the Showboys. Working with Jethro Burns, Homer Haynes, and a few other King stalwarts, Mullican cut some of the tastiest mainstream country of the late 1940s in such records as "Foggy River," "Oh! She's Gone (But Not Forgotten)," "Triflin' Woman Blues," and "Save a Little Dream for Me."

Producer Henry Glover found an ideal collaborator in Moon Mullican, a man who would try just about anything. Their relationship was among the most fruitful producer-artist pairings on King Records. The two co-wrote Mullican's hit, "I'll Sail My Ship Alone," which topped the country charts in 1950. A lilting yet mournful song of lost love, "I'll Sail My Ship Alone" has become a country standard, recorded by hundreds of artists over the years.

Mullican had two more big hits in 1950. Both were covers of hits by black artists: "Mona Lisa," a big pop hit for Nat "King" Cole, and "Goodnight Irene," written and first recorded by Huddie Ledbetter, a blues singer and guitarist better known as Lead Belly.

Mullican joined the cast of the *Grand Ole Opry* in 1951. The next year, while touring together, Moon collaborated with his *Opry* pal Hank Williams on "Jambalaya (on the Bayou)," a reworking of a Cajun hit called "Big Texas." Both men recorded the song. Mullican's record on King didn't do anything, but Williams's version was a top hit of 1952.

The song was published with Williams listed as the sole writer because Mullican reportedly didn't trust King to pay royalties fairly and preferred to receive his share of the money under the table from Williams in a gentlemen's agreement.[2] That worked until Williams's death on January 1, 1953; after that, it probably cost Mullican at least a million dollars in lost income.

Moon's last hit for King came in 1951 with "Cherokee Boogie," an up-tempo romp learned from Chief Redbird, a honky-tonk performer in the Detroit area. This record, alone among the seven major hits he had for King between 1947 and 1951, captures the rollicking, bottle-bouncing boogie of Mullican at his best.

In contrast to many country stars of his era, Mullican was always honest and forthcoming about his love for and debt to black music. He often cited guitarist Joe Jones, a farm laborer Mullican knew in his youth, as a primary influence. Given Mullican's command of black music and his thorough grounding in western swing and country boogie, it's not surprising that so many of his records resonate today as proto-rock and roll or early examples of rockabilly.

Moon could most definitely rock the joint and he was doing it long before Elvis Presley or even Bill Haley. Working with racially mixed bands that often included bassist Clarence Mack, drummer Calvin "Eagle Eye" Shields, and saxophonist Rufus Gore, Mullican helped shape rock and roll with such torrid records as "Well Oh Well," "Pipeliner Blues," "Rocket to the Moon," and "Grandpa Stole My Baby."

Mullican's last session for King, in January 1956, was more self-consciously "rock and roll" and more obviously aimed at the teen market. Glover paired Mullican for the session with Boyd Bennett & His Rockers, a country-turned-rock band that had scored a big pop hit for King the previous year with "Seventeen."

The session produced four sides: "I'm Mad with You," "Seven Nights to Rock," "Honolulu Rock-A Roll-A," and "Rock 'n' Roll Mr. Bullfrog." The latter two were novelty efforts of middling quality, but "I'm Mad with You" and "Seven Nights to Rock" were superb rockers, among the hottest records of Moon's career.

Not that it mattered much. No matter how hard or convincingly he rocked, stardom as a teen idol was just not in the cards for the hard-drinking, portly, forty-seven-year-old piano man. Mullican helped create rock and roll but was just too old to capitalize on it very effectively.

Mullican left King in 1956. He subsequently recorded for Coral, Hall-Way, and Starday, scoring one final hit for Starday with "Ragged But Right" in 1961. In poor health throughout the 1960s, he suffered a fatal heart attack shortly after midnight on New Years' Day 1967.

Moon Mullican's modern legacy is multifaceted. He was a major figure in western swing and postwar country music as well as a forefather of rock and roll. He was an amazingly open-minded and versatile musician, a polished songwriter, and an excellent and expressive singer.

Mullican is arguably the most important and influential piano player in country music history and was a major influence on pianists ranging from Jerry Lee Lewis to Floyd Cramer to Leon Russell. Mullican has not yet been inducted into the Country Music Hall of Fame. That's an almost unbelievable omission for an institution chartered to tell the history of country music.

• • •

Harold "Hawkshaw" Hawkins was another prolific country artist for King, charting six big hits during two stints on the label. Born in Huntington, West Virginia, Hawkins (1921–63) was a genial honky-tonk singer with a taste for the blues who had spent his youth working on radio stations in his hometown and in nearby Charleston.

Hawkins landed in 1946 at WWVA in Wheeling, where he worked on the *Wheeling Jamboree*, an important rival of the *Grand Ole Opry*. Billed as "eleven and a half yards of personality," Hawkins was quite the showman, augmenting his music with "trained horse acts and rope and Australian bullwhip tricks."[3]

Like many country singers of the era, Hawkins was heavily influenced by Ernest Tubb, though Hawkshaw's smooth baritone vocals were more polished than those of the Texas Troubadour. Hawkins hooked up with King during the summer of 1946 and recorded twenty songs by the end of the year. Sixteen were covers of records by Tubb, but none of Hawkins's versions made the country charts.

Hawkins recorded extensively throughout 1947, enjoying a bit of success with "Sunny Side of the Mountain," his radio theme song. He scored big in 1948 with two Top Ten hits, "Dog House Boogie" and a cover of Hank Williams's "Pan-

American." Most of Hawkins's records had relatively minimal instrumentation, but "Dog House Boogie" and its follow up "Back to the Dog House" benefit greatly from backing by Boots Woodall and His Radio Wranglers, an Atlanta western swing sextet that cut four songs for King in 1947.

Hawkins hit the charts again in 1949 with "I Wasted a Nickel," but his career year was 1951. He had three Top Ten country singles during the year, all of them covers: "I Love You a Thousand Ways" (a hit for Lefty Frizzell), "I'm Waiting Just for You" (Lucky Millinder), and "Slow Poke" (Pee Wee King).

Considering Hawkins's natural feel for the blues and his success with such songs as "Dog House Boogie" and "Back to the Dog House," Henry Glover tried to steer him toward more R&B-oriented material, but Hawkins "proved stubborn," according to Glover. "I don't think he really understood what I was after."[4]

Glover maintained that "Hawkshaw could have been a rock singer,"[5] but it's fairly hard to hear that in his King recordings. Despite an occasional flash of rocking attitude on such songs as "Got You on My Mind," "Somebody Lied," and especially "Teardrops from My Eyes" (one of his finest moments), Hawkins was more comfortable with a nice country ballad. At any rate, Glover never really got the chance to rock the Hawk, because Hawkins left King in 1953 and spent the rest of the decade on RCA Victor and Columbia. He joined the *Grand Ole Opry* in 1955.

After a long, dry spell with only one hit to his credit, Hawkins returned to King in 1962. He cut twelve songs in a September session, including the song that restarted his career, "Lonesome 7-7203," a honky-tonk shuffle in the style of Ray Price. It would be Hawkins's first number one hit single, but he wouldn't live to see it happen. Just three days after the record entered the *Billboard* country chart, Hawkshaw Hawkins was killed in a plane crash with Patsy Cline and Cowboy Copas. Nothing else from Hawkins's last session made the charts.

King was never much of a force in western swing, a fabulously American hybrid of fiddle tunes, blues songs, big-band swing, and honky-tonk country that was extremely popular in Texas, Oklahoma, and California. Western swing had waned in popularity from its prewar peak by the time King came to the style, but the label recorded numerous examples of excellent western swing between 1944 and 1955.

Much of King's western swing output was the result of a marathon Nathan recording expedition in California. Nathan "hit Hollywood with all the force of an earthquake" (according to *Tophand* magazine)[6] and set up shop at Universal Recorders. Over the course of roughly a month, Nathan cut dozens of sides with Hank Penny, Red Egner, Leon Rusk, Charlie Linville, Tex Atchison, and several others. It was a most productive trip for Nathan.

Better known for his exceptional work as a sideman and singer with Bob Wills, Spade Cooley, and Tex Williams, Jimmie Widener (1924–2001) cut twenty-four songs for King as a bandleader in 1946. His first two sessions, produced by Merle Travis, were more of a showcase for Widener's singing and guitar playing, but a longer third session produced some exciting western swing.

It's very tasty stuff—classic small-band swing somewhat similar to Bob Wills's MGM recordings—and Widener deserves to be better known for these recordings. The band is red hot, almost a western swing dream team. Lead guitarist Jimmy Wyble, steel guitarist Noel Boggs, trumpeter Truman Quigley, and fiddlers Buddy Ray and Harold Hensley played some of the jazziest, hippest west coast swing ever recorded.

Widener was the ostensible star of the recordings as the lead singer, but he gave his sidemen plenty of room, and they took full advantage of it. Wyble and Boggs, particularly, burn it up on song after song, firing off perhaps the wildest, most bebop-influenced solos in all of postwar western swing.

Tenor banjo player Ocie Stockard (1909–88) is one of the unheralded pioneers of western swing, having played in Milton Brown's Musical Brownies, the first great western swing band, as well as Bob Wills's Texas Playboys, the band that did the most to popularize the style. In between, Stockard led a band called the Wanderers that recorded for Bluebird and OKeh.

In its only session for King, recorded in 1946 in Fort Worth, Texas, Stockard and the Wanderers (actually an all-star band assembled for this session) cut four tracks: a pair of decent songs and two much more interesting instrumentals, "Cowtown Boogie" and "Twin Guitar Polka," both sterling examples of small-band swing featuring fiddle great Cecil Brower and the twin-guitar work of J.B. Brinkley and Lefty Perkins.

Arkansas singer Paul Howard (1908–84) was a country music visionary whose work never quite caught on with the public. Howard was one of the first musicians in the southeast to embrace western swing. He joined the *Grand Ole Opry* in 1940 as a solo singer, but within a few years he was working with a large band that sometimes included as many as ten musicians.

Paul Howard and His Arkansas Cotton Pickers debuted on King in January 1949. Over the course of the next year and a half, Howard recorded ten songs for King. The records didn't do much, despite the presence of such fine musicians as guitarist Jabbo Arrington and steel guitar player Billy Bowman. Howard left the *Opry* in frustration in 1949 and worked for a few years in Texas, Louisiana, and Arkansas before gradually drifting out of the business.

The Light Crust Doughboys is a legendary band in western swing history. Formed in Fort Worth in 1930—two of the group's charter members were Bob

Wills and Milton Brown—the Doughboys recorded extensively, appeared in two Gene Autry movies, and helped Doughboys manager/announcer W. Lee O'Daniel ride the popularity of the band to two terms as governor of Texas.

The Doughboys reformed after the war, though tenor banjo player Marvin "Smokey" Montgomery was the only prewar member still around. The revamped band recorded for King a few times in 1947 and 1948. It's a bit difficult to sort out, because some of the records were labeled the Light Crust Doughboys, some Jack Perry, and some Mel Cox & His Flying X Ranch Boys. There are also five banjo tunes Montgomery recorded in 1947, two of which, "Hear Dem Bells" and "My Old Kentucky Home," were issued in the short-lived "Hillbilly Series" on Federal.

• • •

Dubbed the "Hillbilly Waltz King," North Carolina singer and guitar player Clyde Moody (1915–89) had a distinguished musical career spanning more than fifty years. After an apprenticeship performing and recording with the Happy-Go-Lucky Boys and Wade Mainer's Sons of the Mountaineers, Moody made it to the big leagues in 1940 when he joined the band of *Grand Ole Opry* star Bill Monroe. Moody was the first lead singer to record with Monroe's new band, the Blue Grass Boys, contributing a strong solo vocal on his original song "Six White Horses."

Moody left Monroe's band in 1945, determined to make it on his own. He signed with King in 1947 and had a regional hit with his first release, "Shenandoah Waltz." He subsequently recorded a number of similar efforts: "West Virginia Waltz," "Cherokee Waltz," "I Waltz Alone," and "Carolina Waltz," a Top Fifteen hit in 1948. The record's flip side, "Red Roses Tied In Blue," did even better, entering the Top Ten.

Moody scored another Top Ten hit, "I Love You Because," in 1950. Though he would record more than fifty songs for King before leaving in 1952, he had no more hits. Moody recorded for Decca, Starday, Wango, and Old Homestead after he left King and enjoyed a career revival performing at bluegrass festivals in the 1970s and 1980s.

Singer-songwriter Jimmie Osborne (1923–57) placed three songs in the top ten of the *Billboard* country chart during his time at King. Known as the "Kentucky Folk Singer," Osborne was one of the more traditionally oriented country singers to emerge in the late 1940s. He signed with King in 1947 after gaining a degree of regional popularity performing with the Bailes Brothers on *The Louisiana Hayride*. Osborne had a Top Ten hit with his first King release, "My Heart Echoes," which entered the charts in July 1948.

Osborne recorded primarily three kinds of songs for King: songs about topical events, typified by his biggest hit, "The Death of Little Kathy Fiscus," which reached the Top Ten in June 1949; patriotic songs, including "The Voice of Free America," "Thank God for Victory In Korea," "The Korean Story," and "God Please Protect America," which entered the charts in October 1950; and cautionary songs such as "A Million People Have Died," hailed by *Billboard* as "a first-rate weeper based on the terrible toll taken each year in traffic accidents" and "a must for dee jay shows."[7]

Osborne had no more hits after 1950. He performed and worked in radio for a few years, appearing on *The National Barn Dance* in Chicago and *Midwestern Hayride* in Cincinnati. He then worked as a disc jockey in Kentucky. Apparently depressed about his career, Osborne took his own life in 1957.

Talented guitarist, singer, and songwriter Zeb Turner, whose real name was William Grishaw (1915–78), had one of the first country boogie hits in 1946 with "Zeb's Mountain Boogie" for Bullet Records. He began recording for King in 1949 and had a big hit with his first release, "Tennessee Boogie." Turner recorded a number of boogie and novelty songs for the label through 1953, but only "Chew Tobacco Rag," a Top Ten record in 1951, made much noise.

Zeb's younger brother Zeke Turner (real name James Grishaw) was a mainstay of the King "house band" and one of the first renowned session musicians in Nashville. A pioneer of the electric guitar in country music, Zeke Turner is another largely forgotten influence on rock and roll guitar.

Country music superstar Hank Williams died in the backseat of his Cadillac in the early hours of January 1, 1953. Seven days later, a singer-disc jockey named Jack Cardwell entered a radio station in Mobile, Alabama, and recorded "The Death of Hank Williams" for King.

An original song by Cardwell, it's more listenable than one might imagine. Of course, in this race the prize went to the swiftest, not the most artful, but Cardwell's ode was far better than many similar efforts. Singing in a style heavily influenced by Williams, Cardwell presented a straightforward, respectful account of Hank's last hours.

King was able to get this record recorded, pressed, and released very quickly, giving Cardwell a jump on the competition. His tribute did quite well, placing in the top five on all three of the *Billboard* country charts (measuring sales, radio airplay, and jukebox activity). A *Billboard* review described the record as "a powerful side which should have a strong appeal," adding, "Cardwell chants the number—as a dirge."[8] Cardwell was never able to match the popularity of his breakthrough record, placing only one more record on the country charts, "Dear Joan," a Top Ten hit in 1953.

Country singer Bonnie Lou (born 1924), a star on *Midwestern Hayride* for more than twenty years, was described in a 1953 magazine article as a "young and attractive Swiss yodeler and ballad singer."[9] A native of Illinois, Bonnie Lou (her real name is Mary Kath) came to WLW in 1945 and stayed until 1966, becoming quite well known in the Ohio-Indiana-Kentucky tristate area.

Bonnie Lou began recording for King in March 1953, cracking the country Top Ten with her first release, "Seven Lonely Days," a cover of a pop hit by Georgia Gibbs. In its typically arcane jargon, *Billboard* raved about the record, saying, "The thrush sells it powerfully, showing off a good set of pipes . . . an exciting disk."[10]

Her follow-up release, a novelty called "Tennessee Wig Walk," did even better, peaking at number six on the country charts. Bonnie Lou continued recording for King into the late 1950s. She was a star on WLW-TV through the mid-1960s, performing on *Midwestern Hayride* as well as on several non-country music variety shows.

There were dozens of other country artists who recorded for King and contributed to the amazing diversity of country music sounds documented by the label—Minnie Pearl, Redd Stewart, Bill Carlisle (who had a major hit on King, "Tramp on the Street," in 1948), Curley Fox & Texas Ruby, the York Brothers, Bill & Evalina, the Carlisle Brothers (Cliff and Bill, who had one of King's first hits with "Rainbow at Midnight" in 1946), Esco Hankins, and Bob Newman, a singer from Georgia whose records included "Lonesome Truck Driver's Blues," "Hangover Boogie," "Greetings," and "Phfft! You Were Gone."

Through the purchase of several masters from Four-Star Records, a California label owned by Bill McCall, King was also able to offer albums in the late 1950s by such notable country stars as the Maddox Brothers and Rose, Ferlin Husky, the Wilburn Brothers, T. Texas Tyler, Hank Locklin, Webb Pierce, and Jimmy Dean.

• • •

By the mid-1950s, country music had become a relatively low priority at King. Though King continued to record bluegrass bands and an occasional country singer, the emphasis had certainly changed at the label. Except for three left-field hits—"Drunk Again" by Lattie Moore, "Passing Zone Blues" by Coleman Wilson (both 1961), and Hawkshaw Hawkins's "Lonesome 7-7203" in 1963—and a few bluegrass records, King Records had no more country hits after 1953.

The well had simply gone dry after an amazing run of success. The major labels made it easier for new companies to get established in country music in the 1940s by scaling back their own country efforts. King was one of the first labels to take advantage of this opportunity. But as the new independent labels demonstrated the commercial viability and national popularity of country music, the major labels again became interested. With much more money, the majors were able to outspend the smaller companies for talent, leading to an exodus of artists from the independents to the majors.

At about the same time, Nashville was becoming the center of the country music industry. With the opening of Nashville's first commercial recording studios in the late 1940s, record companies dealing with country music opened branch offices in Nashville. As the record companies came to the city, so, too, did the ancillary parts of the industry: booking agents, promoters, publishing companies and the like. The musicians also came, lured by the opportunities for work playing on recording sessions.

After the country music industry became centralized, it became increasingly difficult for record companies located elsewhere to compete with those based in Nashville. The window of opportunity that opened for the small companies in the 1940s was decisively slammed shut as the major labels regained control over country music. It's no surprise that Nathan decided to focus more of the company's energy on blues and R&B. That music, with rare exceptions, was still so culturally marginalized that the major record companies were not that interested, so a label like King could do quite well.

King Records had a great decade-long run in country music. The label sold millions of records, made a ton of money, changed the sound of country music, and helped to midwife rock and roll. For the ten-year period from 1944 through 1953, King was arguably the most successful independent record company in country music.

King had forty-seven Top Fifteen country hits on the *Billboard* charts, an impressive average of nearly five hit records per year. Of those forty-seven, thirty-six made the Top Ten. Of those, nineteen records climbed into the Top Five. King had three number one country hits during this period: "Blues Stay Away from Me," "Why Don't You Haul Off and Love Me," and "I'll Sail My Ship Alone."[11]

Even more important, however, is the role King Records—and its artists—played in the postwar transformation that forever changed country music. No label better demonstrated in its records the ongoing dynamic of change that was reshaping the music.

Those changes included the move from an instrumental sound based primarily on acoustic instruments to one based primarily on electric instruments, with a heavy dose of the aggressive rhythms of boogie-woogie, which came to country music in the 1940s. There was a new willingness to borrow from other styles of music, particularly blues and R&B. Finally, there was the increased use of "session musicians" and "house bands" for recording.

King rode the brief but important wave of country boogie as well as any label. Records by the Delmore Brothers, Wayne Raney, Moon Mullican, and several other King artists helped define the exciting style, the last of the basic building blocks that went into the foundation of rock and roll. By serving as a laboratory where pioneering electric guitarists like Zeke Turner, Jethro Burns, Roy Lanham, and Al Myers could work out the basic vocabulary of the new instrument, King, again, both anticipated and helped to create the musical revolution that would blow the world apart in a few years.

• • •

Jethro Burns, who was posthumously inducted into the Country Music Hall of Fame in 2001, felt strongly that historians of country music have unjustly neglected Nathan. "I don't think Sydney Nathan has ever gotten the credit he deserves from the industry or anybody else," said Burns. "People talk about these legendary record men like Ralph Peer, Sam Phillips, Art Satherly, and people like that. And they're great men. But right there in Cincinnati, Syd Nathan was a great man, too. He was every bit the pioneer those other guys were."[12]

Ten

RECORD MAN

Ralph Bass and Federal Records

•••

I was a talent scout, I was a promotion man,
I saw the DJs, I went to the branch offices—
as well as producing records. You did everything.
You were a "record man" in those days.

—Ralph Bass

Ralph Bass (1911–97) was one of the true characters among the record producers, A&R men, and talent scouts who came to the fore in the 1940s and 1950s. Although he didn't try to pass for something he wasn't, there was always something different about Ralph Bass, a white man of mixed Jewish-Italian ancestry who crossed the color line and never looked back. Bass was a jive-talking wheeler-dealer, half artist and half con artist. He was a consummate record man.

Bass was full of himself, but seemed to know it, in a way that made his shtick (and self-promotion) more entertaining than irritating. He moved freely between two parallel worlds at a time in America when relatively few people crossed the racial divide. Bass was a pioneering record man, but he was proudest of the role he played in bringing blacks and whites closer together through a common love for music.

As the main man at Federal Records (King's most successful subsidiary label) from 1951 to 1958, Ralph Bass was at the helm for some of the era's greatest hit records, cut by some of the most influential musicians and singers of the 1950s. Among the great artists associated with Bass at Federal are James Brown, Hank Ballard, Billy Ward & the Dominoes, Little Esther, the Platters, Big Jay McNeely, and Jimmy Witherspoon.

Bass also dabbled as a songwriter, usually in a collaborative situation. Among the songs in his modest catalog are such little-remembered numbers as "Be Bop

Wino," "The Last of The Good Rocking Men," and "Quiet Dad." He was more successful with his publishing company, Armo Music, which published the songs of numerous top writers, including Hank Ballard, Jerry Leiber & Mike Stoller, James Brown, Rudy Toombs, Lowman Pauling, Billy Ward, and Ike Turner.

The bulk of this chapter is told through excerpts from a lengthy interview with Ralph Bass conducted April 19, 1984, in Chicago. During the interview, held in his second-floor office above his wife's dance studio on a major South Side street, Bass talked about his career in the record business, touching on such topics as leaving Savoy Records for King, his relationship with Syd Nathan, his "discovery" of James Brown, and the reasons he left King for Chess. Bass's stories were so lovingly tended and told, it seemed a shame to burden them with extra exposition unless absolutely necessary. It's Ralph Bass in his own colorful words.

• • •

"I started with Black & White Records in 1944," began Bass.[1] "Then I went out on my own, with Bop Records, which had Wardell Gray and Dexter Gordon. I had another label, Portrait, which had Erroll Garner on it. This was in L.A. After a year, when I couldn't get my money from the distributors, I went with Savoy, from 1948 to 1951.

"Herman Lubinsky of Savoy had asked me to move to New York to be close to the operation. I didn't like the idea at all, but I was born and raised in New York, so I moved back. Herman had promised me the sun, moon, and stars to move back to New York, and I came to find out he didn't even pay but half of my moving expenses. All this jive, just to get me to come to New York.

"There were so few independent labels at this time, and they were all family affairs, so where could I go? You couldn't get anywhere unless you were family. But they *were* completely dependent on good producers. Irving Green of Mercury Records was in New York, and he grabbed me. He said, 'Let's make contracts up. I'll have them all ready for you. I have to go to Europe first, but when I get back, we'll get to it.' Well, three or four months went by, and I never heard from Irving Green.

"I think the guy in charge of Mercury had something to do with that. He didn't like the way I acted or something. I guess he didn't dig me. But look, babe, I'm in black music. Being white, I had a lot to overcome to gain the confidence of blacks so they would accept me as being for real, not just a jive cat who was gonna take advantage of them. I had to learn the language all over again. I didn't really become a different person, but I acclimated myself to what was happening with blacks in the south.

"Ben Bart of Universal Attractions, which was at that time one of the biggest booking agencies for black talent in the country, said to me, 'Hey, Syd Nathan's in town. Why don't you go see him?' So I went to see Syd at his office there, a building on West 54th Street. Henry Glover was King's A&R man and producer, and he had an office there.

"I met with them and they gave me a proposition. I told them I couldn't wait because I didn't have any money—my money was getting nil. I wanted to quit Savoy so bad, but I couldn't afford to. So, I accepted the proposition. We made papers up that night and signed them. So I left Herman. He couldn't believe his ears when I told him. But I left Lubinsky to go with Syd Nathan [in 1951], knowing I was going from the frying pan into the fire.

"We created a new label, Federal. That was what I wanted, my own label. Everything I produced was to go on my own label, because I had a royalty deal, a production deal. That was why it was so great. I did record some of the acts for King—I did most of Earl Bostic's hits and a session with Bill Doggett and Earl Bostic—but other than that, everything I produced went on Federal. Later on, some of the acts were switched to King from Federal, like James Brown.

"We also started a publishing company [Armo] at the same time. I had fifty per cent [ownership]. These were the things that Lubinsky had promised me, but they never came through. I wanted my own publishing company, because in those days, we wanted to record original material. I never thought songs would be a valuable property later on, especially R&B songs. But I have a song, 'Dedicated to the One I Love,' that was recorded by the Mamas & Papas and it still makes me money."

• • •

Bass spoke of Federal Records as a label created for his production efforts, but that's not precisely the case. Federal actually predates Bass coming to King by at least a couple of months. Federal originally had two divisions, a "Hillbilly Series" and a "Rhythm, Blues & Spirituals Series." Both were active by late 1950. If Bass joined the staff of King in 1951, it seems likelier that he was hired to oversee the newly launched label under the King umbrella.

The first Federal releases were issued in the "Hillbilly Series," thirty singles by such acts as Homer & Jethro, Bill Carlisle, Fairley Holden, and Tex Atchison. These were reissues of relatively unsuccessful King releases, which suggests that Federal was conceived at least in part as a budget label.

As was the publishing company Nathan offered Bass, Federal was a bargaining chip, a way for Nathan to sweeten the deal and lure the talented producer to King. Bass ran the label for the next eight years, producing countless hits along the way.

• • •

"My job at King was to supply the talent and produce them.[2] I practically lived on the road. I lived out of the trunk of my car. That's when I found all those artists for King.

"The James Brown story is a classic. I was in Atlanta. There were two radio stations in Atlanta then that played black music, both of them on Auburn Avenue. One of them had Zenas Sears, who was a big DJ at the time. He was just a great guy, a beautiful cat.

"We had our own branch there and I came there and the branch manager said, 'Hey, I've got a dub I want you to hear.' He played this dub for me and I said, 'Who the hell is that?' I had never heard anything like that. It was so different. My theory as a producer has always been: Let me find someone who's different and at least I have a chance. It might backfire, but at least I have a chance of being different, novel. That was my basic philosophy about finding talent and producing them.

"Anyway, I said to the branch manager, 'Where is this group?' It was a group called the Flames. He said they were in Macon. I got one of the black DJs to go with me and we drove down to Macon. In those days, when you were looking for someone, you went to the nearest radio station. So we went to the station and I introduced myself and told them what I was there for. I said, 'Where can I reach these Flames? Where can I find them?'

"And the cat at the radio station said, 'They are managed by a cat named Clint Brantley,' and he gave me a phone number. In those days, the smaller cities and towns in the deep south always had some black cat who controlled everything across the tracks, you might say. He usually had a big nightclub. Brantley was that guy in Macon.

"Well, they gave me a number for Brantley's home. I called and talked to his wife and told her who I was. His wife said, 'You stay right there and I'll get ahold of him and he'll call you right back.' And he did. I told him who I was. And then he said to me—this is like a James Bond story—'Now at eight o'clock you park your car in front of this barbershop, which is right across the street from the railroad station. When the lights go on and the blinds go up and down, after they go down, you come in.' Now Macon was one of those towns . . . well, an out-of-town white cat could be in trouble in those days.

"At about half past seven we drove to this barbershop and parked the car right in front. Everything was dark. There was nothing open, nothing. The street was absolutely deserted. All of a sudden, the lights went on, the blinds went up and down. I said to the DJ who was with me, 'Hey, man, if I don't come out, if something happens to me, come and get me.' I didn't know what in the hell was happening; it was so strange.

"So I went in and told him who I was. I explained that I'd heard a dub and I was very interested. With that, he pulls out a contract that Leonard Chess [of Chess Records] had sent him. When I worked for Chess later on, Leonard told me he'd never forgive me for taking James Brown away from him. Leonard was supposed to have come down, but the weather was pretty bad. He couldn't make it because of the weather.

"I had about three hundred dollars in my pocket, so I took two hundred out and said, 'Clint, this is for you. Two hundred.' Those days, baby, you know, two hundred was a lot of money. I said, 'But I want to sign them now.' He said, 'We've got a deal.' So he got on the phone and he had the cats come down, the group. I didn't know who the lead singer was. All I knew was that I wanted the group just the way they sang on the dub.

"I told Clint, 'Now I want to be sure this is the same group before I sign my name on the contract. Where can I hear them?' Clint said, 'Well, I've got this big club. You come over tonight.'

"So we went to the club, and James started to sing. Now he must have seen an act named Big Jay McNeely. Big Jay had a thing where he would get on his back and he'd crawl all over the floor on his back blowing his horn, his saxophone. James must have seen this because James got on the floor and did the same thing, crawling from table to table singing this song I'd heard on the dub, which was 'Please, Please, Please.' It was fantastic. So I signed the contract, gave them a copy, and said I'd be in touch.

"I got back to Cincinnati and called the group. I told them to come up to Cincinnati at a certain time and I'd put them up in a hotel. They came up and we did the session. I left right after the session [to go back on the road]. I was in St. Louis when Henry Glover and Andy Gibson, an arranger for King, came in on their way to Hot Springs, Arkansas.

"They said, 'You better call the old man [Nathan] right away. He told us when we found you to tell you you were fired.' And I said, 'Fired? For what? What did I do this time?' They just said, 'You'd better call.' So I did.

"Nathan got on the phone and said, 'What are you on? What kind of shit are you on?' See, everybody in those days thought I was smoking pot because of the crazy things I did. Henry Glover said to me once, 'I'm black, but I won't go in some of the joints you do.' So, I had to be on some shit, right?

"Anyway, Nathan says, 'You gotta be on something, because how could anybody in his right mind record the worst piece of shit I ever heard in my life? Sounds like someone stuttering on a record, all he says is one word.'

"I said, 'Oh, you must mean the Flames and "Please, Please, Please."'

"Nathan said, 'You took all my money, spent all that money bringing that group up here, giving that man two hundred dollars.' I said, 'Is that right? Tell you what, Syd. Put it out in Atlanta.' I had the dub with me and every place I used to go, I'd play it for a bunch of broads and they'd go crazy. They'd go out of their minds. So I knew what I had.

"Nathan said, 'I'm gonna put it out all over the country, not just Atlanta, to show you what a piece of shit this is.' I said, 'Fine. And if it doesn't sell, you don't have to fire me. I quit.' I was so sure of this damn thing. Well, of course, the rest is history.

"Now the aftermath of the story is that Syd never discussed how great this record was and what a great job I had done. He could never do that. But I was in the studio there one day, waiting for somebody to do a session. Syd came blustering in with some other cat who was evidently not in the record business. I could hear it all because of Syd's loud voice. Syd said to the guy, 'You know why we're so successful here at King Records? Because we don't do things like anybody else. I'm gonna show you what I'm talking about.' And with that, he went to the record player and put on a copy of 'Please, Please, Please.'"

• • •

"Syd gave me a free hand with Federal.[3] The only time he ever hit the ceiling was with James Brown, when Syd thought I'd wasted all his money. He had a terrible temper. Oh, my God. He'd break out and his blood pressure would go sky high. But I did whatever I wanted. That was the thing I admired about Syd. I had a free hand.

"I went wherever I wanted. I used to flip a coin to see where I'd be going. Once I was at a motel in Texas and the manager asked where I was I going next, in case any mail came. I said, 'I don't know. Let's see.' And I flipped a coin. I never knew. I just played it by ear.

"I'm half Jew and half Italian and I went to a Baptist school for four years. My second wife is black. I have a black daughter and two white sons. I have tolerance for all cultures coming from that kind of background.

"I would never sign an artist unless they could write [songs] as well as sing. If it was a group, someone in the group had to write songs. That was my number-one rule. For example, Hank Ballard of the Midnighters. Hank wrote practically all of the material. I might have thrown some ideas at him, like the one time I changed the title from 'Sock It to Me, Mattie' to 'Work with Me, Annie,' but Hank wrote most of the songs.

"I wanted—depended upon—talented singers who could write. Nobody came to us with songs in those days. Why do you think I was on the road looking for talent? All this talent, especially in the deep south, they never saw a record company. I mean, the artists themselves could barely find the record companies, never mind the songwriters who were writing the kind of stuff I could use.

"Someone came to me with a dub of Billy Ward and the Dominoes. They had been on TV, on the Ed Sullivan show or Arthur Godfrey or something [actually, it was Arthur Godfrey's CBS radio program, *Talent Scouts*[4]], won some contest. I listened to them and I said, 'No, I can't use them.' They were singing some pop song. Billy Ward was writing pop music, not R&B. They didn't sound like a black group to me. But the guy was very persistent, so I finally told him to bring them by. This was at the King office in New York.

"Ward, and Rose Marks, the woman who managed the group and invested a lot of her money in them, brought the group over. I listened to them sing. The lead singer was very legitimate. But I pointed to another cat in the group and said, 'Let me hear you sing lead.' When I heard him, Clyde McPhatter, I said, 'My God, *there's* your lead singer.' And when I heard the bass singer, Bill Brown, I said, 'And there's your other lead singer.'

"So I said to Billy Ward, 'Here's what I want you to do. Buy these records and listen to them and write me some material like that.' And I mentioned several groups that were hot right then in black music. I said, 'You write songs like that and I'll sign you.' He said, '*That's* what you want? You got a deal.'

"Syd Nathan gave me this. He said when you hear somebody sing, and nothing happens to you, forget it. But if someone starts singing, and you feel the blood coming up into your arms, and shit, and you get all emotional, that's it!

"Another thing I learned from Syd is that no producer can stay hot or stay cold forever. I remember one time I had a string of no hits. We were walking around Harlem, and I was feeling down, real down. Syd said, 'Ralph, no producer can be a hundred percent. None in the world. A great baseball player, a great hitter, hits three hundred. If you hit three hundred for me [three successes in ten attempts], you'll be doing great.'"[5]

• • •

To the producer of some of King's greatest "dirty" songs, the controversy over dirty R&B records was a tempest in a teapot. To make his point, Bass recounted a television appearance he made in the early 1950s.

"I was in Los Angeles, living there again and running the branch office," remembered Bass.[6] "All of a sudden, white kids were buying black records for the first time. There were a lot of radio stations that wouldn't play 'Work with Me, Annie.' There was a big TV personality in L.A. who had this show where he'd exploit the headlines and make a big issue out of something that maybe contradicted the norms of society. He called me and said, 'Would you like to come on and defend yourself?' I said, 'Sure, why not?'

"There was some politician running for some office, and a woman with her young daughter, maybe eleven years old, and the head of the P.T.A. They were all against me.

"So I got on the show and I said, 'Look, when it comes to something where white people don't understand the language used, they immediately think in the worst terms. They don't think in humorous terms, they just think it's nasty.' "Making Whoopee" is all right, it's cute, but when a black person says the same thing, it's nasty.'

"I turned to the little girl and asked her, 'Do you know what the words are to "Work with Me, Annie"? She said, 'No, not really.' I said, 'Well, why do you like the record?' She said, 'I like the beat.'"

• • •

"I left King in 1958.[7] I was here in Chicago and I had an overture, an indirect overture, from Leonard Chess. And I figured my operation with Syd . . . well, I was losing something with Syd. I thought he was doing things behind my back. It didn't feel like he was on my side anymore. I had to get away, to start fresh. I felt I was stagnating at King. So, I got a better deal from Leonard Chess and I went over to Chess Records. Simple story."

Bass worked as an A&R man and producer until 1976 for Chess Records, the premier Chicago blues label. During nearly two decades at the label, Bass produced records by Muddy Waters, Howlin' Wolf, Sonny Boy Williamson, and many others. After leaving Chess, Bass continued recording and producing on a freelance basis, working with such blues artists as Magic Slim, Jimmy Johnson, and Sunnyland Slim. Ralph Bass was inducted into the Rock and Roll Hall of Fame in 1991. He died March 5, 1997.

THE SIXTY-MINUTE MEN

Rhythm & Blues Vocal Groups on King Records

• • •

You couldn't do a good R&B radio show in
the 1950s without playing King records.
—Bill "Hoss" Allen, WLAC, Nashville, Tennessee

The line is short and straight from the R&B vocal groups of the 1940s and 1950s back to the black gospel quartets of a decade or two earlier. Quartets such as the Golden Gate Quartet, the Soul Stirrers, and the Harmonizing Four inspired the Ink Spots (with the very influential lead singer Bill Kenney), the Mills Brothers, and such seminal groups as the Delta Rhythm Boys and the Five Red Caps. These highly skilled vocal harmony groups of the 1940s secularized the music of the quartets and brought the sound to the masses.

Next came the "bird groups"—the Ravens, Orioles, Crows, Larks, Robins, Flamingos, Penguins, and so on. These groups had much in common with their gospel and pop forebears. Mostly male, they sang quartet-style harmonies, usually had four to six members ("quartet" in the gospel music context refers to the style of harmony rather than the actual number of singers), and the best of the groups had both a great lead singer and a booming bass singer.

The bird groups *sounded* gospel but were sold as R&B and (with luck) pop. This was no accident, as Charlie Gillett pointed out in *The Sound Of The City:* "Between 1948 and 1952 the potential connections between the emotions of gospel singing and the expectations of adolescent listeners of popular music occurred to various singers, record company executives, and composers. Indirectly and directly, gospel styles and conventions were introduced into rhythm and blues—

and constituted the first significant trend away from the blues as such in black popular music."[1]

King never snared the true high flyers of the bird group genre, but snagged a portion of the market with recordings by the Ravens and the Swallows. The Ravens scored a big R&B hit in 1948 with "Bye Bye Baby Blues," King's first hit with a secular black vocal group. That success opened the floodgates for the many groups that followed.

The Ravens was a Baltimore group built around bass singer Jimmy Ricks, one of the most distinctive singers in the history of R&B and the major influence on all subsequent R&B bass singers. The Ravens represented something new. By "breaking with the pop-oriented sounds of the Mills Brothers, the Ink Spots, and the Delta Rhythm Boys and introducing a bluesier approach that influenced such later groups as the Dominoes, the Drifters, and the Temptations,"[2] the Ravens were in the vanguard of post-war R&B.

In 1946, the group joined forces with R&B impresario Ben Bart. Besides managing the group, Bart also recorded it for his tiny label, Hub Records. The group cut six songs for Hub in June, including "Bye Bye Baby Blues." Early the next year, the Ravens re-recorded all six songs for Bart, possibly because of a change in the group's membership. Bart sat on the records, though, and the group landed a contract with National. The Ravens had several big hits for National, including "Old Man River."

Syd Nathan purchased the Hub recordings by the Ravens in June 1948. King's first Ravens release, "Bye Bye Baby Blues," was a Top Ten R&B hit. Because he had only six songs by the group (albeit two versions of each), Nathan carefully rationed the Ravens material. Three of the remaining songs were released on King singles, but each was paired with an instrumental effort by another artist. None sold as well as "Bye Bye Baby Blues."

That was the extent of King's involvement with the Ravens, but it convinced Nathan that there was money to be made with vocal groups. King tested the water with the Ravens, and the results were highly encouraging. That success led directly to the Dominoes, the Midnighters, the 5 Royales, and all the other groups that made history with King.

● ● ●

If church-going folks had been shocked by Roy Brown's mixing of blues and gospel music, they were outraged by Billy Ward and the Dominoes. The group looked like a gospel quartet and had the drive, energy, and virtuoso singing of a great gospel quartet. That was part of what made the group's "Sixty Minute Man" so scandalous. This record wasn't just banned in Boston—it was banned from radio airplay practically everywhere. Despite that (or because of it), "Sixty Minute Man" was the biggest R&B hit of 1951 and probably the biggest R&B record of the first half of the 1950s.

Born in 1921 and raised in Philadelphia, Billy Ward was something of a child prodigy as a composer. After wartime service in the Army, Ward studied at Juilliard and then set up shop in New York as a singing teacher, pianist, songwriter, arranger, singer, and gospel quartet coach. He was one of the primary forces in the blending of gospel music and blues that reshaped R&B in the 1950s.

As a leading vocal coach in Harlem, Ward was working with several outstanding young gospel singers when he decided to form a secular group in 1950. After a false start or two, he formed a group called the Ques with four of his students: Clyde McPhatter, Bill Brown, Charlie White, and Joe Lamont. Renamed the Dominoes, the young quartet conquered the R&B world within months of its creation.

Success came almost immediately. With Ward playing piano, the Dominoes won an amateur show at Harlem's Apollo Theatre, a legendarily tough crucible of talent. That victory earned them a spot on Arthur Godfrey's radio show, *Talent Scouts*, which the group won with a four-part harmony version of "Goodnight, Irene," a big hit at the time. Rene Hall, an arranger and talent scout for King, signed the group for the label.

Despite Ralph Bass's colorful anecdote (related in Chapter 10), Ward likely didn't need to be told that his stars were lead singer Clyde McPhatter and bass singer Bill Brown. Ward knew what he was doing; he handpicked this group for maximum commercial impact. As for Bass's complaint that the Dominoes sounded like a pop group, that aspect of them was by design. Ward's dream for his group was mainstream pop music success of a level that few black entertainers had then achieved. Ward *wanted* the group to sound pop, but if the label wanted R&B, well, it could do that, too.

The Dominoes first recorded in November 1950, cutting four songs for King's new subsidiary label Federal. "We were very frightened in the studio when we were recording," remembered lead singer Clyde McPhatter.[3] "We had patterned ourselves after the Ink Spots because I had such a high voice, but I just didn't believe in trying to sound like Bill Kenney [lead singer of the Ink Spots], and that's how we started the gospel stuff.

"Billy Ward was teaching us the song, and he'd say, 'Sing it up.' I said, 'Well, I don't feel it that way' and he said, 'Try it your way.' I felt more relaxed if I wasn't confined to the melody. I would take liberties with it, and he'd say 'That's great, do it that way.'"

The group's debut single, "Do Something for Me," cracked the R&B Top Ten and the Dominoes took off. The group returned to the studio in December and recorded two songs, including "Sixty Minute Man," a showcase for the exceptional bass singer Bill Brown. The record was released in March 1951. The trouble began about ten minutes later.

Double-entendre blues songs are a tradition dating back to the dawn of the recording industry. But "Sixty Minute Man" crossed some invisible line and unleashed a firestorm of criticism and condemnation from politicians, religious leaders, and media pundits. The record—a ribald tale of a "mighty, mighty man" known as "lovin' Dan"—*was* pretty explicit for 1951. The self-proclaimed "Sixty Minute Man" broke it down for those keeping score: fifteen minutes each of "kissing," "teasing," and "squeezing," followed by a climactic quarter-hour of "blowing my top." Well, now.

The real problem with "Sixty Minute Man" was that it was among the first raunchy R&B records to be purchased by thousands of white kids. What had been merely risqué was suddenly beyond the pale—an unmistakable sign of society's moral decline. The record rocketed up the R&B chart, spending a total of thirty weeks there, including an astounding three and a half months in the top position. The record also crossed over to the pop chart, where it peaked at number seventeen. As have countless artists before and since, the Dominoes learned that controversy is not necessarily bad for sales.

The Dominoes contained three of the most gifted and identifiable R&B singers of the 1950s. The first was basso Bill Brown, who provided lead vocals on "Sixty Minute Man" and such records as "Chicken Blues" and "Love, Love, Love." The second was Clyde McPhatter, a gospel-tinged tenor from Durham, North Carolina. McPhatter was only sixteen years old when the Dominoes began recording, but his powerful and emotional singing made an instant connection with the fans.

Clyde McPhatter (1933–72) sang lead on most of the early hits of the Dominoes, including "Do Something for Me," "I Am with You," "That's What You're Doing to Me," "Have Mercy Baby" (another huge hit, with twenty weeks on the R&B chart, ten at number one), "I'd Be Satisfied," "The Bells," and "Don't Leave Me This Way."

With his "dramatic tenor style, filled with effortlessly soaring glides, fluttering sobs, cascading melismas, and great rhythmic invention,"[4] McPhatter helped lay the foundation for soul music. He was a tremendously influential singer; Jackie Wilson, Smokey Robinson, and Ben E. King are just three of the vocalists who followed McPhatter's lead in mixing gospel and secular styles. As Ben E. King said, "It all came together in Clyde. He could sing the blues, but he had that gospel sound since he came up in church."[5]

Billy Ward was a superb judge of talent, but he was also a stern taskmaster. He had apparently picked up a taste for regulations and discipline in the Army, and more than one musician complained, as bass singer Dave McNeil did, that Ward "tried to run his group like a squad in the Army."[6] Except that Ward's troops had to down a mandatory glass of warm milk at bedtime. That was the rule.

It was inevitable that conflicts would arise between Ward and the individual Dominoes. There were several areas of friction. Some were relatively minor: Ward was prone to introducing McPhatter as his younger brother, "Clyde Ward," and after "Have Mercy Baby" hit it big, the group became Billy Ward & the Dominoes, which nettled the singers.

The financial complaints were more serious. Each of the Dominoes was paid a flat weekly salary, which meant they benefited little from the huge hits and lucrative coast-to-coast touring. They even had to buy their own on-stage "uniforms." The profits were to have been invested on behalf of the Dominoes, but several group members have said they know nothing about that. Ward also served as the group's co-manager (along with his business partner, Rose Marks), which would seem to be an obvious conflict of interest.

And then there were Ward's rules. Ward was certainly not the first or the only bandleader to have a system of rules, regulations, and fines to keep group members in line. James Brown was infamous for his tight discipline in the 1960s and 1970s, and many black gospel quartets had formal rules for themselves. But Ward was apparently a martinet's martinet.

In addition to the nightly glass of warm milk, there were rules and fines covering a variety of infractions. Facial hair was not allowed, nor was talking to the chauffeur or members of the backing band. Unshined shoes earned a fine. If a group member left his hotel room at night, it was a $50 fine; the fine was doubled if one member knew of another member's absence and didn't report it to Ward.

Tenor singer Charlie White was the first to flee, leaving the Dominoes in 1951 to start his own group, the Checkers. Bill Brown left in early 1952 to join White. Brown's replacement, Dave McNeil, lasted only about seven months before he left to join the Army, which pretty much says it all about the environment within the group.

Finally, in April 1953, McPhatter quit to form *his* own group. Ward always claimed that he fired McPhatter, and that may be true because Ward had a replacement groomed and ready to take over: Jackie Wilson, a native of Detroit and a former Golden Gloves boxer. The third great singer to pass through the Dominoes, Wilson (1934–84) was one of the most exciting R&B performers of the 1950s and 1960s. While his claim that he could "out-sing McPhatter" is arguable, Wilson certainly kept the ball rolling by singing lead on such hits as "You Can't Keep a Good Man Down," "Until The Real Thing Comes Along," and "I'm Gonna Move to the Outskirts of Town."

The Dominoes enjoyed a profitable association with legendary disc jockey Alan Freed. Often credited with coining the term "rock and roll," Freed supposedly had his "eureka" moment (at least according to Ward) when he first heard Lovin' Dan boast "I rock 'em, roll 'em, all night long" in "Sixty Minute Man."

Freed booked the Dominoes for his March 1952 "Moondog Coronation Ball," the first large-scale concert he promoted. Although a riot at the oversold Cleveland Arena prevented the Dominoes from performing, the group did get to perform at the "Moondog Maytime Ball" a few months later and at Freed's "Second Annual Moondog Birthday Party" and "Holiday Ball" the following year.

In June 1954, Ward announced that the Dominoes were leaving for Jubilee Records, despite a contract with King that still had a year to run. Even if Nathan thought the group had run its hitmaking course (which he did), he wasn't about to let one of his acts walk out on a contract. King sued and won, and the Dominoes were forced to stay at King until the following June.

Ward still had pop ambitions for the Dominoes, and the group's post-King recordings for Decca and Liberty were in that vein. The Dominoes had a few hits during the late 1950s ("Stardust" was the biggest), but the group also recorded such schlock as "Hawaiian Wedding Song" and "When Irish Eyes Are Smiling." By this time, the Dominoes weren't even mentioned on some of the albums; the billing was now the Billy Ward Orchestra and Chorus.

Clyde McPhatter and Jackie Wilson both survived being fired by Ward. Shortly after leaving the Dominoes, McPhatter signed with Atlantic Records and formed the Drifters. One of the most successful groups of the decade, the Drifters had such huge hits as "Money Honey," "What'cha Gonna Do," "Honey Love," and "White Christmas." McPhatter went solo in 1955 and had a productive stint on Atlantic.

Jackie Wilson was fired by Ward in 1957, at which point he launched a highly successful solo career. He racked up a number of big hits for Brunswick Records in the next few years, including "Lonely Teardrops," "Baby Workout," and the exquisite "(Your Love Keeps Lifting Me) Higher and Higher."

During the five years the Dominoes recorded for Federal and King, the group set a new standard for R&B vocal groups that was hard to top. In McPhatter, Wilson, and Bill Brown, the Dominoes had three of the best singers in R&B. Several of the group's hits, most notably "Sixty Minute Man," have attained classic, even iconic, status.

However harsh his methods and discipline, Ward coaxed great performances from his singers, with nine Top Ten R&B hits between 1951 and 1953 to show for it. The Dominoes may have hated Billy Ward at times, but they sure sang for him. Clyde McPhatter and Jackie Wilson were inducted into the Rock & Roll Hall of Fame in 1987. The Dominoes will surely join them one day.

• • •

The Midnighters—Detroit's first great R&B singing group—couldn't buy a hit in its early days. The talent was definitely there; only the hits were missing. After signing with Federal in 1951, the group cut song after song without a hit. Of their first nine records, only "Get It" sold appreciably.

But instead of giving up, Henry Glover and, later, Ralph Bass patiently worked with the group. They hit paydirt in 1954 with a massive hit on the group's tenth single, a song written by Hank Ballard called "Work with Me, Annie."

The Midnighters story begins with a young group of singers in Detroit called the Royals. Organized in 1950 by baritone singer Charles Sutton, the group included Henry Booth, Sonny Woods, and Lawson Smith (who was drafted a year later and replaced by Hank Ballard). The quartet was augmented by songwriter, arranger, and guitarist Alonzo Tucker, a man several years older than the others.

In 1951, the Royals won an amateur talent contest at the Paradise Theater in Detroit. Besides the $25 first prize, the group caught the ear of bandleader Johnny Otis, at the time a roving talent scout for King. Otis told the young singers he thought they could make records, and that if they signed a one-year management deal with him, he'd get them a contract with Federal. The Royals signed, and Otis delivered.

The Royals recorded four songs for Federal in January 1952, four more in May, and four more in November. Nothing much happened with any of the resulting records, though the group's first session was notable for introducing Johnny Otis's song "Every Beat of My Heart," which resurfaced in 1961 as the hit that launched Gladys Knight & the Pips.

Hank Ballard (1936–2003) joined the group shortly after its first session. By the spring of 1953, Ballard was the group's primary lead singer and songwriter. At about the same time, Alonzo Tucker gave the guitar-playing job to Arthur Porter, who was replaced within about a year by Cal Green, a hot Texas guitarist and arranger. Also, from 1954 on, the Royals were produced exclusively by Ralph Bass.

The change in producers paid immediate dividends with the January 1954 recording of "Work with Me, Annie." The Royals had not met Bass before this session because the producer had been on the west coast since 1951. As Bass remembered it, "Hank Ballard came in with a song to record.[7] The title was 'Sock

It to Me, Mattie' ["Mary" in other tellings], but it was nasty. I said, 'Hank, that's too nasty, man. We can't do the song with that title because nobody will play it.' So I was trying to think of a title we could use.

"I had gone out on the road with Little Esther Phillips and Johnny Otis. He had asked me to manage Little Esther after I had all those first hits with Esther on Savoy and she was the hottest thing in the country. I wanted to see the south through the eyes of a black person, not through the eyes of a white person, so that's why I went.

"Anyway, there used to be a word they used called 'work.' If they were in a club and there was a dancer or musician performing great, they'd say, 'Work with it.' Or we'd be on the bus and we'd get to a town and see a pretty girl on the street, they'd lift up the window and say, 'Work time.' Finally, [the title] came to me: 'Work with Me, Annie.'"

It seems odd that Bass thought a new title would solve the problems with the song, as its lyrics contain the now-infamous "Annie please don't cheat/give me all my meat" and "let's get it while the getting is good." Bass also knew, of course, that "work" was more than "a word they used," that it was a common black slang term for sexual intercourse. The song was recorded and quickly released. If "Sixty Minute Man" was the epitome of double-entendre humor, "Work with Me, Annie" came right to the point, with no ambiguity whatsoever.

The record was banned immediately by most radio stations from coast to coast. Needless to say, the record shot straight to the top of the *Billboard* R&B chart. Despite universal condemnation, the record spent twenty-six weeks on the chart in 1954, buoyed by jukebox play, word-of-mouth publicity, and the always potent allure of the forbidden.

The controversy was more intense than it had been three years earlier with "Sixty Minute Man," but there was one similarity—the "problem" was as much with the audience as the song. According to R&B researcher Marv Goldberg, "'Work with Me, Annie' probably had more to do with introducing white teenagers to R&B than any other song. It wasn't the first crossover R&B hit: 'Sixty Minute Man' had crossed over in 1951, and the Crows' 'Gee' crossed over in 1954. [But those] were the cracks in the dike; 'Annie' was the floodwaters let loose!"[8]

By the spring of 1954, the music industry was in a tizzy. A group of New York-area DJs banded together in the Metropolitan Disk Jockey Club and Association of Broadcasters and announced their intent to boycott dirty records and to pressure the labels to stop releasing them.[9] DJs in other cities avoided releases from certain labels (such as King and Federal). To Peter Potter, the host of CBS's *Juke Box Jury*, "All rhythm and blues records are dirty and as bad for kids as dope."[10]

The massive success of "Annie" inspired countless sequels, answer songs, songs about Annie's relatives, gender-reversal songs, even songs for white kids in which "work" received a euphemistic downgrade to "dance."

In a story that may be apocryphal, a Los Angeles DJ supposedly played "Work with Me, Annie" and then quipped, "If you think this one is great, you should hear their version of 'Annie Had A Baby.'" Of course, there was no such song, but so many orders for the record came into King that Henry Glover and Syd Nathan sat down and wrote (or were at least credited with writing) "Annie Had a Baby." A much wittier song than "Work with Me, Annie," it's actually a fairly perceptive look at the changes in a young couple's life after the birth of a baby.

The Royals were suddenly rechristened the Midnighters in April 1954. Nathan made the change without consulting any of the Royals, and some group members resented the new name because of perceived racial implications. Nathan said he made the change to avoid confusion between the Royals and the 5 Royales, which suddenly mattered to him because he was trying to lure the 5 Royales away from Apollo.

The Midnighters followed "Work with Me Annie" with another Hank Ballard original, "Sexy Ways," a huge R&B hit that peaked at number two on the charts. Further hits came in quick succession: "Annie Had A Baby" (number one on the R&B chart), "Annie's Aunt Fanny," "Henry's Got Flat Feet (Can't Dance No More)," and "It's Love Baby." All but "Henry" were Top Ten R&B hits.

Listening to the Midnighters, it's obvious that Hank Ballard was influenced by Clyde McPhatter, though Ballard also idolized country singer Gene Autry. Ballard was not as smooth as McPhatter, but the young Detroiter, only seventeen when he wrote and sang "Work with Me, Annie," had a distinctive and powerful voice and an engaging style. Besides, where McPhatter was an R&B and pop vocalist, Ballard was a rock singer—one of the first and part of a new breed. In the words of Cliff White, the Midnighters "were briskly transformed from old to new wave" by Ballard.[11]

After "It's Love Baby" in 1955, the Midnighters went into a slump. The group continued to record, but only "Tore Up Over You" and "In the Doorway Crying" made much impact. After a bit of retooling, the group reemerged in 1958 on King as Hank Ballard & the Midnighters. The catalyst for the group's rebirth was a song Ballard wrote called "The Twist." Nathan reportedly did not like the song (Ralph Bass was gone by now and working for Chess) and agreed to release it only as the B-side to "Teardrops on Your Letter."

"Teardrops on Your Letter" was a Top Five R&B hit, but "The Twist" also did respectably, reaching number sixteen on the R&B chart in 1959. Perhaps influenced by the Top Five success of the group's "Finger Poppin' Time," Nathan decided to re-release "The Twist" in the summer of 1960. His decision probably also took into account the fact that Hank and the group continued to perform "The Twist" (and a little dance they made up to go with it) to wild response at their gigs.

Whatever Nathan's motivation, his intuition was correct, and the record rose to number six on the chart. It was a big enough hit that Dick Clark, the unctuous and clean-cut young host of the *American Bandstand* television show, put aside his personal disdain for the group (he found their music "dirty") and invited the Midnighters to appear on his hit program. It was a golden opportunity for the group.

Except that the Midnighters never made it to Philadelphia for the show. There are numerous stories (many of them scandalous and all of them entertaining) claiming to explain why the Midnighters missed the most important gig of their career. At any rate, they missed it.

That wasn't a big problem for Clark because guests on *Bandstand* "lip-synched" along with their records instead of actually singing. Being the resourceful operator he was, Clark recruited young Ernest Evans, a local amateur singer and mimic, to take the stage and lip-synch along to Ballard's singing on the record.

Clark hustled Evans into the studio the next day, recorded a note-for-note copy of the Midnighters' record (even appropriating Ballard's peculiar "ee-ahh" vocal tic), and rushed it onto the market. As Ballard said, "They did an absolute clone."[12]

Released on Parkway as being by Chubby Checker (a play on Fats Domino), this copy of "The Twist" quickly eclipsed Ballard's original, thanks to Clark's incessant promotion of the Checker record.

The Midnighters placed several more hits in the R&B Top Ten over the next year or two, including "The Hoochi Coochi Coo," "The Float," "The Switch-a-Roo," "Nothing But Good," and "Lets' Go, Let's Go, Let's Go." The hits dried up after 1961 and Ballard was working as a solo by the end of the decade, often as part of the James Brown revue. Ballard's last hit on King, "How You Gonna Get Respect (If You Haven't Cut Your Process Yet?)" in 1968, was produced by Brown and credited to Hank Ballard & the Dapps (a Cincinnati rock band).

Ballard recorded sporadically through the 1970s for a variety of small labels and even made a few country records. He had assembled a new group of Midnighters by the mid-1980s and toured with the group to rave reviews. In 1990, Hank Ballard was inducted into the Rock & Roll Hall of Fame.

On stage at the San Francisco Blues Festival in the mid-1990s, Hank Ballard & the Midnighters enthralled the huge audience, not as an "oldies" act but as a sharp-looking, slick-dancing, hard-rocking group that whipped the crowd into an absolute frenzy. For at least a moment, it felt as though forty years had fallen away. The biggest ovation of the show came when Ballard, with a wide grin on his face, introduced "a romantic ballad about a little girl named Annie." Hank Ballard died in 2003.

• • •

After the Dominoes and the Midnighters, the most successful R&B group on King was the Charms, which had five Top Ten R&B hits between 1954 and 1957. Organized by a Cincinnati high school student named Otis Williams (not the Otis Williams who later sang with the Temptations), the Charms recorded prolifically for King and its subsidiary DeLuxe, cutting nearly 100 songs over a ten-year period.

One of the very few acts on King actually from Cincinnati, the Charms took a roundabout route to the label. In 1952, Nathan forged a business alliance with a Florida record man named Henry Stone, who owned the labels Rockin' and Glory. In the deal, Nathan "transferred" Roy Brown and Dave Bartholomew from DeLuxe to King and then turned DeLuxe over to Stone as an outlet for Stone's production efforts. Glory and Rockin' closed up shop, and the labels' releases were selectively reissued on DeLuxe and eventually on King LPs.

The Charms was the first act Stone recorded for DeLuxe. The Charms didn't have much luck initially. Things changed suddenly in the fall of 1954, when the Charms' release of "Hearts of Stone," a cover of a record by the Jewels, outsold the original and made it to the top of the R&B chart.

The Charms' next hit was a successful cover of the Five Keys, "Ling Ting Tong," which entered the Top Ten early in 1955. About six weeks later, "Two Hearts, Two Kisses (Make One Love)" also dented the Top Ten. "Ko Ko Mo (I Love You So)" and "Whadaya Want" made a bit of regional noise.

By the end of 1955, the Stone-Nathan partnership had run aground. In December, Stone started Chart Records and took the Charms with him, but not Williams. Williams continued to record for DeLuxe, first as Otis Williams, then as Otis Williams and His New Group, and finally as Otis Williams and the Charms. Williams hit it big with "Ivory Tower" and "United," and also had smaller hits with "That's Your Mistake," "Gum Drop," and "Don't Wake Up the Kids." From 1960 through a final session in July 1962, the group's recordings were issued on King. After a hiatus of several years, Williams staged a comeback in 1971 with *Otis Williams and the Midnight Cowboys*, a country album recorded in Nashville with an all-black country band. The album sank like a stone.

The Swallows, a vocal quintet from Baltimore, had Top Ten R&B hits on King in 1951 and 1952, "Will You Be Mine" and "Beside You." Not to be confused with the Chicago-based Swallows (which became the Flamingos, probably the only black Jewish vocal group in 1950s R&B), these Swallows formed in 1946. As three of the group members played instruments in addition to singing, this was one of the few "self-contained" bands in early R&B.

Signed by Henry Glover to King, the Swallows recorded four songs in April 1951 featuring lead singer Eddie Rich. The band's first release, "Will You Be Mine," made it into the R&B Top Ten. "Eternally" and "It Ain't the Meat (It's The Motion)" were both minor hits, but the Swallows next cracked the Top Ten in 1952 with a song written and sung by Herman "Junior" Denby, "Beside You." From then on, Denby did most of the lead singing in the group, giving the Swallows a cooler, bluesier sound.

The Swallows left King in 1953 and began a downward spiral into oblivion. Denby quit the group soon after it left King and returned to the label for a solo session in 1954 before being drafted into the Army. In a great it-could-happen-only-at-King postscript, the Swallows resurfaced on Federal in 1958 with a country-oriented sound. A single featuring the new approach, a cover of country singer Don Gibson's "Oh Lonesome Me," was released. It failed to chart, as did the remainder of the group's Federal releases. The Swallows' last release for Federal, "Itchy Twitchy Feeling," generated only minor interest.

Although virtually all the R&B vocal groups of the 1950s were influenced by gospel quartets, the 5 Royales, a group from Winston-Salem, North Carolina, actually *was* a gospel quartet. Organized in the late 1940s as the Royal Sons by Johnny Tanner and Lowman Pauling, the group developed a reputation as church-wrecking performers. The Royal Sons soon came to the attention of Apollo Records.

The group began recording in 1951. At the second session, someone asked if the group knew any R&B songs. One of the tastiest guitarists on the gospel circuit, Pauling was also a gifted songwriter and—now that you mention it—he had a couple of songs that might work. One of them, "You Know I Know," was a big enough regional R&B hit that it forced the group into a decision.

The gospel-singing Royal Sons were history. The group was now a full-bore R&B outfit called the 5 Royales ("pronounced roy-ALS, not ROY-als," according to Johnny Tanner[13]). The 5 Royales hit it big almost immediately, with four Top Ten R&B hits in 1953: "Baby Don't Do It," "Help Me Somebody," "Crazy, Crazy, Crazy," and "Too Much Lovin'." For a year, the group ruled R&B. Then the hits stopped.

The 5 Royales left Apollo in 1954 and signed with King, but the group's first singles on King didn't go anywhere. Finally, in 1957, the Royales had a regional hit in "Tears of Joy." Later that year, an energetic treatment of Lowman Pauling's original song "Think" took the group back into the Top Ten for a final visit.

"Dedicated to the One I Love" (1958) and "The Real Thing" (1959) were the 5 Royales' last hits for King. "Think" and "Dedicated to the One I Love" became R&B and pop standards, thanks to cover versions by James Brown in the first case, and the Shirelles and the Mama & the Papas in the latter.

The 5 Royales exerted an influence on other performers that was vastly out of proportion to the group's chart success. By combining the disparate but related strains of doo-wop, blues, and gospel, the 5 Royales served as a vital bridge between the R&B of the 1950s and the soul music that emerged in the 1960s.

Pauling's exciting blues-drenched guitar playing touched many a young picker, including legendary Stax session guitarist Steve Cropper in Memphis.[14] The Royales' wild stage show, centered around the raw, impassioned lead vocals of brothers Johnny and Eugene Tanner, likewise had a huge impact upon countless groups, most notably James Brown and the Famous Flames. As Brown said of Pauling's song "Think," "Soul really started right there, or at least my kind did."[15]

Pauling also had a brief "solo" recording career on King in 1960 and 1961, recording as El Pauling & the Royalton as well as teaming with singer/pianist Royal Abbit. The 5 Royales left King in 1963 and broke up a few years later.

When tenor singer Charlie White left the Dominoes in 1951, it was announced in *Billboard* that he would be both joining the Clovers (a successful group on Atlantic) and recording as a solo for Atlantic.[16] Although that eventually happened, it took about a year and a half for White to make it to the Clovers. As soon as Nathan heard White was leaving the Dominoes, Nathan asked him to form a new group to record for King. White agreed and organized the Checkers.

Within a few months, bass singer Bill Brown had also fled Billy Ward's discipline in the Dominoes and joined White in his new group. The Checkers first recorded for King in June 1952, and though the group recorded twenty-one sides over the next two years for King, nothing made the national charts.

Charlie White left early in 1953 and finally joined the Clovers. Under Brown's leadership, the Checkers created a bit of regional noise in 1954 with "White Cliffs of Dover" and a bit more with the double-sided hit "House with No Windows" and "Don't Stop Dan," in which Brown revived his Lovin' Dan persona. A talented group that never quite put it together, the Checkers disbanded in 1955.

Every label in history has occasionally misjudged talent, and the Platters was "one that got away" from King. Signed by Ralph Bass, the Los Angeles-based group began recording for Federal in 1953, cutting sixteen sides over the next two years. "Love All Night," "Maggie Doesn't Work Here Anymore," and "Tell the World" were minor hits in California in 1954 and 1955, but nothing clicked nationally.

Then, in 1955, a group called the Penguins had a massive hit with "Earth Angel." Mercury Records wanted the group for its roster. The Penguins' manager, Samuel "Buck" Ram, told Mercury it could have the Penguins only if the label also signed another of Ram's groups, the Platters. Desperate to get the Penguins, Mercury agreed. The Penguins never had another big hit. The Platters became the most successful black vocal group of the 1950s, producing twelve Top Twenty hits for Mercury, including the classics "Only You" and "The Great Pretender."

YOU GIVE ME FEVER

Solo R&B Singers on King Records

• • •

Willie John's songs were about knowin',
then missin'. Kind of missin' makes me scream.
Willie John did not scream it. No. But you could
hear it. To me it was very loud.

—James Brown

Henry Glover called Little Willie John "the artist of all artists," and though he laughed when he said it, Glover wasn't kidding. "He was in a class all to himself," Glover told writer Steve Tracy.[1] "He was a really truly great singer. I would say that blues came so natural to him that he was just a master at that and no one living during that day could touch him. He had some of the greatest blues gymnastics and voice gyration that you could ever dream of a person having."

Unfortunately, William John (1937–68) was also, as Glover put it with admirable restraint, "a headache."[2] Little Willie John hit it big at a young age, flamed out early, and came to a bad end, dying in prison serving a sentence for manslaughter. His recording career lasted only nine years, but he still became a major star, known for his huge hit "Fever" and eleven other Top Twenty R&B hits. James Brown has hailed Little Willie John's pioneering efforts, calling John "a soul singer before anyone thought to call it that."[3]

John was born in Camden, Arkansas, but grew up in Detroit. He was a precocious talent who began his career while still a young boy with a gospel quartet called the United Four, which also included Willie's sister, Mable John (a successful singer in her own right, with recordings on Motown and Stax and as one of Ray Charles's Raelettes). By the age of fourteen, Willie was a seasoned performer. His voice was hip, powerful, and yearning, all at the same time.

As noted earlier, the Royals/Midnighters had been "discovered" in 1951 at a talent contest at the Paradise Theater in Detroit. Talent scout Johnny Otis had actually recommended three acts from the contest to King, but Nathan accepted only the Royals, passing on both Jackie Wilson and Little Willie John.

John performed in Detroit clubs before going on the road with bandleader Paul Williams in 1954, belting out "The Hucklebuck" with a big voice that belied his young age and diminutive stature. John also recorded his first single, "Mommy, What Happened to the Christmas Tree?" By the summer of 1955, however, he was in New York, fired by Williams and needing money. In desperation, he went to see Henry Glover at King's branch office.

"I think his success was just written in the cards," Glover recalled. "Willie John came into my office. I heard Willie John at five o'clock and I was so impressed with him that at eight o'clock I had musicians in the studio and I recorded him. 'All Around the World' had just been released that day [by Titus Turner]. I picked the record up, covered it, and changed the arrangement completely."[4]

"All Around the World"—with its immortal chorus of 'Well, if I don't love you baby/grits ain't groceries/eggs ain't poultries/and Mona Lisa was a man'—was John's first release on King. Featuring crisp guitar fills by Mickey Baker and a lusty sax solo by Willis "Gatortail" Jackson, the record was a big hit, spending four months on the R&B charts, peaking at number six. It was a good showcase for John's muscular yet supple voice, and it got his solo career off to a rousing start.

Willie John was one of the greatest singers of the 1950s. He was also one of the most copied vocalists of the era: singers from James Brown to Al Green have cited John as a primary influence. Still, some critics have downplayed his contributions and importance because John's singing lacked the showy virtuosity of such contemporaries as Clyde McPhatter, Jackie Wilson, or Roy Brown.

But that misses the point because John was not trying for that kind of sound. John was a power singer. His aim was to nail the listener to the wall, even with a ballad, and he usually succeeded. "He could go head to head with any singer in his field," said Hank Ballard. "Willie could cut another singer to pieces with his blues ballads."[5]

The follow-up to "All Around the World," a ballad titled "Need Your Love So Bad," made the R&B Top Five. John did his best work in his first three years on King, when he recorded under the direction of Henry Glover. A sympathetic and astute producer, Glover recorded John in New York with such top-shelf musicians as Willis Jackson and Hal Singer (tenor sax), Mickey Baker, Kenny Burrell, and Bill Jennings (guitar), as well as in Cincinnati with Ray Felder and Rufus Gore (tenor sax), Edwyn Conley (bass), and John Faire (guitar).

Willie John hit a home run with his fourth single for King, "Fever," a song co-written by Otis Blackwell. The record was John's only number one single, his first appearance on the pop charts, and the definitive version of a song that became a classic through recordings by Peggy Lee, Elvis Presley, and others. As James Brown once said, "'Fever' will beat what any dictionary tell you about soul."[6] John's original record (most fans will want to avoid the version with a garish, overdubbed string section) is a slice of smoldering sexual passion. When he sings "You give me fever," the room heats up.

Willie John had all the tools as a singer—awesome power and range, dynamics, hip phrasing, and an innate musical sophistication—and the hits piled up in the early years. "My Nerves," "Do Something for Me," and "I've Got to Go Cry" all charted by the end of 1957. None was as big as "Fever," however, which led the powers-that-be at King to begin tinkering with John's sound.

Prior to this transformation, Little Willie John was a powerhouse blues singer, belting out ballads and shuffles as effectively as anyone on the circuit. On records such as "All Around the World," "Suffering with the Blues," "Need Your Love So Bad," "Are You Ever Coming Back to Me," and the sublime "Home at Last," John's mighty vocal chops make for compelling listening almost half a century later.

Beginning in 1957, though, one can hear a distinct change in John's records, as King started aiming them more at the pop market. It started with the addition of the wordless, cooing vocal choruses that were all the rage back then and moved on to hideously inappropriate overdubbed string sections, as on "Fever." The nadir is probably the big hit "Sleep" from 1960, in which an overcaffeinated string section of six violins does battle with a cheesy roller-rink organ. It went Top Ten, but it's hard listening.

Despite being saddled with lightweight material and lame production, John still managed the occasional great vocal—"Look What You've Done to Me," "You're a Sweetheart," "All My Love Belongs to You," "Inside Information," and "Leave My Kitten Alone"—though his vocals were increasingly just one piece in the overly busy arrangements. In fairness to King, the approach worked commercially, with John scoring a number of hits between 1957 and 1961, including "Talk to Me, Talk to Me," "Tell It Like It Is," "Let Them Talk," and "Spring Fever."

King dropped Little Willie John in 1963, two years after his last hit, "Take My Love." One of the biggest-selling artists of the 1950s was a has-been at age twenty-five, but John's life had begun to unravel. He had been busted for possession of marijuana in 1961, and heavy drinking had worsened the epileptic seizures John had suffered since childhood. In August 1964, John was arrested in Miami for assault.[7] He jumped bail and headed for the west coast.

By October, John was in Seattle. He got into an argument at an after-hours club and stabbed a man to death. Although the testimony at the trial suggested self-defense—the other man was much bigger and had started the fight by punching John in the mouth—John was convicted of manslaughter, reduced from the original charge of second-degree murder. He again jumped bail and disappeared. He was arrested several months later, in May 1965, and returned to Seattle.

Legal proceedings and hearings managed to delay the inevitable for almost a year, but finally Little Willie John was sent to the state penitentiary in Walla Walla to serve an eight-to-twenty-year sentence. John told his friend James Brown he wouldn't survive prison. He was right. He didn't make it two years.

Syd Nathan kept in touch with Willie John after his legal problems started. In a 1965 letter, Nathan wrote about his worsening health and his feeling that he wasn't long for this world. Nathan was right about that, but the end came soon for Willie John, too. He died on May 26, 1968, the victim of pneumonia, a heart attack, or a severe beating, depending on which source one believes. Little Willie John was only thirty when he died.

Little Willie John is not exactly forgotten today—his version of "Fever" is on countless R&B anthologies, and his songs have been covered by the Beatles, Fleetwood Mac, the Blasters, and numerous others—but he may well be the most overlooked pioneer from the early days of rock and soul music. Willie's vocals, from his desperate pleading to his hoarse, wailing roar, helped shape what came to be called soul music in the 1960s.

Just as John's singing had been shaped by big-band vocalists and gospel singers (especially Sam Cooke, Julius Cheeks, and Claude Jeter), so was John a tremendous influence on such leading soul singers as Wilson Pickett, Aretha Franklin, Otis Redding, and, of course, James Brown. As usual, Brown said it best: "The man left his mark. On my music, on lots of singers who understand how to sing with *feelin'*."[8] Little Willie John was inducted into the Rock & Roll Hall of Fame in 1996.

• • •

R&B in the 1950s was mostly a male preserve, but there were a few talented and determined women who made their marks as singers and musicians during this time. The first to do so on King was Annisteen Allen (1920–92), a soulful singer born in Illinois and raised in Toledo, Ohio.[9] Allen was a big-band singer in the style of Ella Fitzgerald when she was hired in 1945 to work with the Lucky Millinder band, the outfit that provided King with so many early R&B artists.

Allen's given name, Ernestine, apparently reminded Millinder of his Alabama hometown, Anniston, so Millinder combined the two words and rechristened his new singer "Annisteen." The moniker stuck, and it was not until Allen's final recording session, in 1961, that she used her real name on a record.

Allen made her recording debut late in 1945 for King's subsidiary label Queen. Backed by Millinder band mates Bull Moose Jackson, Panama Francis, Hal Singer, and Sir Charles Thompson, Allen cut six songs, including such romantic fare as "I Know How to Do It," "More, More, More," "I Want a Man (Who's Gonna Do It Right)," and "I've Got Big Bulging Eyes for You."

Millinder used to introduce Allen onstage as "a red-hot tamale from San Antonio," and she was all that as a singer. She toured and recorded with the Millinder band through 1954, recording for King as a member of the band and for Queen and King as a solo singer. Allen sang on such Millinder hits as "(Ah Yes) There's Good Blues Tonight," and "I'm Waiting Just for You." She was also one of the first artists to record for Federal, cutting four songs in January 1951 and two more in October of that year.

Things started well for Allen in 1953, when her records began appearing on King, and she had the biggest hit of her career, "Baby, I'm Doin' It." The song was a brassy answer to the 5 Royales' hit on Apollo, "Baby, Don't Do It," and it cracked the R&B Top Ten. Despite that success, King released her after only one more session.

Allen signed with Capitol in 1954; she also recorded for Decca and several tiny labels later in the decade. Her swan song was her finest work on record, a 1961 album called *Let It Roll* with the King Curtis band. It was her only album. She left show business shortly after.

In addition to his work as a talent scout for King, musician and bandleader Johnny Otis was a fixture on the Los Angeles R&B scene. He toured extensively with an outstanding revue, the Rhythm and Blues Caravan, which featured at various times many of his "discoveries"—the Robins, singer Mel Walker, Johnny Guitar Watson, and a young woman, barely a teenager, really, who performed as Little Esther.

A native of Texas who was living in Los Angeles when she began performing, Esther Mae Jones (1935–84) was once the youngest person to have a number one R&B hit record, "Double Crossing Blues" in 1950. She had another number one, "Release Me," in 1962. And she had a Top Ten hit in 1975, "What a Diff'rence a Day Makes." In between were long periods of musical inactivity caused by her heroin addiction.

Little Esther was only thirteen when she recorded "Double Crossing Blues" on Savoy with the Johnny Otis Orchestra. She sang on an amazing five *more* Top Five R&B hits in 1950, including chart toppers "Mistrustin' Blues" and "Cupid's

Boogie." Savvy (or at least experienced) beyond her years, Esther was one of the stars of the hottest R&B act in the country, at a time when her peers were just starting high school.

When Ralph Bass left Savoy for Federal, Little Esther was one of the acts who went with him. Bass wasted little time in getting Esther into the studio, recording four songs in January 1951. "The Deacon Moves In," on which Esther was joined by the Dominoes, was a sizable regional hit. A mildly risqué duet with Mel Walker, "Ring-a-Ding-Doo," was a bigger hit, reaching number eight on the R&B charts.

Little Esther recorded sixteen songs for Federal in 1952, a wide-ranging bunch of cuts that included two duets with Little Willie Littlefield, two duets with Bobby Nunn of the Robins, and another regional hit in "Aged and Mellow." She also made a guest appearance on "Ooh Midnight," a Federal single by Pete "Guitar" Lewis (of "Chocolate Pork Chop Man" fame). Her final session in March 1953 produced the best known of her Federal records, the oft-reissued "Cherry Wine."

Though she recorded thirty-some songs for Federal, only "Ring-a-Ding-Doo" was a national hit. This seems puzzling, as Little Esther was working with the same producer and musicians that she had at Savoy, and the Federal records had essentially the same sound as the Savoy hits. Despite her young age, Esther had a distinctive, sassy voice and a unique sense of timing and phrasing. Her scratchy alto was well suited to the material she recorded, but, for whatever reasons, Little Esther was not as successful on Federal as on Savoy.

When Esther resurfaced in 1962 with her chart-topping cover of the country hit "Release Me," she was known as Esther Phillips. She claimed to have taken her new surname from a Phillips 66 gas station sign. Phillips had one more moment in the spotlight in 1975, when "What a Diff'rence a Day Makes" made both the pop and R&B charts. "Diff'rence" was a fitting coda to a bizarre up-and-down career. Little Esther died in 1984 at the age of 48.

Lula Reed is almost unknown today, but she was a prolific and successful recording artist in the 1950s with a number of R&B hits, including the original version of the classic "I'll Drown in My [Own] Tears" (transformed into an R&B classic by Ray Charles). Her electrifying, right-on-the-edge-of-shrill voice is a bit of an acquired taste, but there are quite a few winners in her catalog of nearly fifty records for King and Federal.

Other than the facts that she was born in Port Clinton, Ohio,[10] in (possibly) 1927,[11] and that she came up through gospel music, surprisingly little is known about Reed's life. She apparently began her recording career on King in late 1951 when she recorded two songs as the vocalist with the Sonny Thompson band. The songs—"I'll Drown In My Tears" and "Let's Call It A Day"—are among Reed's finest recordings, and both were Top Ten R&B hits in the summer of 1952.

After one more session as a member of Thompson's Chicago-based band, she moved out front as a "solo" act, though she would continue to record and tour with the Thompson band throughout her career. She and Thompson married at some point.

Reed had a handful of regional hits in 1954 and 1955, most of them written and produced by Henry Glover, including "Bump on a Log," "Watch Dog," "Your Key Don't Fit It No More," and "Rock Love." She also did a two-song gospel session in 1952, as well as a four-song gospel session in 1954. After a final session in August 1956, Reed and Thompson left King for a stint on the Chess subsidiary label Argo.

Not much came from that association, and by 1961, Reed was back at King, recording now for Federal, which Sonny Thompson had been running since Ralph Bass' departure. Reed did some of her best work on Federal. Her voice had deepened a bit and she was now a most convincing blues singer. "I Got a Notion" and "I'm a Woman But I Don't Talk Too Much" from 1961 are superb blues records, and probably the best of her King/Federal sides. She also recorded four duets with blues guitarist and singer Freddie King the following year that were released on a King album called *Boy—Girl—Boy* (the other "boy" being Sonny Thompson).

Lula Reed recorded for the Tangerine label a year or two later, but she disappeared from the radar screen soon after. Her King and Federal records deserve to be better known, as the best of them hold up very well as solid, enjoyable R&B and blues.

Just as Sonny Thompson's band was the vehicle for Lula Reed, the Todd Rhodes band was a platform for a number of female singers over the years, mostly young women from the Detroit area. Three of them recorded with Rhodes during his time on King: Kitty Stevenson, Connie Allen, and LaVern Baker. Stevenson did not sing on any of Rhodes' hits, but Connie Allen, a singer who had worked previously with Paul Williams' band, sang on one of King's classic "dirty songs," "Rocket 69" from 1952.

LaVern Baker (1929–97) did much better for herself, becoming one of the biggest R&B stars of the decade. Unfortunately for Syd Nathan, her big hits came on Atlantic. Born in Chicago but based as an adult in Detroit, the young singer recorded as Bea Baker and Little Miss Sharecropper for Columbia, OKeh, RCA Victor, and National.

By the early 1950s, Baker was working with the Todd Rhodes band. She sang on two of the band's 1952 King hits, "Pig Latin Blues" and "Trying." The latter song especially shows the church-rooted vocal power and promise that led Baker's manager to steer her to the greener grass at Atlantic Records, where she had seven Top Ten R&B hits during 1955 and 1956 alone, including "Tweedle Dee" and "Jim Dandy." She recorded on Atlantic through the mid-1960s and also starred in two of Alan Freed's low-budget rock and roll movies. She was inducted into the Rock and Roll Hall of Fame in 1991.

Atlanta-born singer Annie Laurie, who was working in New Orleans in the postwar years, had two different relationships with King, first in the late 1940s and again a decade later. After working with a couple of jazz territory bands, Laurie joined the smaller band of New Orleans pianist and singer Paul Gayten in 1947. She recorded four songs fronting the band for DeLuxe and had a Top Ten R&B hit with her first single, "Since I Fell for You." She recorded nearly twenty songs throughout the remainder of 1947, but nothing else made the charts.

When Nathan completed his takeover of DeLuxe in 1948, the Braun brothers, the former owners of DeLuxe, started a new label, Regal. Laurie went with the Brauns to Regal and had two more Top Ten hits in 1949 and 1950. Regal went out of business, and Laurie eventually returned to DeLuxe in 1956. It was a good move because she had the biggest hit of her career the following year, "It Hurts to Be In Love," which hit number three on the R&B chart. "If You're Lonely" made the Top Twenty in 1960, but that was the only other hit from her second stint on DeLuxe. Laurie reportedly retired from secular music not long after that and devoted her magnificent voice solely to church work.

Finally, a salute to the rest of the women who were singin' it and bringin' it on King, Federal and DeLuxe—Lil Greenwood, Tiny Topsy (whose 1957 Federal record of "Miss You So" is blues screaming at its best), Little Miss Cornshucks (not to be confused with Little Miss Sharecropper), Lynn Davis, Beverly Ann Gibson, Mabel Scott, Juanita Nixon, Alice Rozier, Fluffy Hunter, and Cora Woods.

• • •

Between Little Willie John in the 1950s and James Brown in the 1960s, there wasn't much spotlight left over for other male R&B singers at King. A handful of singers recorded hit singles, but none was able to score a second hit for King. Some went on to solid post-King careers; others were never heard from again. With styles ranging from hard R&B to proto-soul, these men helped keep the groove going.

The earliest of them was a singer from Philadelphia named Earl (Connelly) King, whose recording of "Don't Take It So Hard" was a Top Ten hit in 1955. Earl King (not the New Orleans blues guitarist and singer of the same name) was remembered by Henry Glover as "a very good blues singer based on the church, with which, of course, there is a very close tie. The line of demarcation is so thin that you can almost say that they are the same."[12] Recording primarily in New York with Glover producing, King cut twenty songs between 1955 and 1959. Besides "Don't Take It So Hard," only "Big Blue Diamonds" gained much attention.

The New Orleans-born, Buffalo-raised soulman Donnie Elbert had a respectable run of hits in the 1970s on the All Platinum label, but he first made the charts in 1957 while recording for DeLuxe. Elbert recorded about twenty songs for DeLuxe, but only "What Can I Do" in 1957 made the charts. King later released the material on an album, *The Sensational Donnie Elbert Sings*.

It didn't make the national charts, but the wackiest record of this bunch was "Davy, You Upset My Home" by Joe Tex. Long before his hits for Dial in the 1960s and 1970s, Tex spent two years on King. He cut "Davy" at his first session, held in September 1955 in New York.

The song is a tuneful, bouncing R&B rant against American folk hero Davy Crockett—not the real-life frontiersman and politician, but the one portrayed by Fess Parker on the enormously popular three-part Walt Disney television event in 1955. The larger-than life figure of Davy was causing problems for the song's narrator.

For starters, his "baby" was buying "Davy Crockett this and Davy Crockett that," including the requisite coonskin hat. Second, and more troubling, his baby had compared him to Davy Crockett and found the singer a bit, well, lacking. Not only had he failed to "kill him a bear when he was only three," to quote the TV show's theme song, he had yet to "fight through no Indian war." Now that's cold.

Sydney Nathan, circa 1940s. Photo courtesy of © Gusto Records, Inc.

Sydney Nathan, circa late 1950s. Photo courtesy of © Gusto Records, Inc.

Grandpa Jones, King's first successful recording artist. Photo courtesy of © Gusto Records, Inc.

The Delmore Brothers, Alton (*left*) and Rabon (*right*), the greatest duo in country music history. Photo courtesy of © Gusto Records, Inc.

Syd Nathan with some of his early artists, circa 1947–48; Syd Nathan (*fourth from left*), Bull Moose Jackson (*fifth from left, seated*); others unidentified. Photo courtesy of © Gusto Records, Inc.

Henry Glover. Photo courtesy of © Gusto Records, Inc.

Henry Glover and Syd Nathan. Photo courtesy of © Gusto Records, Inc.

Syd Nathan and associates at Coin Machine Industries Convention in Nashville, 1947; Syd Nathan (*left*), Al Miller (*third from left*), others unidentified. Photo courtesy of © Gusto Records, Inc.

Wynonie Harris, Mr. Blues.
Photo courtesy of © Gusto
Records, Inc.

Homer & Jethro at WLW, Cincinnati; Jethro Burns (*left*), Homer Haynes (*right*). Photo courtesy of © Gusto Records, Inc.

A busy day at the King pressing plant, circa late 1940s. Photo courtesy of © Gusto Records, Inc.

Bill Doggett and Syd Nathan with one of Doggett's gold records, circa 1956; (*left to right*) Bill Doggett, Clifford Scott, Billy Butler, Shep Shepherd, Syd Nathan. Photo courtesy of © Gusto Records, Inc.

Moon Mullican, the King of the Hillbilly Piano Players, posing here with a guitar for some reason. Photo courtesy of © Gusto Records, Inc.

Syd Nathan and Hank Ballard.
Photo courtesy of © Gusto
Records, Inc.

Little Willie John.
Photo courtesy of © Gusto
Records, Inc.

Sonny Thompson and Lula Reed. Photo courtesy of © Gusto Records, Inc.

Don Reno and Red Smiley. Photo courtesy of © Gusto Records, Inc.

The Stanley Brothers: Ralph (*left*), Carter (*right*). Photo courtesy of © Gusto Records, Inc.

Freddie King with his Gibson
Les Paul. Photo courtesy of
© Gusto Records, Inc.

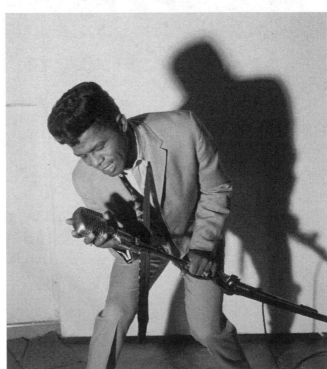

James Brown, the Hardest-
Working Man in Show
Business. Photo courtesy
of © Gusto Records, Inc.

James Brown turning on the charm. Photo courtesy of © Gusto Records, Inc.

Syd Nathan and Hal Neely presenting a gold record to James Brown for his single of "I Got You (I Feel Good)," 1966; Nathan (*left*), Brown, Neely (*right*). Photo courtesy of © Gusto Records, Inc.

James Brown and Syd Nathan, 1966. Photo courtesy of © Gusto Records, Inc.

EVERY TIME I FEEL THE SPIRIT

Black Gospel Music on King Records

• • •

I do not pastor a church, because the church is in
the heart of men. I evangelize wherever I am.

—Reverend Claude Jeter, The Swan Silvertones

It wasn't always Saturday night at King Records. Religious music, especially that
of black Americans, was an important part of the King mix from the earliest
days of Queen Records until King sputtered to a halt in the early 1970s. This was
entirely consistent with Nathan's oft-stated goal of making music for "the little
man." Gospel music was also a niche in which King could prosper, as the major
record companies were largely uninterested in the music.

Black gospel records on King fit into three categories: gospel quartets, small
groups of usually four to seven singers who sang old hymns and spirituals in four-
part *a cappella* harmony; gospel choirs, much larger vocal groups patterned after
the "mass" choirs assembled each year at the National Baptist Convention; and
everything else, including solo singers, duets, steel guitarists, singing preachers,
preaching singers, organists, and Elder Charles Beck, a traveling evangelist who
played trumpet to accompany his singing.

Of the many quartets that recorded for King and its associated labels, the best
known was the Swan Silvertones. Led for thirty years by Claude Jeter, one of the
greatest voices of the twentieth century, the Silvertones recorded forty-five songs
for Queen and King between 1946 and 1951. The group's later, harder-edged gospel
recordings for Specialty and Vee-Jay are more highly esteemed by modern critics,
but it was the Silvertones' work for King that established the group nationally.

These records featured superb tight-harmony quartet singing and are fascinating as a portrait of a quartet, and a style of music, in transition.

Claude Jeter (1914–2009) was born near Birmingham in Jefferson County, Alabama, ground zero for black gospel quartet singing in America. He moved to Kentucky as a child and was working as a coal miner in West Virginia by the late 1930s.[1] In 1938, he organized a quartet called the Four Harmony Kings, which changed its name a few years later to the Silvertone Singers to avoid confusion with the better-known Kings of Harmony. A final name change to the Swan Silvertones came in 1942 when the group began singing on a Knoxville radio program sponsored by the Swan Bakery Company.

The Silvertones maintained a stable line-up during the group's five-year stay on King. In addition to Jeter on first tenor and lead vocals, the group included baritone John Myles, tenor/lead Solomon Womack, bass Henry Brossard, and (beginning in 1950) tenor/lead Percell Perkins. Womack and Perkins were "shouters," leather-lunged foils for Jeter's smoother approach.

Jeter was an extraordinarily gifted singer, a trailblazer who deeply influenced countless other singers, including Al Green, Ray Charles, Sam Cooke, and Curtis Mayfield, to name just a few. Jeter was the master—past, present, and probably future—of the falsetto. Jeter claimed his falsetto, which he called a "lyric tenor," was simply a way to reach notes he couldn't hit with his natural voice. More revealing was his comment, "When you were up against fellows like the Pilgrim Travelers and Blind Boys, you needed something special to grab Grandma."[2]

A *Washington Post* concert review noted that Jeter began a song "in his hearty tenor, dropped suddenly into his deep rumbling bass, and then, after a perfect, punctuating pause, answered himself with an unearthly strong and pure falsetto . . . It was as if he were a one-man gospel trio."[3] This was in 1986, when Jeter was seventy-two years old. Imagine him at the peak of his powers. He wrecked more than a few churches in his prime.

The Silvertones first recorded in July 1946, cutting eight songs for Queen. The group's debut record, "I Cried Holy" and "Go Ahead," sold quite well, but none of the subsequent releases did much. Twelve songs were recorded at the group's next session in December 1947. The Silvertones had four more sessions for King before leaving in 1951 to record for Specialty.

Jeter was in later years dismissive of the Silvertones' King recordings. "They only wanted hillbilly-style gospel," he complained. "They didn't care too much for the real gospel."[4] In fairness to Nathan and others at King, Jeter didn't much care for hard gospel either when he first encountered it in the 1940s. "I used to think all that screaming was a disgrace,"[5] he said. Such disapproval was not uncommon within the church community.

When the Swan Silvertones started out in the late 1930s, the most successful (and most imitated) group was the Golden Gate Quartet. The Gates featured what was called "jubilee" singing, a closely blended four-part harmony style not unlike that of barbershop quartets. Jubilee singing was a precise style, in which diction, phrasing, enunciation, and seamless harmonies were of vital importance. The material tended to consist of spirituals and older "folk" music in the public domain. Most of the quartets performed without instrumental accompaniment. Excessive emotionalism was discouraged.

That began changing in the 1940s, as the fervent, nakedly emotional music from the Pentecostal fringes moved into the mainstream of black religious and cultural life. Though the differences between the jubilee quartets and the gospel quartets that replaced them seem a bit obscure to the nonenthusiast, the change was fundamental. Reflecting its roots in Pentecostal and "holiness" churches, the gospel music that developed in the 1940s and 1950s was highly charged, hard-edged, passionate, exciting, and emotional to the core.

Some quartets made a smoother transition to the new style than others. A solid Baptist who initially found the new gospel sound a "disgrace," Jeter was a flexible and pragmatic man who faced the challenge head-on with two smart decisions. The first was hiring singer Solomon Womack, a gospel shouter of lacerating power who brought plenty of edge to the Silvertones' sound. Jeter called Womack "the best lead I ever had."[6] The second was hiring a guitarist in the late 1940s, making the Swans one of the earlier groups to add instrumental support on a regular basis.

Womack and Jeter singing together was something special. On songs in which they trade the lead vocal ("Working on a Building," "I Cried Holy," or "All Alone," for example), the contrast and interplay between the swinging, silky voice of Jeter and the rough, window-rattling tenor of Womack is astounding, almost scary. As one critic noted, "They are not for the weak of heart."[7] Jeter's solo showcases—"Toll the Bell," "All Night, All Day," "I've Tried," and "Careless Soul," in which Jeter *hums* more soulfully than most men sing—are essential listening for anyone interested in the origins of soul singing.

Jeter's opinion notwithstanding, the records made by the Swan Silvertones for King constitute an undervalued treasure. While not the "real gospel" Jeter apparently wanted, the records are musically exciting, highly enjoyable for their beautiful *a cappella* harmonies, and historically important as a snapshot of an evolving gospel group caught "midway between jubilee and modern quartet."[8]

The Swans' King material has been available only sporadically over the past half century. It was issued in the late 1950s on three LPs (*Spirituals*, *Volumes 1, 4, and 7*) and reissued in the 1960s as *The Nation's Favorite Singers, A Fine Collection of Songs of Faith* and *Songs You'll Remember Forever,* respectively. An album on Gusto in the late 1970s contains sixteen of the group's best songs. Early in 2005, the British label Acrobat issued all forty-five songs the Silvertones cut for King on a two-CD set, *The Swan Silvertones: 1946–1951,* with complete session annotation and notes by Opal Louis Nations.

The Swan Silvertones left King in 1951 for a two-year association with Specialty Records before reaching its pinnacle on Vee-Jay in the late 1950s and early 1960s. The Silvertones' 1959 recording of "Mary Don't You Weep" is rightly regarded as a gospel classic. Jeter left the group in 1963 and became an ordained minister. His forays out of retirement were infrequent but noteworthy. Jeter's 1988 album, *Yesterday and Today,* and his 1989 appearance on the network television program *Sunday Night* struck like lightning. His majestic voice still brought strong men to their knees.

Whereas the Swan Silvertones established an effective soft-hard dynamic with Reverend Jeter and his shouters, the Spirit of Memphis Quartette alternated hard with harder and hardest. The Spirit of Memphis had three of the most powerful singers in postwar gospel in Silas Steele, Jethro "Jet" Bledsoe, and Wilbur "Little Ax" Broadnax. In seven sessions between 1949 and 1952, the group (which dropped the Quartette from its name in the late 1940s) recorded thirty-two songs for King, a body of work gospel scholar Anthony Heilbut calls "among the most beautiful quartet records in this style."[9]

The Spirit of Memphis had roots extending back to the 1920s (the group's name was a play on the name of Charles Lindbergh's airplane, *Spirit of St. Louis*), but the group known to modern listeners came together when Silas Steele joined in 1948. A gospel music pioneer, Steele was a veteran of the Famous Blue Jay Singers, whose "preacher shouts may be the most impassioned of any quartet lead on records."[10] Heilbut wrote of Steele's singing that "the voice is thunder and wonder itself, the Burning Bush in song."[11]

Steele joined an outfit that was loaded with talent. In addition to Bledsoe and Broadnax, the group included Earl "Doc" Malone, Theo Wade, James Darling, and Robert Reed. They had an uncanny tightness. "We knew the range of each other so well," Steele said. "I could always depend on Ax to pick up a note where I left off. A split second before I finished, he got it. We understood each other just that closely."[12]

The group was democratic in the studio. Bledsoe, Steele, Broadnax, and basso Earl Malone alternated lead vocals on the King records, creating a variety of group sounds, all of them intense. For sheer excitement, it's hard to top the songs where Steele and Broadnax both cut loose—"If Jesus Had to Pray," "Calvary," "Jesus, Jesus," and "Every Time I Feel the Spirit" (with Bledsoe on third lead).

The group had a hit record from its first session, "Days Passed and Gone," featuring Bledsoe and Steele on lead. This record had a big impact on the group, as Bledsoe told Kip Lornell in 1982. "[That] was the record that really introduced us on King Records. Silas Steele was preaching on that record. Nobody had ever heard anything like that! We got that record out there . . . and that's what sold us throughout the country. Silas was a great singer and showman . . . They criticized me for letting him do that type of thing on a record, 'cause nobody wasn't doing no preaching when [we] made the record."[13]

Preaching songs were a relatively small part of the group's repertoire, which tended to consist of jubilee-style arrangements of traditional material. Like the Swan Silvertones, the Spirit of Memphis was moving from a jubilee orientation to more of a gospel approach. The group certainly had the right singers for the new style in Steele, Bledsoe, and Broadnax. The songs pairing Steele and Bledsoe ("Days Passed and Gone," "Automobile to Glory," "God's Got His Eye on You," "That Awful Day," "The Atomic Telephone," and "Toll the Bell Easy") are enormously powerful and compelling.

Reportedly dissatisfied with the financial situation at King,[14] the Spirit of Memphis left in 1952, after a final session in October yielded the popular single "Lord Jesus, Parts 1 and 2." The group started recording for Peacock in 1953, staying with the Houston-based label through the late 1960s.

Based in Durham, North Carolina, the Four Internes consisted of Nick Allen, Alonzo Eubanks, Theodore Freeland, Joseph Davis, and Raymond Davis, with Harold White on piano. The group signed with Federal in 1951; its first single, which also included the singers Blind Mary and Baby Shirley, was issued as the Interne Quartet. As the Four Internes, the quartet recorded nearly two dozen songs for Federal, including a cover of Don Reno's bluegrass standard "I'm Using My Bible for a Roadmap."

The sound of the Four Internes is unlike that of any other gospel act in the King catalog. Neither sweet jubilee harmonizing nor intense gospel shouting, the group's sound was hip and sophisticated, a creative fusion of old and new. The Internes added their own touches, including distinctive original material, harmonic ideas borrowed from such pop acts as the Mills Brothers, unusual arrangements, and a piano-bass-drums rhythm section that would have been right at home on some of King's R&B records.

Between December 1951 and the end of 1955, the Four Internes cut twenty songs for Federal. The group made a few hard gospel records ("Going Back to Jesus," for example), but where the Internes really shone was on such original songs as "Do You Know Him," "Count Your Many Blessings," "New Born Again," and "I'm Troubled." Those records, which still sound fresh after fifty years, have a swinging ease to them that is scandalously close to danceable. It's somewhat surprising that the Four Internes didn't make more of a mark with its unique, innovative sound. It probably didn't help that the group was about twenty years ahead of its time.

Though they didn't record as much or achieve as much national success as the Swan Silvertones, the Spirit of Memphis, or the Four Internes, dozens of gospel quartets tried their luck at King or one of its associated labels. In the earliest days, on Queen, the quartets included the Harmoneers, the Southern Harps, the Jubalaires, and the Gospel Trumpeteers.

The main figure in the Gospel Trumpeters was Willie Eason, a veteran street-corner musician (known at the time as "Little Willie and His Talking Guitar") and arguably the first electric steel guitarist in gospel music. Eason is today hailed as "the father of gospel steel guitar"[15] and a pioneer of the "Sacred Steel" movement that moved into the secular spotlight in the late 1990s with records on Arhoolie and other labels.

Formed in 1946 in Baltimore by Joseph Johnson, the Trumpeteers recorded nine excellent jubilee-style songs for King in 1949 and 1950. Also known as the CBS Trumpeteers because of the group's two-year network radio program in the late 1940s, the quartet had eight songs released, the most exciting of which were "The Sun Didn't Shine," "This Is a Mean World," and "Lay Down My Heavy Burdens."

The Flying Clouds, the leading quartet in Detroit during the 1940s and 1950s, recorded four songs for King in 1950. Alternating the hard lead vocals of Joe Union with the more understated singing of John Evans, the Flying Clouds had an interesting, dynamic sound, but never made much of an impact outside the Motor City.

Other important quartets had equally fleeting associations with King, often lasting just long enough to record a single or two. The Sensational Nightingales, featuring the awesome lead singing of Julius Cheeks and Paul Owens, recorded five songs for King in 1949, of which four were issued. King also leased or purchased masters by the Famous Blue Jay Singers, the Shelley Quartet, and the Jewel Jubilee Singers. Through its affiliation with the Glory label, King distributed records as well by such southern acts as the Ford Gospel Singers, the Miami Soul Stirrers, and the Spiritual Harmonizers.

• • •

During the 1950s and 1960s, the quartet was supplanted by the "mass choir" as the gospel music ensemble of choice among fans and record companies. This movement had been building since the late-nineteenth century, when student singing groups toured the country to raise money for new black colleges and universities in the south. The most prominent was the Fisk Jubilee Singers, a group from Fisk University in Nashville that toured widely between 1871 and 1903.[16]

On a local level, choirs became a standard part of the religious landscape, appearing first in holiness churches and spreading in the 1920s to Baptist and Methodist churches. Boosted by the endorsement of the National Baptist Convention, gospel choirs crossed denominational boundaries with ease and had gained tremendous popularity in black churches by the 1940s.

Only a few gospel choirs recorded in the late 1940s. King recorded the most popular of those groups, the Wings Over Jordan Choir, and had a sort of backdoor relationship with another, the great Los Angeles choir headed by Professor James Earle Hines.

The Wings Over Jordan Choir, organized by Reverend Glenn T. Settle in 1935, was the first great choir of the modern media age. A visionary thinker, adept promoter, and early proponent of what came to be called black pride, Settle was the pastor of Gethsemane Baptist Church in Cleveland. His choir, which included members from his church as well as other local churches, began broadcasting a weekly radio program, *The Negro Hour*, designed "to address the Negro community and introduce the non-Negro to the Negro experience."[17]

The program went national in 1938, broadcasting every Sunday morning on the CBS network. *Wings over Jordan*, which included inspirational talks by such distinguished black guests as Langston Hughes, Mary McCloud Bethune, and Adam Clayton Powell, was a huge hit. With its unique blend of spiritual singing, positivism, and pride, the program was a rare network offering for black families, and the Wings Over Jordan Choir developed a huge and devoted audience as a result of its radio exposure. The program ran for a decade on CBS and won numerous honors, including the prestigious Peabody Award, for its contributions to American life.

At the peak of its popularity when it began recording for Queen, the Wings Over Jordan Choir cut twelve songs with conductor Frank C. Everett in June 1946. The songs were all issued on Queen singles and then reissued on King when Queen was phased out. Several of the records, including "Swing Low Sweet Chariot," "Old Ship of Zion," "Deep River," and "When You Come Out of the Wilderness," sold quite well. All twelve songs were later issued on a King LP, *Deep River*.

The choir returned to the studio one more time, in 1953, to record another twelve songs for King. "When I Have Done the Best I Can," "Trying to Get Ready," "I've Been 'Buked," and "I Cried And Cried" were released as singles, and several other songs were released on extended-play singles (EPs). The entire session was released on one of King's first LPs, *Amen*.

Usually containing between thirty and forty singers, the Wings Over Jordan Choir recorded spirituals, hymns, and newer gospel songs. The group's soloists, including Olive Thompson, Albert Meadows, Louise Jones, Martha Spearman, Cecil Dandy, and Esther Overstreet, were highly skilled, and many became stars in their own right. The group's most famous soloist, Paul Breckenridge, recorded six songs in 1947 for King as Paul Breckenridge and the Four Heavenly Knights.

Disbanded in the mid-1950s, the Wings Over Jordan Choir has never received the credit it deserves as an enormously popular musical act and longstanding, nationally prominent cultural institution. Not only was the choir the first full-time professional black choir in America, its CBS radio program was the first independently produced national program created by black artists.[18] As Reverend Settle had hoped, the choir appealed to not only blacks but also white radio listeners and record buyers. For many listeners, the Wings Over Jordan Choir was their introduction to black culture and religious music.

The choir of the St. Paul Baptist Church in Los Angeles was the second great choir associated with King. Organized in 1947 and sometimes known as the Echoes of Eden Choir, this ensemble was directed by Professor James Earle Hines, a magnificent baritone vocalist. Working with pianist Gwendolyn Cooper Lightener, Hines shaped the Echoes of Eden into what one scholar calls "the premier gospel choir in the nation" and "the most fully developed gospel choir of the first decade of the Golden Age [of gospel music.]"[19]

Featuring such singers as Sallie Martin, Cora Martin, and Erie Gladney, the choir first gained notice outside Los Angeles with a Sunday evening radio program that could be heard in "seventeen states with an audience of one million people (the largest audience on the West Coast)."[20] With that kind of radio exposure, recording was a logical step for the choir. The group signed with Capitol and had a big hit in 1948 with "God Be with You."

That same year, the choir, or part of it, recorded fourteen songs for the Sacred label. Billed as Prof. J. Earle Hines and the Goodwill Singers, the group included Hines, Lightener on piano, Gladney, Ruth Black, and others. This material was leased to DeLuxe, which issued it on seven singles. Hines and the choir had three subsequent DeLuxe singles, but none had much commercial impact.

Professor Hines made an impact, however, inspiring a generation of Los Angeles singers. One of the youngest members of the St. Paul's choir was a five-year-old prodigy named Jamesetta Hawkins. Years later, as Etta James, she was a major R&B star, but she never got over her awe of the flamboyant Hines. "He had a voice like God," James recalled. "He'd raise his hands up high, the red silk robe flowing down his arms, and I'd swear the man had wings. I wanted to fly like that; I wanted to sing like him."[21]

• • •

The rest of the gospel acts on King, Federal, and DeLuxe make up a wonderfully diverse cast of characters. There was a gospel organist, Alfred Bolden, and preachers such as the Reverend J.B. Crocker and the Reverend Abraham Swanson XII who recorded three-minute sermons. Vocal groups of all sizes, including the Patterson Singers, the Ambassadors of Philadelphia, and the Kingdom Bound Singers, were part of the blend. Male solo singers such as Robert Anderson, Professor Harold C. Boggs, and Reverend John T. Highbaugh cut a number of popular records, as did Sister Bonnie Bradford and other female solo singers.

Three of the most interesting of these acts were Baby Shirley, the Spiritual Consolers, and the Reverend A. Johnson. Baby Shirley was a thirteen-year-old singer from Durham, North Carolina, when she cut several sides for Federal in 1951, recording solo with just piano accompaniment, as well as with Blind Mary (aka Thelma Bumpess), with the Interne Quartet, and with Thelma Bumpess & the Royalettes. Baby Shirley kept at it and attained international stardom in the 1960s and 1970s as Shirley Caesar. Caesar has won several Grammy Awards, is a member of the Gospel Music Hall of Fame, and has been called "the most popular gospel singer since Mahalia Jackson."[22]

One of the last great duets of the early days of gospel music was the Spiritual Consolers, the husband-and-wife team Sullivan and Iola Pugh, based in Miami. Sullivan sang lead and played electric guitar, and with Iola singing harmony, the couple's countryish sound was about as down-home as any in postwar gospel. The Pughs sang straightforward songs of mother, home, hearth, and old-time religion.

The couple recorded four songs for DeLuxe in Miami in 1953. Only one single of the duet was released, "Wade in the Water" and "How Long Has It Been Since You've Been Home." The Pughs recorded five or six more songs the following year, but nothing was issued from the session. The Consolers (the first part of the name was dropped at some point) achieved stardom later in the decade on Nashboro, but the template for their fascinating, mesmerizing sound was in place from the beginning.

Not much is known about the Reverend Anderson Johnson, but the electric guitar-playing, singing preacher recorded some blistering gospel sides in 1953 for Glory, the Florida label in which King had an interest. Best known for his ferocious recording of "God Don't Like It" (of which *Billboard* perceptively noted, "This could get as much action in the straight R&B field as in the spiritual market"[23]), Johnson recorded roughly a dozen songs. All but four were released as singles on DeLuxe. He apparently never recorded again.

Elder Charles Beck, an itinerant preacher associated with the Church of God in Christ, recorded for a number of record companies beginning in the 1930s. In a 1956 letter to the *Cleveland Call & Post*, he set forth a bit of his theology. "When it comes to the church," he wrote, "I believe there should be rhythm. I have it in my church in Buffalo. I play the trumpet, vibes, sax, bongos, Hammond organ, piano, and many instruments."[24]

Elder Beck cut only four numbers for King, in July 1950, but they are all keepers. Recorded "live" in front of an enthusiastic congregation, the four songs, especially "Shouting with Elder Beck," provide a revealing glimpse into a world that was almost completely unknown to most Americans in 1950.

HOW MOUNTAIN GIRLS CAN LOVE

Bluegrass Music on King Records

•••

> I know what's wrong with bluegrass.
> It ain't got no sex in it.
> —Sydney Nathan

In 1946, only one band was playing the music that would come to be called blue-grass: Bill Monroe and His Blue Grass Boys. By the early 1950s, probably a few dozen bands, of varying levels of professionalism and spreading throughout the southeast and such northern states as Ohio, Michigan, and Indiana, were playing bluegrass.

Monroe bitterly resented these groups "stealing" his personal music, but the successful bands soon created distinctive sounds and identities of their own. Two of the best of these "first generation" bluegrass bands recorded extensively for King. One was called Don Reno, Red Smiley, and the Tennessee Cut-Ups; the other was the Stanley Brothers and the Clinch Mountain Boys.

The most prolific and commercially successful bluegrass band on King was Don Reno, Red Smiley, and the Tennessee Cut-Ups. From the band's first recording session in 1952 through Smiley's retirement in 1964, Don Reno and Red Smiley comprised one of the great partnerships in bluegrass. They recorded more than 250 songs for King and had two hit singles in 1961—"Don't Let Your Sweet Love Die" and "Love, Please Come Home"—a rarity for bluegrass bands then or now.

The creative spark within the band was Don Reno (1927–84), arguably the most talented individual in the history of bluegrass. Born in Buffalo, South Carolina, Reno was a first-rate songwriter, with almost five hundred songs and tunes to his credit, including all but three of the first sixty songs Reno & Smiley recorded for King. Dozens of his songs are still performed today, including "I Know You're Married but I Love You Still," "Country Boy Rock and Roll," "I'm Using My Bible for a Roadmap," "Maybe You Will Change Your Mind," and "No Longer a Sweetheart of Mine."

Reno's versatility as a singer was hard to match. He usually sang superb tenor harmony to guitarist Red Smiley's lead vocal, but Reno sang lead on numerous songs and, when needed, he sang all the harmony parts as well: bass, baritone, tenor, and high baritone, with a skyrocket of a falsetto on top of that.

An instrumental virtuoso, Reno had few peers on any given instrument and none when it came to all-around chops. He is best known as a jazzy, innovative, sophisticated banjo picker, but as bluegrass writer Bill Vernon once noted, Reno "knew more music farther up the necks of more stringed instruments than any of his contemporaries."[1] In addition to banjo, Reno played guitar, mandolin (using finger picks and a three-finger picking style), and bass on various records.

Most scholars rank Reno second only to Earl Scruggs in terms of popularity and influence among banjo players. Reno and Scruggs both came out of a robust regional stringband scene in western North Carolina, an area that was home to a unique "three-finger" banjo picking method created in the 1930s. Reno and Scruggs refined that regional style and took it to new heights. Reno had the first shot at taking it national.

Bill Monroe had not found the banjo picker he could hear in his head until he met Don Reno in 1943. Monroe offered him a job on the spot, but Reno had just enlisted in the Army. He told Monroe he'd take the job if he failed his pre-induction physical. He passed with flying colors and shipped out shortly thereafter, ultimately landing in China. Two years later, Monroe finally found, in Earl Scruggs, the banjo picker he was seeking.

Don Reno and Arthur "Red" Smiley (1925–72) first recorded in 1951 as members of the Tennessee Buddies, the band of fiddler Tommy Magness. The band recorded four songs for Federal, but Syd Nathan was more impressed by Reno and Smiley than he was by the veteran Magness, who ended up not even playing fiddle or singing on his own records. The group disbanded shortly after this session.

Reno and Smiley started working together as partners and entered the King studio for their first session in January 1952, recording sixteen selections, all Reno originals. This was an especially fruitful session, producing several songs ("The Lord's Last Supper," "I'm Using My Bible for a Roadmap," "Drifting with the Tide," and "Gone, Long Gone") that have become bluegrass standards. "I'm Using My Bible for a Roadmap" was the biggest hit from the session.

The "classic" Reno and Smiley band, one of the tightest, most exciting bluegrass bands of the era, came together in 1955 with the addition of bass player John

Palmer and fiddler Mack Magaha. Based in Virginia for most of this period, Reno and Smiley worked on the *Old Dominion Barn Dance* radio show in Richmond and had a daily television program in Roanoke.

The band maintained a busy recording schedule. Though these were lean times for bluegrass, King released a steady stream of Reno and Smiley singles in the late 1950s and early 1960s. The band's first three albums, *Sacred Songs, Banjo Instrumentals,* and *Instrumentals and Ballads,* all released in 1958, contained cuts recorded between 1952 and 1956.

"Jimmy Caught the Dickens (for Pushing Ernest in the Tubb)," the band's third Top Thirty single in 1961, was released as being by Chick and His Hot Rods, the band's comedic alter egos. Silly as it was, the record gave Reno and Smiley something no other bluegrass band except Flatt and Scruggs ever had: two singles simultaneously in the top thirty of the *Billboard* country chart (the other was "Love, Please Come Home").

Red Smiley left the band in 1964. He returned for occasional reunions in the next few years, but his health was failing and he died in 1972. After Smiley retired, Reno partnered briefly with fiddler Benny Martin and then with Bill Harrell, a singer and guitar player from Maryland. Reno and Harrell first recorded in November 1967 and cut three albums over the next two years: *A Variety of New Sacred Gospel Songs, All the Way to Reno,* and *I'm Using My Bible for a Roadmap.* Fittingly, Don Reno and Red Smiley were inducted together into the Bluegrass Hall of Honor in 1992.

• • •

In contrast to Reno and Smiley, who began their career on King Records, the Stanley Brothers were established bluegrass stars when they arrived at King in 1958. The Stanleys—lead singer and guitarist Carter and tenor singer and banjo player Ralph—had been among the first musicians to follow the path blazed by Bill Monroe, beginning their recording career in 1947 on Rich-R-Tone. They subsequently recorded for Columbia, Mercury, and Starday and had attained a fair degree of renown by 1958.

The Stanley Brothers had the most mountain-oriented and old-time sound of any of the major bluegrass bands. The brothers were born (Carter in 1925 and Ralph in 1927) in southwestern Virginia, a hotbed of country music activity in the 1920s and 1930s. The brothers were already accomplished musicians by the time they first heard Bill Monroe, and bluegrass seemed a natural progression from the music they had grown up playing.

The Stanleys produced one of the first great bluegrass albums in the fall of 1958. Usually referred to by its catalog number, King 615, because it lacks an actual title, the album contains twelve songs, all but one written or co-written by Carter or Ralph. Many of them—"How Mountain Girls Can Love," "The Memory of Your Smile," "Your Selfish Heart," "Love Me Darling Just Tonight," and the banjo tunes "Clinch Mountain Backstep" and "Train 45"—are still widely played today. It's among the most important albums in the history of bluegrass.

According to the liner notes to the 1963 album *Folk Concert*, the Stanley Brothers had been rejected by King in 1946, when the band sent an audition tape to Syd Nathan. Reportedly, Carter received "a nice letter from Mr. Nathan telling the boys to practice harder, to learn more about their musical heritage and in a few years come back and see him."[2] When they finally signed with King twelve years later, the Stanleys enjoyed a good relationship with Nathan.

"Everybody always said they dreaded Syd," recalled Ralph Stanley, "and said he was a pretty hard cat to clean after, you know, and pretty hard to get along with. But as far as the Stanley Brothers was concerned, he was number one with us. He cooperated with us. He was plain-spoken and he would tell you just what he thought.

"As far as I know, he was strictly honest with us. We were well satisfied with our royalty statements. And if we needed an advance, we always got it from Syd. An advance against your royalties, you know. He'd accommodate you. I don't have a thing to say against Syd Nathan."[3]

Stanley said Nathan gave them plenty of space in the studio: "He sort of A&R'd the first couple of sessions. But he saw that we didn't really need that and he pretty much left us alone. We more or less recorded them the way we wanted to on King. There was one time he wanted us to do an album with just two guitars, rhythm guitar and lead guitar, and a bass. So we did. It was a gospel album. All except for that album, we used the instruments we wanted to."[4]

As prolific as they were as songwriters, Carter and Ralph Stanley simply couldn't write enough songs while touring to fill a couple of twelve-song albums each year. When the brothers ran out of original songs, Nathan, as the owner of several publishing companies, had plenty of choices for the band to consider.

"Sometimes we had our [original] material ready and we just went in and recorded it," says Stanley. "Other times, we went in and didn't know what we were going to record. Syd would have some material for us, some songs, and it would be in an altogether different style to what we did. But we learned it and recorded it in our style right there on the spot, in the studio. We did several songs that way."[5]

The Stanley brothers were certainly cooperative. If Nathan wanted them to try something, they gave it their best shot. And if Carter and Ralph felt silly covering an R&B hit by Hank Ballard, as they did in 1960 with "Finger Poppin' Time," or recording cornball comedy songs such as "He Went to Sleep and the Hogs Ate Him," they trusted Nathan's commercial judgment. When asked if the band minded recording the Hank Ballard cover, George Shuffler, who played bass on the cut, said, "Naw, they didn't care. Old man Syd thought it'd sell records and that's what we was up there for."[6]

From the Stanleys' perspective, they had no reason not to try Nathan's ideas. "During the 1950s," Ralph Stanley explained, "things were bad. Bluegrass music got sort of down. There wasn't too much demand for it. Rock and roll had took over and our record sales were way down. It was a bad time."[7]

The most significant change to the Stanley sound while the band was on King was the addition of lead guitar to the instrumental mix. Using guitar as a lead instrument was rare in bluegrass and it gave the band an even more distinctive sound. From the late 1950s on, the band's recordings increasingly featured guitarists Bill Napier, Al Elliott, and George Shuffler, with a reduced role for the fiddle, mandolin, and, on occasion, even Ralph's banjo.

King had some success promoting the Stanley Brothers as a "folk" act within the folk music revival. Thanks to such albums as *Folk Song Festival, Folk Concert,* and *Spotlight on Country Folk Music* and an attempt to record more "folk music" (as that was understood by Nathan and others at King), the Stanleys enjoyed a high profile in the folk and college market. The all-instrumental album *The World's Finest 5–String Banjo,* popular with that same audience, helped establish Ralph Stanley as one of the most influential banjo players in bluegrass.

The final Stanley Brothers session for King was held in September 1965. The band did twenty-two recording sessions for King in all, cutting nearly two hundred songs and tunes on seventeen albums, seven of them all-gospel albums. In addition to Carter and Ralph Stanley, the King records featured such musicians as Ralph Mayo, Chubby Anthony, and Art Stamper (fiddle); Al Elliott, Curley Lambert, and Earl Taylor (mandolin); and lead guitarists Bill Napier and George Shuffler.

Carter Stanley died in 1966, silencing one of the great bluegrass duets. His death left younger brother Ralph, not yet forty years old, in an awkward position. Carter had always been the one out front—the leader of the band, the lead singer, the emcee, the public face and image of the Stanley Brothers. As Ralph confided to biographer John Wright, losing Carter was like "losing his right arm . . . At the time he died, I really didn't know what to do. I didn't know how the people would take to it without him."[8]

Stanley put together a new band and contacted Nathan to ask whether King was interested in recording the band. Nathan was agreeable, replying, "Why not?

The Stanley Brothers have done really well for us and who knows, you might do better."[9]

Ralph Stanley and the Clinch Mountain Boys recorded three albums for King, *Brand New Country Songs, Over the Sunset Hill,* and *Hills of Home.* Compared to the Stanley Brothers, the sound was rougher-edged, more lonesome, with even more of an old-time feel to the music. The fans loved the new sound and readily accepted Ralph Stanley as a bandleader. He became a major attraction at the bluegrass festivals that were springing up in the late 1960s and early 1970s.

Stanley remained a potent draw on the bluegrass circuit into the new century, and enjoyed an improbable career upswing in 2000 with the release of the film *O Brother, Where Art Thou?* The bluegrass and old-time soundtrack album, which featured Stanley's chilling *a cappella* version of "O Death," was a surprise hit, selling more than six million copies. The improbable became unbelievable when Stanley won the Grammy Award in 2001 for "Best Male Country Vocal Performance," the only time a bluegrass singer has ever won that award.

In the bluegrass hagiography, the Stanley Brothers rank at the top with Bill Monroe and Flatt & Scruggs in terms of popularity, influence, and historical importance. The Stanley Brothers' recordings on King constitute a fundamental part of their legacy, as the brothers recorded far more material for King than for any other label. Furthermore, the King albums were readily available throughout the 1960s, 1970s, and 1980s, while the Stanleys' recordings on other labels were mostly out of print.

The Stanley Brothers had only one hit on the *Billboard* charts, a 1960 novelty called "How Far to Little Rock" (a variant of the 19th-century minstrel routine "Arkansas Traveler"), but the duo's contributions to American music are incalculable. The Stanley Brothers were inducted into the Bluegrass Hall of Honor in 1992. Syd Nathan joined them in the Hall of Honor fourteen years later, in 2006.

• • •

In hindsight, 1960 wasn't the best time to form a bluegrass band. Times were tight for bluegrass; even Bill Monroe had trouble keeping his band on the road. But Charlie Moore, a singer from South Carolina, and Bill Napier, a multi-instrumentalist from Virginia, forged ahead anyway. By the time their seven-year partnership ended, Moore and Napier had cut nine albums for King, making the group one of the most recorded bluegrass bands of the decade.

Moore and Napier (a veteran of the Stanley Brothers band in the late 1950s) first recorded for King in December 1962. All fourteen of the songs from that session were released on the album *Folk 'n' Hill,* though the first single, pairing the novelty songs "Country Twist" and "Sing Along with Mitch," was issued for some reason on Bethlehem, a King-affiliated label usually reserved for jazz releases.

Despite recording nine albums, Moore and Napier have never received much critical attention, perhaps owing in part to their propensity for recording cornball songs such as "Sing Along with Mitch," "Ballad of Big Fred," or "Guitar Pickin' Truck Driver." A related factor is that Moore and Napier, in contrast to bluegrass acts of the 1940s and early 1950s, were album oriented. Those albums were often thematic, and the results were decidedly mixed.

An album that worked was *Songs by Moore & Napier for All Lonesome Truck Drivers*. Songs about truck drivers were enjoying a vogue in country music at the time, and Moore and Napier carved out their own little bluegrass niche. Several of these songs—"Long White Line," "Pinball Blues," "Bluegrass Truck Driver," and "Truck Driver's Queen"—rank among the band's best recordings. A thematic album that didn't work, on the other hand, was *Country Music Goes to Viet Nam*, a warmed-over pastiche of war songs dating back to the American Revolution.

Moore and Napier were at their best on bluegrass gospel music. Their stand-out gospel cuts include "Gathering in the Sky," "Our Fathers Had Religion," "I Believe in the Old Time Way," and "Shout and Sing," and they had two quite satisfying all-gospel albums, *Country Hymnal* and *Gospel and Sacred*.

One of the first bluegrass bands to record for King was Shannon Grayson & His Golden Valley Boys, which cut four gospel quartets in 1950: "I Like the Old Time Way," "Let Me Travel Alone," "Since His Sweet Love Has Rescued Me," and "I'm Gonna Walk On." Grayson was a pioneering North Carolina banjo picker who used a three-finger picking style similar to that of Earl Scruggs and Don Reno. He is perhaps best known for his work with Bill and Cliff Carlisle in the 1930s and 1940s and for his later work with the Briarhoppers.

Guitarist Jimmy Martin and mandolinist Bobby Osborne, two of the most talented and dynamic musicians in bluegrass history, entered the King studio in August 1951. They had just left the Lonesome Pine Fiddlers to form their own band, Jimmy Martin, Bob Osborne, and the Sunny Mountain Boys. The four songs they cut ("My Lonely Heart," "She's Just a Cute Thing," "Blue Eyed Darling," and "You'll Never Be the Same") are among the best bluegrass records from the era. The partnership between the strong-willed musicians imploded, however, and the two singles are all that's left to suggest what might have been.

Martin carried on with the Sunny Mountain Boys, while Bobby Osborne teamed with his banjo-playing younger brother, Sonny, in the Osborne Brothers. Both bands became quite popular. Bobby Osborne, Sonny Osborne, and Jimmy Martin have all been inducted into the Bluegrass Hall of Honor.

Leon Jackson, who wrote "Love Please Come Home," a big hit for Reno & Smiley in 1961, also made a few records with Johnny Bryant and the White Oak Mountain Boys. Jackson, Bryant, and the band did one session for King in 1956, cutting seven songs. Five were released as singles or on compilation albums on Audio Lab, King's "budget" LP label. "White Oak Mountain Breakdown," "Rocky Roads," and "Buttahatchee" are solid instrumentals featuring Bryant's banjo picking, but "Go Find Another Man," "So Goes My Heart," "This Heart's Been Broken Before," and the original version of "Love Please Come Home" are more interesting and quite enjoyable.

Although Bill Monroe was certainly unique in the way he synthesized different musical elements into bluegrass, he was not alone in leading a country stringband that used fiddle, mandolin, banjo, and guitar. King recorded several of these acts, including the Bailes Brothers, King's Sacred Quartet, and brothers J. E. and Wade Mainer. Though their music was rooted in pre-bluegrass styles, these groups fit in the story here as well as anywhere.

The Bailes Brothers, a West Virginia band that featured four Bailes brothers (Walter, Homer, Johnny, and Kyle), had recorded for Columbia and been on the *Grand Ole Opry* in the mid-1940s. The group achieved its greatest fame in the late 1940s, as members of the *Louisiana Hayride* radio program in Shreveport. King's association with the Bailes Brothers started in 1947 or 1948, when King began issuing songs the group had recorded for radio transcriptions.

Sixteen of those recordings were issued on singles and four were reissued on an Audio Lab LP, *Avenue of Prayer*. The remainder of that album came from 1953 sessions in which Walter and Johnny Bailes and band cut another sixteen songs, including "That's What We Need," "There's a Difference in Religion and Salvation," "God's Hand Rules the World," "Goodbye Hallelujah I'm Gone," and "I'll Run All the Way."

Johnnie Wright and Jack Anglin, working as Johnnie & Jack and the Tennessee Mountain Boys, had one of the hottest country acts of the 1950s, with hits on RCA and tenure on the *Grand Ole Opry*. The group, which included Wright's wife, future country superstar Kitty Wells, began its recording career in 1947 with sessions for Apollo and King. For King, the group (Johnnie, Jack, Ray Atkins, and Clyde Moody[10]) recorded six songs as King's Sacred Quartet. With simple guitar and mandolin accompaniment, the recordings resemble those of the Brown's Ferry Four, which was probably the point. The songs, all released as singles, included "Turn Your Radio On," "He Will Set Your Fields on Fire," "This World Can't Stand Long," and "I'll Be Listening."

Fiddler J. E. Mainer and his younger banjo-picking brother Wade Mainer were the core of the leading country music stringband of the late 1930s, Mainer's

Mountaineers. The brothers parted ways in 1936, when Wade left to form his own band, the Sons of the Mountaineers. Both bands played an energetic style that has been called "protobluegrass,"[11] and both were very successful and influential in the Carolinas.

Both Mainers revived their careers after the war, each recording separately for King in the early days of the label. In three sessions during 1946, J.E. Mainer, again fronting Mainer's Mountaineers, recorded twenty-four songs for King. Most were released as singles; sixteen were reissued in 1960 on *Good Ole Mountain Music*.

Wade Mainer first recorded for King in 1947, cutting twelve songs, mostly gospel or sentimental "heart" songs. He did two further sessions in 1951, recording influential versions of such songs as "That Star Belongs to Me," "Dreaming of a Little Cabin," and "The Girl I Left in Sunny Tennessee." Much of his material from this time was collected on an album in the early 1960s, *Soulful Sacred Songs*.

The Mainer brothers were among the older blues and country musicians "rediscovered" during the folk music revival of the 1960s. Wade returned to King in 1961 and cut twelve songs, half of which ended up on *Soulful Sacred Songs*. J.E. Mainer and the Mountaineers went into the King studio two months later and recorded sixteen songs and tunes; twelve were released later that year on *A Variety Album*.

Bluegrass fans had something to cheer about at the close of 2004: the release of *The Best of King and Starday Bluegrass*. The four-CD set, compiled and annotated by Gary B. Reid, contains 100 songs and tunes from the King and Starday archives, 50 from each label. The two CDs devoted to King provide a good overview of the label's bluegrass efforts. The best of the bunch are the four cuts recorded by Bobby Osborne and Jimmy Martin in 1951.

• • •

Syd Nathan's most significant contribution to bluegrass was his advocacy of the guitar as a lead instrument. It wasn't appreciated at the time and he still hasn't received due credit for it, but Nathan is as responsible as anyone for introducing the lead guitar to bluegrass recordings. Working in the King studio, guitarists Don Reno, Bill Napier, and George Shuffler helped liberate the guitar from its strictly defined bluegrass role as a rhythm instrument, raising it to solo-taking parity with the banjo, mandolin, and fiddle.

Don Reno was playing lead guitar on records as early as 1954, and the Stanley Brothers' King records from 1959 on featured the lead guitar more than any other instrument. That was because of Nathan. As Ralph Stanley said of him, "He didn't care too much about the five-string banjo and he didn't care too much about the fiddle. Syd was responsible for us starting to use the lead guitar."[12]

According to his son Dale Reno, Don Reno often said, "I'm not a banjo picker, I'm a guitar player. I just play the banjo 'cause I have to."[13] Don started playing guitar at age nine and soon became a protégé of Arthur "Guitar Boogie" Smith, from whom Reno learned everything from swing to country fiddle tunes. Although Reno wasn't the first person in bluegrass to play melody on a guitar—that honor probably goes to Earl Scruggs or Joe Stuart, both of whom finger-picked guitar accompaniment on gospel songs—Don Reno *was* the first great lead guitarist in bluegrass.

Reno was the first guitarist in bluegrass to take linear, melody-based solos over the rhythm section, the same as the fiddler or banjo player would. Beginning in 1954 with a pair of instrumentals, "Double Banjo Blues" and "Reno Ride," and several gospel songs ("Family Altar," "Jesus Is Waiting," "Jesus Answers My Prayers," and "Get Behind Me Satan"), Reno blazed a trail that guitarists are still exploring fifty years later.

Reno's best showcases as a lead guitarist were *Country Songs* and *Hymns and Sacred Songs*, both recorded in 1959. The first album was a significant departure from the Reno and Smiley norm in two respects: the material—covers of earlier King records by Grandpa Jones, the Delmore Brothers, the York Brothers, and others—and the instrumentation—two guitars, upright bass, and snare drum.

Surprisingly, Nathan had to talk Reno into doing this session. "Syd had had great success with the Delmore Brothers," explained Reno, "and he knew I could play this type guitar. He conceived the idea that this type of guitar could sell again. I didn't want to do it because I was featuring the banjo. I'd given up featuring guitar a few years earlier. It didn't seem to sell then, so I decided to just play banjo. I was against it but he sweet-talked me into doing the two albums."[14] The reward was the duo's highest-charting single, "Don't Let Your Sweet Love Die," a cut from *Country Songs.*

The Stanley Brothers employed several lead guitarists during their King years. The most significant was George Shuffler, a native of Valdese, North Carolina. Shuffler joined the band in the late 1950s as a bass player, but made the biggest impact as the band's lead guitarist in the 1960s. His major contribution was his introduction of "cross-picking," a style of playing in which one uses a pick to duplicate the feel and momentum of a banjo "roll," which a Scruggs-style player produces with a thumb and two fingers. Mandolinist Jesse McReynolds developed the style, but when it came to guitar, George Shuffler was the main popularizer of the technique.

"Everybody was trying to pick a guitar like a mandolin," Shuffler told John Wright. "So I started using that cross-picking on it. Cross-picking, you do with a flat pick what most people do with a banjo roll … You're crossing backwards and forth on three strings. You're playing your own melody and harmony, too … You get your left hand in some of the awfullest positions. You look down and you think it's broke sometimes.

"It's just a homemade thing [worked out by] Jesse McReynolds and I, when we were together … And they didn't like it, Carter and Ralph didn't. Chuck Seitz was the engineer at King, and I guess Chuck gave me more encouragement than anybody did on it. [He said,] 'Go ahead and put in on the record and let the chips fall where they would.'

"And it was guitar and it soothed old man Syd Nathan there a little bit, enough to, well, to keep the contract a-going. Then after I got to doing it, why, I liked it and I noticed the crowd liked it. It seemed like the overall thing fit them. Ninety percent of the time they was just Carter and Ralph and myself on the road. And I could fill in more with three or four strings going.

"So I would pick it and Carter, he would say, 'Well, why don't you change? Get off that roll. Get off that lick you're doing there. Do something else. You want to play it like a mandolin.' I would go ahead and do it irregardless because I thought that it fit better than anything [else] I could put behind them."[15]

Shuffler was right. He was also, fortunately, even more stubborn than his bosses and prevailed in this dispute. Despite the initial objections of Carter and Ralph Stanley, Shuffler's cross-picking became an integral element of the band's sound and helped set the group apart from its contemporaries. Ralph Stanley kept the sound alive when he formed his own band, and he continues to employ a Shuffler-style lead guitarist as of this writing. The picking style is common in bluegrass today, heard on recordings by countless guitarists. It's another little piece of the King Records legacy.

LET'S HAVE A NATURAL BALL

The Blues on King Records

• • •

Hearing Freddie King was what started
me on my path. He taught me everything
I needed to know.

—Eric Clapton, guitarist

The success of Mamie Smith's 1920 recording of "Crazy Blues" proved that an audience existed for the blues. From that point on, record companies large and small would look to the blues as a source of artists, songs, and records. Syd Nathan made money with blues in his record-store days, so it is not surprising that King was an early and important force in postwar American blues.

King's most successful blues artist was guitarist and singer Freddie King,[1] who influenced a generation of blues and rock guitarists. The label also recorded important guitarists Albert King, John Lee Hooker, and Lonnie Johnson; singers Jimmy Witherspoon, Eddie Vinson, and Gatemouth Moore; and singing pianists Champion Jack Dupree, Charles Brown, Memphis Slim, and Little Willie Littlefield.

A native of New Orleans, Alonzo "Lonnie" Johnson (1889–1970) gained national acclaim in the 1920s as one of the first hot jazz guitarists. His playing from this period is simply astounding, particularly the duets he recorded with white jazz guitarist Eddie Lang (recording as Blind Willie Dunn).

Johnson was on King in the middle of his extraordinarily long recording career, which extended from 1925 to 1967. He cut more than seventy songs for the label in a variety of styles and settings. His early King records featured his vocals backed by just his guitar or by a trio of Johnson's electric guitar, piano, and bass. On later sessions, he quite comfortably fronted hard-driving, jumping R&B outfits drawn from the Todd Rhodes and Tiny Bradshaw bands.

Format didn't matter to Johnson. Whether playing with a trio, as he did on "Falling Rain Blues," or a horn-dominated quintet, as on "Friendless Blues," Johnson was a strong singer and a brilliant guitarist with a sharp, stinging tone and an imaginative approach.

"Tomorrow Night," a million-selling chart-topper and the biggest R&B record of 1948, was Johnson's most spectacular hit for King. A mellow ballad that had been a pop hit in 1939, "Tomorrow Night" was recorded at Johnson's first King session, in December 1947, as King was stockpiling masters for the upcoming recording ban.

Johnson had three more big hits during his tenure in Cincinnati: "Pleasing You (As Long As I Live)" in 1948, "So Tired," (1949) and "Confused" (1950). Being a King artist, he also covered the Delmore Brothers' classics "Blues Stay Away from Me" and "Trouble Ain't Nothing but the Blues."

The seven-piece Todd Rhodes band backed Johnson on some of his most dynamic recordings, cut in June 1952. While it is difficult to even imagine most of Johnson's 1920s contemporaries in this position, Johnson fills the role with considerable élan, absolutely nailing a trio of powerhouse originals, playing electric guitar and singing on "Can't Sleep Any More," "You Can't Buy Love," and "I'm Guilty."

The hits fell off for Lonnie Johnson as R&B moved from solo singers to vocal groups. He made his final records for King in 1952 and retired, his long career seemingly at an end. But Johnson was "rediscovered" in 1960 and became one of the major figures of the early 1960s "blues revival." Johnson made a triumphant tour of England and Europe and recorded a series of successful albums. He was pushing eighty but could still deliver the goods. Lonnie Johnson died in 1970, an underappreciated master of American music.

Legendary blues singer John Lee Hooker had little use for contracts early in his career. As would many musicians of the time, Hooker would make records for any company that asked. He would record any time, any place, as long as the money was right. According to blues DJ Hoss Allen, "John Lee Hooker was known to do as many as four or five sessions a day under different assumed names."[2] It was inevitable that Hooker would wind up on King.

Hooker (1920–2001) was born and raised in Clarksdale, Mississippi. Living in Detroit by the mid-1940s, Hooker launched his recording career in 1948 with Bernie Besman, a local record distributor and owner of the Sensation label. Besman heard something in Hooker's ultra-primitive music and wisely decided to record him without any accompaniment other than Hooker's guitar. Besman leased Hooker's first recordings to Modern, a Los Angeles label that had a huge hit with Hooker's first single, "Boogie Chillen." Modern followed with such hits as "Hobo Blues" and "Crawling King Snake Blues."

At about the same time as he started working with Besman, Hooker also linked up with local entrepreneur Joe Von Battle, who recorded Hooker on four songs in December 1948. Von Battle leased *his* songs to King, which paired "Black Man Blues" and the instrumental "Stomp Boogie" on a 1949 single credited to "Texas Slim," one of the many aliases Hooker used in a half-hearted attempt to disguise his instantly recognizable sound. He also used Delta John, Johnny Williams, John Lee Booker, the Boogie Man, Johnny Lee, Little Pork Chops (really), and Birmingham Sam & His Magic Guitar.

Although Hooker's King single didn't sell as well as "Boogie Chillen," it sold enough that Nathan bought or leased another eight masters from Von Battle late in the summer of 1949. These were all released as singles. King issued sixteen songs by Hooker in 1949 and 1950; some were reissued later with overdubbed drums and bass. The entire output was collected on the albums, *John Lee Hooker Sings the Blues* and *Highway of Blues* (on King subsidiary label Audio Lab).

The King recordings of John Lee Hooker contain some of the most unassimilated music in modern blues. Hooker spooled out an endless boogie of simple yet hypnotic guitar work that seldom included more than a couple of chords. Above that backing, Hooker sang, moaned, and shouted what one writer has called "blank verse mood pieces."[3] It's raw, intense music that feels oddly untethered to any particular time or place, with its powerful combination of electric guitar, a cheap amplifier turned up to eleven, and metal bottle caps affixed to the bottoms of Hooker's stomping shoes.

Hooker found stardom on Vee-Jay in the late 1950s and matured into one of the towering figures of modern blues. Though his King records are not as well known as his Modern singles, they are equally valuable and instructive as the formative work of a singular artist.

Guitarist and singer Albert King cast a huge shadow across the postwar blues scene, and not just because he stood 6'4" and weighed well over two hundred pounds. Born in Indianola, Mississippi, King (1923–92) was one of the most important electric guitarists in blues, a huge influence on such players as Eric Clapton, Jimi Hendrix, Otis Rush, Buddy Guy, Stevie Ray Vaughan, Robert Cray, and Jimmy Page.

The mainstream rock world first became aware of Albert King in the late-1960s through such records as "Born Under a Bad Sign" and "Crosscut Saw." But King made his recording debut in 1953 when he cut a single while he was playing drums for Jimmy Reed in Chicago.

After moving to St. Louis in the mid-1950s, King formed a band and started working the vibrant local club scene. He recorded a few singles for Bobbin in 1959, but given the label's limited distribution, few people outside St. Louis heard them. That changed in 1961 when Bobbin sold or leased four masters to King Records.

The label released the Albert King material on a pair of singles and had a big hit with the first, "Don't Throw Your Love on Me So Strong." The record entered the *Billboard* R&B chart in December 1961, eventually reaching number fourteen, the best chart showing of King's career. Another single followed in 1963, but it was the release later that year of the album *The Big Blues* that properly introduced the new guitar sound King had created over the past five years.

Blues fans, other guitarists especially, sat up and took notice. Although King's guitar playing showed signs of his early influences—"I always liked three people: T-Bone Walker, Lonnie Johnson, and Blind Lemon Jefferson," he told writer Bill Dahl[4]—King had worked out a stunning new voice for the electric guitar, with "a plethora of barbed-wire licks,"[5] phrases, and fills that instantly became part of the standard vocabulary of blues and rock guitar.

"Let's Have a Natural Ball," an audacious reworking of T-Bone Walker's "T-Bone's Shuffle," is a good example of King's new sound. The song starts with a driving, bebop riff copped from jazz pianist Horace Silver and then, over the course of two titanic guitar solos, King cuts loose—a loud, aggressive, searing, stinging, slashing blend of taut, ragged phrases and the almost unbelievable string bending for which King became famous. His bravura playing was showcased on several other songs, including "I've Made Nights by Myself," "I Get Evil," and "Travelin' to California."

As Daniel Jacoubovitch has written, Albert King was not a guitar virtuoso, just a guitar master: "Compared with the guitar styles of the other two widely influential blues 'Kings'—B.B. and Freddy—Albert's is the simplest and nastiest. B.B. and Freddy have more moves, but Albert beats them both on the number of ways he can bend and squeeze varied expression from just a few licks."[6] On top of all that, he was a superb blues singer, with a powerful baritone voice.

The records Albert King made later for Stax are what made his reputation, but *The Big Blues* (reissued as *Travelin' to California*) is where the story began. It's almost impossible to overstate Albert King's impact upon guitarists of the 1960s and 1970s. Wayne Jackson of the Memphis Horns called King "probably the most influential guitar player that ever lived."[7] That's only a slight exaggeration.

Eddie "Cleanhead" Vinson (1917–88) was a better saxophonist than singer, but it was his singing that sold records. Vinson made his name working with trumpeter Cootie Williams in the early 1940s. Vinson had his first big hit, "Cherry Red Blues," in 1944, which led to a solo deal with Mercury, where he had such hits as "Old Maid Boogie" and "Kidney Stew Blues."

Born in Houston, Vinson came to King in 1949. His first session produced the hits "Ashes on My Pillow" and "Somebody Done Stole My Cherry Red," which made it into the R&B Top Ten. Vinson had a distinctive if unusual singing style, ending most lines with (in Tony Russell's eloquent phrase) "a whooping falsetto like a piglet's squeal."[8] Several of Vinson's King records sold quite well; among his other hits for the label were "I'm Gonna Wind Your Clock" (1950) and "Person to Person" (1953).

Vinson (whose nickname reportedly came from an ill-fated experiment with hair straightener that left him bald) recorded twenty-four songs for King between 1949 and 1952. All were issued on singles, and eight eventually turned up on an album, *Battle of the Blues, Volume 3*.

Jazzy blues singer Jimmy Witherspoon (1923–97) also recorded twenty-four songs for the King labels. Witherspoon was a far better singer than Vinson, sophisticated but powerful and very versatile. In six recording sessions in 1952 and 1953, Witherspoon cut everything from cool west coast blues to proto-rock and roll.

Witherspoon was born in Arkansas but moved to Los Angeles in his teens. The young singer caught on with bandleader Jay McShann in 1944. "Spoon," as he was called, worked with McShann for three years, making more than forty records with the band.[9] Thanks to several hits—"Ain't Nobody's Business" was the biggest—Witherspoon went out on his own in 1949, signing with Modern.

In 1952, Ralph Bass brought Witherspoon to Federal, where he was paired with the Maxwell Davis band for his first two sessions. Several good records of solid blues came out of the sessions, including "Foolish Prayer," "Two Little Girls," and "The Day Is Dawning," but nothing clicked commercially.

Two more unproductive sessions inspired Bass to try something radically different for the fifth session in October 1953—matching Witherspoon's powerhouse singing with the Lamplighters, an R&B vocal group that also recorded for Federal, and a band that included several members of the Johnny Otis group.

The four records from this session are the most interesting Witherspoon cut for Federal. "24 Sad Hours" and "Sad Life" display his early gospel training and sound like a powerful gospel quartet singing secular material. "Just for You" and "Move Me Baby" are rock and roll in all but name. "Move Me Baby" is especially fine, with Spoon giving Hank Ballard a run for his money. When those records failed to chart, the writing was on the wall. Witherspoon left Federal after one more recording session. He eventually found a congenial home in jazz, where his blues-based singing was appreciated for the marvel it was.

• • •

Throughout the 1960s and 1970s, there was one tune every blues guitarist had to know—"Hide Away" by Freddie King, arguably the most popular blues guitar instrumental of all time. If a guitar player couldn't play the tune, the gig went to one who could.

"Hide Away" is an irresistible pastiche of unlikely elements: a slide guitar riff from Hound Dog Taylor, a bit of Henry Mancini's theme for *Peter Gunn*, some stop-time chords learned from Robert Jr. Lockwood, and a chunk of Jimmy Mc-Cracklin's "The Walk." Freddie King recorded the instrumental at his first recording session for Federal in 1960. The record launched both King's career and a whole generation of electric guitar players.

Freddie King (1934–76) was born in Gilmer, Texas, where he learned his first guitar chords from his mother and an uncle. King moved to Chicago when he was sixteen, and it was there that he developed his distinctive guitar style. "I picked up the style between Lightnin' Hopkins and Muddy Waters," King explained, "and between B. B. King and T-Bone Walker. That's in-between style, that's the way I play, see. So I plays country and city."[10]

King was a Texas bluesman as well as a member of the same "West Side" school of gritty Chicago blues that produced incendiary guitarists Buddy Guy, Otis Rush, Magic Sam, and Luther Allison. King was already a guitar player when he moved north, but he honed his chops in Chicago under the tutelage of Jimmy Rogers and Eddie Taylor (best known for their work with Muddy Waters and Jimmy Reed, respectively). King's guitar playing was a unique synthesis of the two blues styles.

King made his first local records in 1957, but his recording career began in earnest when Sonny Thompson signed him to Federal in 1960. At his debut session in Cincinnati in August, Freddie cut six songs. The session showcased his superb singing; "Hide Away" was the sole instrumental. The first single, "You've Got to Love Her with a Feeling" and "Have You Ever Loved a Woman," sold especially well for a blues record, entering the bottom reaches of the *Billboard* pop chart.

A second four-song session was held in January 1961, kicking off a torrid, almost unbelievable stretch for Freddie King. By the time the year had ended, King had placed six records on the *Billboard* R&B chart: "See See Baby," "Christmas Tears," "I'm Tore Down," "Hide Away," "Lonesome Whistle Blues," and "San-Ho-Zay."

The last four were Top Ten R&B hits; the last three crossed over to the pop chart, as well. It was the biggest year of King's career.

It was also when King's guitar playing came to overshadow his singing, a change he never really welcomed. The transformation happened almost by accident. His second Federal single was "I Love the Woman" backed by "Hide Away." A few DJs flipped the record over, liked what they heard, and played "Hide Away" on the air. Suddenly, "Hide Away" was sitting at number five R&B and number twenty-nine pop, and Nathan was demanding more guitar instrumentals.

Freddie King answered the call, recording eight instrumentals in April 1961 and three more in July. The label then released an all-instrumental album, *Let's Hide Away and Dance Away with Freddy King*. His first album, *Freddy King Sings*, now widely regarded as a blues classic, had been released a few months earlier. Both albums contained two Top Ten hits, but it was the instrumental records that really clicked.

Among the most fervent fans of these instrumentals were surfers and surf music aficionados in southern California. Nathan noticed that a disproportionate number of the sales for the "Hide Away" and "San-Ho-Zay" singles, and later the instrumental album, came from the west coast. He rewarded this avid new audience in 1963 with an album created just for them, *Freddy King Goes Surfin'.*

With its new title and surfing theme, it probably took a few listens before some of these new fans realized why the music sounded familiar. They had, in fact, just purchased a copy of *Let's Hide Away and Dance Away with Freddy King* in a new cover, with new song titles, overdubbed clapping, and crowd noise added between the cuts to make it sound like a "live" recording.

A world away, in England, an ardent group of young guitarists including Eric Clapton, Jeff Beck, Peter Green, and Jimmy Page memorized every lick and song by Freddie King. Clapton says that King's "I Love the Woman" was his first exposure to electric blues guitar. Clapton was so smitten that he bought a Gibson Les Paul electric guitar because King was pictured with one on a record cover. "Hide Away," "Have You Ever Loved a Woman," "You've Got to Love Her with a Feeling," and "I'm Tore Down" have long been part of Clapton's repertoire.

After Freddie King's red-hot year in 1961, no one would have predicted that he would never have another hit, but that's what happened. His sudden and complete fall from commercial grace remains mysterious. A 1984 *Goldmine* article mentioned "a partial blacklist of King [Records] product" on radio because the label "upset some leading black deejays during the mid-'60s,"[11] but no details were provided.

Freddie King felt there were two problems. The first was an overemphasis on instrumentals, which he often viewed as little more than album filler. King ruefully noted that after "Hide Away" became a huge hit, "everybody forgot about the vocals . . . just thought I played guitar, that was it."[12] He also faulted the label's lack of promotion of his records. He wasn't wrong when he complained that King Records in the early 1960s put most of its muscle behind James Brown.

King had three recording sessions in 1962, cutting twenty-one tracks plus four duets with Lula Reed. King moved back to Texas in 1963 and subsequently put most of his efforts into touring, playing in blues and rock clubs to great acclaim. He had a nine-song session in 1963 and a twelve-song session in 1964.

Federal released Freddie King singles on a regular basis through 1964, including "The Bossa Nova Watusi Twist" and "Bossa Nova Blues" from Freddie's third album, *Bossa Nova and the Blues*. That album was just about the last straw for Freddie King, who recorded only once more for Federal, a four-song session in 1966 that included guitarist Lonnie Mack, another young Freddie King acolyte.

By the time he left in 1966, Freddie King had recorded seventy-two songs and tunes and had five albums on King to his credit. He also played on sessions for Smokey Smothers, Hank Marr, and Lula Reed, with whom he cut four pop-oriented duets, among them "Do the President Twist," a 1962 record that attempted to cash in on not only the twist dance craze but also the popularity of John Kennedy.

Freddie King recorded at the King studio in Cincinnati, working with producers Sonny Thompson, Andy Gibson, and Gene Redd. "It was cool, you know," King explained. "Long as Syd Nathan would stay out of the studio, it was nice. Like the first hit, all those things like 'Hide Away' and 'Have You Ever Loved a Woman,' 'You've Got To Love Her with a Feeling,' that whole instrumental album, Syd wasn't nowhere in the studio. He was upstairs . . . I was doing exactly what I wanted to do . . . And then Syd got smart, you know, he came down, and he's gonna put some more stuff in there."[13]

Among Nathan's contributions were the nonsensical titles he gave to King's original tunes. As Freddie remembered, "'Hide Away' and 'Just Pickin',' I think those are the only two I named. I made 'em all, you know, wrote all the tunes, but the studio put the names to 'em. Some of them, I don't even know . . . They said 'Swooshy,' you know. I'd listen to it and not even know what he's talkin' about. They got some heck of a names in there."[14] Other good ones were "Sen-Sa-Shun," "San-Ho-Zay," and "King-a-Ling."

King finally had enough and left. "See, the reason I quit recording for King," he said, "[was Nathan would] try to tell me what to do. He sit behind a desk all day, and you out there playin' for the public . . . This guy who sit behind the desk all day don't see how the people dance, how they react when you play. When you walk in to record, he says, 'Here, sing this!' He don't ask you if you like the record. So I quit. I'm not gonna record for nobody that's gonna tell me what to sing."[15] And that was that.

King made two albums for Cotillion and worked with Leon Russell on three rock-oriented albums for Russell's label, Shelter. King next moved to RSO for a pair of albums. And then Freddie King, a robust, vital man in the prime of his life, suddenly died in 1976. He was only forty-two.

One study of blues between 1942 and 1982 has called Freddie King "the most brilliant post-B.B. King electric blues guitarist."[16] To appreciate King's mastery of the electric guitar, listen to his second all-instrumental album on King, *Freddy King Gives You A Bonanza of Instrumentals*, released in 1965. *Bonanza* contains several catchy, hook-laden tunes ("Manhole," "Nickel Plated," and "King-a-Ling"), but three cuts truly illustrate King's greatness as a guitarist.

The first is "Freddy's Midnite Dream," a gorgeous slow blues that would have fit perfectly on one of Roy Buchanan's better albums from the 1980s. There is nothing else quite like it in Freddie King's wide-ranging catalog. Those who know King only from "Hide Away" will be surprised by the majesty and grace of this beautiful tune.

"Low Tide" and "Remington's Ride" are described by one critic as "among the most awesome [performances] in blues guitar history."[17] King's playing was based on long, fluid, improvised lead lines patterned after Charlie Christian and T-Bone Walker, and these tunes gave him ample room to stretch out and show what he could do.

"Remington's Ride," written by steel guitarist Herb Remington, has been covered by many artists, but no one has torched it quite like Freddie King. The record starts out tame enough with a straightforward statement of the melody, but then King cuts loose with an extended barrage of searing, single-string soloing, some of the most exciting he ever recorded. It's a command performance.

"Low Tide," six minutes of blues guitar improvisation without a single chorus where King could catch his breath, is even more impressive. The tune amounts to an advanced tutorial in modern blues guitar playing, as King romps along tossing off phrases, riffs, and ideas as if there were no tomorrow. If it's not his finest moment as a guitarist, it's awfully close.

With the advantage of perspective, it's easy to hear how much Freddie King influenced late 1960s and early 1970s rock guitar—especially that coming from England. Colin Escott calls King "the man who defined modern blues-based rock guitar,"[18] and echoes of King's playing can be heard in the music of dozens of bands from the era, including the Rolling Stones, Led Zeppelin, the Yardbirds, John Mayall's Bluesbreakers, Cream, the Jeff Beck Group, and Fleetwood Mac.

The veteran British producer Mike Vernon was awed the first time he heard Clapton. "It had a huge effect on me," says Vernon. "His sound was so far ahead of anything I'd come across before. Later, I found out that . . . I simply hadn't heard Freddie King. Eric benefited from the fact that no one else had heard Freddie either . . . You look at some of Freddie King's TV appearances and have to ask how in God's name he wasn't more successful."[19]

Guitarist and singer Otis "Smokey" Smothers never came close to stardom, but for a period in the early 1960s, he had one of the most talked-about albums of the day. *Smokey Smothers Sings The Backporch Blues*, released in 1962, is highly coveted by collectors today as one of the rarest of blues albums. Forty-five years ago, it was an unexpected blast of down-home blues that took everyone by surprise.

As were many of his contemporaries, Smothers (1929–93) was from Mississippi. He moved to Chicago when he was seventeen. After several years of playing around town, he joined Howlin' Wolf's band in 1956. Smothers was signed by Sonny Thompson to record for Federal in 1960.

Smothers entered the King studio in Cincinnati for a twelve-song session in August. He was accompanied by guitarist Freddie Jordan, drummer Phillip Paul, and Freddie King, who was in town for his own first session for Federal. King was not scheduled to play on Smothers' session, but as Smothers later explained, it just worked out that way. "I was already recording when he come there," said Smothers. "He didn't rehearse with me. Me and him just played."[20]

As King remembered it, his services were needed because he knew Smothers' music and the studio guitarist did not. "See, they had a cat there to play, Freddie Jordan, playing behind Smokey," said King. "He was a studio man. The cat didn't know what Smokey wanted, so I walks in, and I told 'em, 'Oh, man, I know what he wants.' I told 'em I'd play behind him because I knew what he wanted. So it was no problem."[21]

The 1962 release of Smothers's album on King caught the attention of the blues world. At a time when the usual Chicago blues band featured electric guitars, electric bass, harmonica, piano, and drums, the spare, rural feel of Smothers's album was unexpected. With Freddie King supplying exquisite guitar work throughout, the record was a perfect showcase for Smothers's laconic vocals. It was a sublime piece of work, but it sold poorly.

Smothers returned to Cincinnati for another recording session in 1962, cutting four songs. The strangest of the bunch was "Twist with Me, Annie," a reworking of the Midnighters' hit and perhaps the most low-down twist record ever made. Without Freddie King playing guitar, the music from this session is less exciting than the earlier material, and the resulting Federal singles failed to make much noise.

When it came to bizarre professional twists and turns, few musicians could compete with pianists Champion Jack Dupree and Memphis Slim. Both men had lengthy and productive musical careers, both were memorable characters, both spent years in Europe as expatriates, both recorded for a bewildering array of small labels, and both recorded some outstanding blues for King.

William "Champion Jack" Dupree (ca. 1909–92) was born in New Orleans, raised in the same orphanage as Louis Armstrong, and musically schooled in the brothels and speakeasies of the city's infamous Storyville district. By the mid-1930s, Dupree was earning his living as a boxer (hence the hyperbolic nickname Champion Jack). Deciding it was safer to pound the piano, Dupree made his recording debut in 1940 for OKeh.

Dupree recorded prolifically for a variety of small labels in the 1940s and early 1950s, often working with guitarist Brownie McGhee and harmonica player Sonny Terry. Like John Lee Hooker, Dupree held a general disdain for recording contracts and, also like Hooker, used some wonderful pseudonyms, including Lightnin' Junior, Brother Blues, and Meat Head Johnson. He signed with King in 1953.

Over the next three years, Dupree cut two dozen songs for King, including such sizzlers as "Mail Order Woman," "Stumbling Block," "Let the Doorbell Ring," and "Big Leg Emma's." He also recorded in a more archaic style on such songs as "Me and My Mule" and "That's My Pa." Most of Dupree's recordings were issued on singles, and sixteen were collected on the album *Champion Jack Dupree Sings the Blues.*

The self-proclaimed "last of the barrelhouse piano players" enjoyed his only chart success on King with "Walking the Blues," a Top Ten R&B hit in 1955. This unlikely hit, an exceedingly relaxed piano blues with spoken lyrics, was credited to Dupree and "Mr. Bear" (singer Teddy McRae). Besides his own recordings, Dupree also played piano on King recordings by Little Willie John and Piney Brown.

Born in Memphis as Peter Chatman, the pianist known as Memphis Slim (1915–88) was an important blues musician of the late 1940s and 1950s and a key figure on the European blues scene of the 1960s. After youthful stints as a hobo, bootlegger, and juke joint entertainer, Slim was in Chicago by the late 1930s, where he began a fruitful association with the popular singer-guitarist Big Bill Broonzy.

A disciple of pianist Roosevelt Sykes, Memphis Slim formed his band the House Rockers in the mid-1940s and soon began recording. Besides being an exceptional pianist, Slim was one of the funniest people ever to record serious blues. His performances, and even his records, often featured as much storytelling as actual singing, but Slim's charisma and sense of humor made it work.

Slim's first singles on Federal, cut between 1946 and 1948, had been purchased from Miracle. These featured Slim's regular band and included such hits as "Nobody Loves Me," "Lend Me Your Love," and "Messin' Around," which topped the R&B charts in 1948. His only King session, in January 1949, produced eight songs, including "Mistake in Life," "Slim's Boogie," and "A Letter Home," that were later issued on the misleadingly titled album, *Memphis Slim Sings Folk Blues*.

For those who think all blues is raunchy, rural, or primitive, one name serves as a rebuttal: Charles Brown. The Texas-born pianist and singer was the epitome of urbane musical sophistication. With his classically grounded piano work and laid-back singing, Brown (1922–99) was something of a rarity—an elegant bluesman. He was a huge influence on Ray Charles, Amos Milburn, and Fats Domino.

Working with Johnny Moore's Three Blazers and later his own trio, Brown was one of the biggest stars of the late 1940s and early 1950s, with such top-selling records as "Drifting Blues," "Black Night," and "Seven Long Days." By the time he came to King in 1960, however, the hits were several years behind him. His luck was about to change.

Brown was playing a club in Newport, Kentucky, just across the river from Cincinnati. "Syd Nathan heard I was down there," Brown recalled. "He knew that I had had success with 'Merry Christmas Baby' [recorded for Exclusive in 1947]. He said, 'Can you come up with another Christmas number?' I went in the studio and came out with 'Please Come Home for Christmas.'"[22]

"Please Come Home for Christmas" was Brown's first hit in eight years. The record has become a holiday perennial and will likely be remembered long after Brown's superb blues recordings have been forgotten. Brown accepted that. "If the kids today never hear about you any other time of the year," he said, "they know that at Christmas time they're gonna hear Charles Brown. At least I have that going for me, along with Bing Crosby."[23]

Pianist and singer Little Willie Littlefield is best known as the first person to record the classic rock song "Kansas City," but he deserves more than that because he was an excellent piano player (and influence on Fats Domino). The fourteen sides Littlefield cut for Federal in 1952 and 1953, featuring his rolling piano work and tenor saxophonists Maxwell Davis, Wardell Gray, and Rufus Gore, make one wonder about their complete lack of commercial success.

Born in Texas in 1931, Littlefield started playing piano at a young age and was playing the blues clubs in Houston by the time he was in his teens. He signed with Modern in 1949 and had a big hit with his first release, "It's Midnight." Two more hits followed in quick succession. Even so, Modern dropped Littlefield from its roster, and Ralph Bass snapped him up for Federal.

Littlefield's first Federal session yielded "K.C. Lovin," as it was originally called. Littlefield claimed he wrote the song and sold it to the songwriting team of Jerry Leiber and Mike Stoller, but that seems doubtful given Leiber and Stoller's talents and prodigious output. If Littlefield's assertion *is* true, the sale was a spectacularly bad move for him financially, because the song has been recorded (as "Kansas City") by hundreds of artists since Wilbert Harrison took it to the top of the pop charts in 1959.

Besides "K.C. Lovin'" and the similar-sounding follow-ups "Miss K.C.'s Fine" and "Goofy Dust Blues," Littlefield's Federal output included such solid senders as "Blood Is Redder Than Wine," "The Midnight Hour Is Shining," and two instrumentals, "Sitting on the Curbstone" and "Jim Wilson's Boogie," named for King's Detroit branch manager. Discouraged by poor sales, Littlefield left Federal in 1954.

Kansas-born singer Arnold "Gatemouth" Moore was an active recording artist in the late 1940s. A veteran of such 1920s and 1930s touring troupes as Sammie Green's Down in Dixie Minstrels, the Rabbit Foot Minstrels, and Ida Cox's Darktown Scandals, Moore did not at first care for the blues, telling an interviewer, "I am one of the ultra-men blues singers. I am not accustomed and don't know nothing about that gut-belly stuff in the joints. I put on tuxedos, dressed up, sang intelligent, and tried to give voice instead of singing."[24]

When that failed to provide much of a living, Moore turned to the blues. He made his recording debut in the early 1940s and came to King in 1947 when Syd Nathan heard him at a Cincinnati club and offered him a contract. Moore's first effort for the label, in typical King fashion, was a cover of a country song, "I'm a Fool to Care." Moore had three recording sessions for King in 1947, cutting twenty-eight songs, of which eighteen were released. None of the singles did anything, but Moore's confidence remained unshaken.

As he explained to Johnny Otis, "Without a doubt, and I'm not being facetious, I'm the best blues singer in the business with that singing voice. Now I can't wiggle and I can't dance, but telling a story, I don't think them other boys are in my class."[25]

Moore's first King singles found him "giving voice," but he was more effective as a blues shouter, albeit a restrained one. His better records include "Highway 61 Blues," "I Ain't Mad at You," and "Hey Mr. Gatemouth." Moore became an ordained minister in 1949 and sang only gospel music for the rest of his career.

THAT AIN'T NOTHIN' BUT RIGHT

Rockabilly and Rock and Roll on King Records

• • •

Bluegrass rock, that's what it really was.
Bill Monroe music and colored artists'
music is what caused rock 'n' roll.

—Charlie Feathers

Rock and roll was the ultimate musical mongrel, a cultural amalgamation that borrowed freely from virtually every genre of American music that had come before—gospel, western swing, bluegrass, blues, jazz, and pop. Because King was active in most of those styles, the label was a natural for rock and roll.

Not many people did more than Ike Turner to shape American music in the 1950s. He was a guitarist, pianist, talent scout, bandleader, record producer, songwriter, and behind-the-scenes fixer. Turner did it all and he did it well.

Izear Luster "Ike" Turner (1931–2007) was born in Clarksdale, Mississippi. With his band the Kings of Rhythm, Turner was playing juke joints throughout the Mississippi delta by his high school years. After the Kings recorded "Rocket 88" in 1951—the record was credited to Jackie Brenston and the Delta Cats—Turner became a very busy man.

Five years later, when he signed with Federal in 1956, Turner was a red-hot bandleader. With Turner on electric guitar, Raymond Hill and Eddie Jones on tenor sax, Jackie Brenston on baritone sax and vocals, Jesse Knight Jr. on bass, and singers Billy Gayles and Clayton Love, the Kings of Rhythm may well have been the hottest touring blues, R&B, or rock band in the country. The Kings ruled the St. Louis club scene.

Of the group's singers, Billy Gayles had the best opportunity for individual success, with eight songs issued on singles. Although none made the national charts,

Turner's original "I'm Tore Up" made considerable noise as a regional hit. Gayles was a versatile, distinctive vocalist who took good advantage of a big voice. The best of his Federal cuts –"I'm Tore Up," "Just One More Time," and "No Coming Back"—should have been big hits.

As the voice on one of the first great rock and roll records, Jackie Brenston has a curiously anonymous kind of immortality—many people know the record, "Rocket 88," but probably not one in one thousand could name the singer. Shortly after "Rocket 88" topped the R&B chart in 1951, Brenston quit the Kings of Rhythm, formed his own band, bought a bus, and hit the road.

He found to his disappointment that one can ride a hit, even a big hit, only so long. After a couple of years on his own, Brenston returned to the sideman role, working with Amos Milburn and Johnny Otis. By 1955, Brenston was back with Turner, playing baritone sax and taking the occasional vocal. He had one session in 1956, which produced two solid Federal singles but no hits.

The Kings of Rhythm, billed as "Ike Turner and His Orchestra," had a six-song session in 1957 with Clayton Love on vocals. The two instrumentals and four songs are illuminating as to Turner's mindset at the time. Turner was a born bluesman, but he had one eye on the pop charts as he wrote material for the band. It shows.

"Trail Blazer" and "Rock-a-Bucket" are uptown sax instrumentals that rival Earl Bostic and anticipate Bill Justis's chart-topper "Raunchy." In "She Made My Blood Run Cold," Turner seems to be trying for the same commercial niche as the humorous story-songs of the Coasters. "Do You Mean It" and "The Big Question" could have been contenders with a bit of luck.

Turner had come up as a pianist, but by 1956 he was primarily playing electric guitar. His guitar of choice was the Fender Stratocaster, one of the first production guitars equipped with a device to produce vibrato, known variously as a tremolo arm, whammy bar, or twang bar. Turner didn't really know how to use the tremolo, so he winged it, with spectacular—and spectacularly bizarre—results. Before Link Wray or Duane Eddy, Ike Turner had created one of the first instantly recognizable guitar sounds in rock and roll.

Turner was not subtle in his use of vibrato, and to some, his playing was too gimmicky. But Turner was trying hard to stand out from the pack of rock and roll guitarists, and his forceful, creative, and almost deranged playing certainly accomplished that. He was an original as a guitarist, "abusing the whammy bar to within an inch of its existence blasting forth gut-wrenching solos that still defy sane description some 45 years later."[1]

Though he was only twenty-five years old, Ike Turner was a veteran record producer, musician, and bandleader at the time of his Federal sessions. His biggest hits were still to come, but even at this stage, Turner's crossover vision was beginning to take shape. These records capture a moment in time right before a young singer named Annie Mae Bullock—better known as Tina Turner—joined, and forever changed, the Kings of Rhythm. By 1960, the band had evolved into the Ike and Tina Turner Revue, a hyper-kinetic and sexually charged extravaganza that took the R&B and rock worlds by storm, scoring such hits as "A Fool in Love," "It's Gonna Work Out Fine," and "Proud Mary" between 1960 and 1974.

Ike Turner was an innovator who fully deserves his spot in the Rock & Roll Hall of Fame. Blues singer Little Milton Campbell is on target when he asserts, "Without him, none of the music that you hear today would be the same. He helped Sun start out, and that was only the beginning of the things he didn't get credit for."[2] Turner was one of the primary architects of modern R&B, blues, rock, and soul music.

If talent were all it took, Charlie Feathers (1932–98) would have been a superstar. Instead, Feathers is a classic example of the "can't-miss talent" who missed, several times. He missed on Sun and on several small, obscure labels. And he missed on King, though the eight songs Feathers cut for King in 1956 and 1957 form the core of his modern reputation. It's earthy and deeply crazed rockabilly or, as Feathers himself described it, "some tough goddamned stuff."

Feathers was born outside Holly Springs, Mississippi. As did many of his generation, Feathers developed a musical aesthetic in which race was meaningless. He listened to the *Grand Ole Opry* and was particularly keen on Bill Monroe and Hank Williams. He also loved blues singers, especially Howlin' Wolf and Junior Kimbrough, a sharecropping neighbor who taught Feathers how to play the guitar.

By 1950, Feathers was living in Memphis and hanging out at the Sun Records studio on Union Avenue. He watched the endless parade of blues singers and guitarists entering the studio and hoped for his own chance to record. Feathers always pointed out that he was established at Sun long before Elvis, which he was, in a loitering kind of way. He also claimed that he pretty much taught Elvis the rockabilly style.

Feathers finally got his chance at Sun in 1955, several months after Presley made his debut. Sun head Sam Phillips saw Feathers as a country singer rather than a rocker and recorded Feathers in the country style, while also relegating him to the subsidiary label Flip for most of his singles. Unfortunately, Feathers was hard country at a time when country was going soft. His records flopped.

Miffed that Phillips refused to record his original rock song "Tongue-Tied Jill," Feathers took the song to Sun's crosstown rival Meteor and recorded it there. A truly inspired performance by Feathers, the single wasn't a hit, but it got enough local attention to attract King producer Louis Innis, who promptly signed Feathers.

Feathers and his band, the Musical Warriors, drove to Cincinnati in August 1956 for their first King session. With Feathers on rhythm guitar and vocals, Jerry Huffman on electric guitar, Jody Chastain on upright bass, and drummer Jimmy Swords added for the session, the Warriors tore it up, cutting four of the best rockabilly sides ever. "One Hand Loose," "Can't Hardly Stand It," "Bottle to the Baby," and "Everybody's Lovin' My Baby" are just about perfect—raw, hard-edged, frantic, impassioned hillbilly rock.

Feathers sings like a man who knows this is his last shot at the big time. The records, in Peter Guralnick's words, are "full of nonsense syllables, falsetto shrieks, glottal stops, and unabashed good fun."[3] King probably saw Feathers as its Elvis, but Feathers is far more gone on these cuts than Elvis ever was. The sheen of psychotic menace gracing the languid "Can't Hardly Stand It" is particularly nice.

Neither single did much, so for Feather's next session, in January 1957, Innis decided that if you couldn't beat Elvis, you could at least copy him as closely as possible. RCA was in the process of "sanitizing" Elvis at that time, so that was the plan for Feathers as well. Innis booked the Musical Warriors into RCA's Nashville studio, augmented them with a black vocal group imitating the Jordanaires, and cut four more songs.

Though a bit less exciting than the earlier singles, these records were quite good, too. With the right break (or skillfully applied payola), "Too Much Alike" or "When You Decide" could have been major hits. Neither made the national charts. Feathers drifted away to other labels and other ventures, frustrated by the whole experience.

When asked about them in the mid-1970s, Feathers was dismissive of his King recordings. "Aw, they was never right. We just didn't have the sound. I was dissatisfied with all of them, every one. You just can't figure those things."[4] Feathers added that moving from Sun to King "was like getting out of a Cadillac and into a Ford."[5]

Bitterness aside, that statement makes little sense. The Sun studio had its virtues, and Sam Phillips was a master at using "slapback" echo, but Feathers' records on King sound better than his records on Flip/Sun. King used reverb instead of "slapback," but the bass and drums practically explode from the speakers. A very present "live" sound was one of the King studio's trademarks.

"That old King studio had a terrific sound," said Henry Glover. "It had a very high ceiling, maybe twenty-four feet, and the control room protruded into the studio in a V-shape like the bridge of a ship, so the engineer could see in front and to the side of him.

"I [hired] an engineer by the name of Eddie Smith, who was a very good technical man. He stayed with King for about twelve years . . . Everything was done at one time. There was no multitracking; you would continue making cuts until you got every instrument, every voice on the tape. That was considered your final mix."[6]

Sam Phillips called Feathers "a little difficult,"[7] and that's significant coming from a man who regularly dealt with such characters as Jerry Lee Lewis and Ike Turner. Sam's brother Tom Phillips said that Feathers "had the talent" but "had to pretty much have his own way. King promoted him pretty good, but he didn't like the way they did, and he just let them know."[8]

The records Feathers cut for King in 1956 and 1957 didn't make him much money and didn't make him a star. They did, however, make him a legend. Those records are hailed today as rockabilly masterpieces. Along with "Tongue-Tied Jill," they are the essence of Feathers' greatness.

Peter Guralnick described Feathers in *Lost Highway* as a "sometime ambulance driver, stock car racer, semi-pro ballplayer, shuffleboard hustler, and rockabilly legend."[9] What seems truly remarkable is that Charlie Feathers was too raw, too rough, and too stubborn for rock and roll. Now *that* is something worth celebrating.

Not all rock and roll from the 1950s was surly rebellion. One of the enduring songs from the era is "Seventeen," a paean to adolescent femininity as light and frothy as cotton candy. Recorded for King in 1955 by Boyd Bennett and His Rockets, the song has sold millions of records over the years and appeared on countless anthologies.

As did many first-generation rockers, Boyd Bennett (1924–2002) started out as a country singer. Born in Alabama and raised in the Nashville area, Bennett came to King after a failed audition for Columbia. Bennett cut four country songs at his first King session in 1952. It was almost two years before Bennett returned to the studio, and when he did, he was still searching for a musical identity.

As Boyd Bennett & His Southlanders, the group cut four songs in November 1954. The results were pretty bad—the ersatz Dixieland of "Little Ole You All" is dismal, but it pales beside "Waterloo," an overblown cha-cha that is pure corn. This session was hardly encouraging, but then something happened.

"We started playing rock and roll music," explained Bennett. "We discovered that American kids were listening to so-called race music stations in those days. The black stations were playing the old soul music, and we discovered that the high school kids were listening to that type of music in their bedrooms when their parents weren't listening."[10]

The new rocking sound was promptly showcased on a single that paired "You Upset Me Baby" and "Poison Ivy." Another change was a more with-it name for the group—the Rockets. But Bennett had to fight Nathan to record the song that became his biggest hit.

"I had brought 'Seventeen' into him as a dub," said Bennett, "and handed it to him and said, 'Syd, I want to record this song.' He listened to about half of it and then threw it in the wastebasket and said, 'That's crap. Don't bring stuff like that to me.'"[11]

Bennett told Nathan he was recording "Seventeen" or nothing. Nathan reluctantly agreed to his demand, but then refused to release the record. When Nathan went on vacation, Bennett approached Henry Glover, who agreed to release the single. It broke quickly. As Bennett said, "From the day we released it, I never changed my shoes except to take a shower. I was on the road for six weeks."[12]

"Seventeen" was a huge hit, among the biggest of 1955. It made the Top Ten on both the pop and R&B charts in *Billboard,* reaching number five on the pop chart, and spawned covers by the Ames Brothers, the Fontane Sisters, and others. It was Bennett's moment in the sun. He returned to the charts later in the year with "My Boy Flat Top" (a male "Seventeen") and in 1956 with a cover of "Blue Suede Shoes."

Bennett and the Rockets recorded steadily into 1958, recording more than fifty songs for King. The hits were scarce, but the band recorded some decent cuts in the style of Bill Haley—"Boogie at Midnight," "Hit That Jive, Jack," "Everlovin'," and "Mumbles Blues," among others. The band also backed Moon Mullican on a 1956 session.

Wesley Erwin "Mac" Curtis was born in Fort Worth, Texas, in 1939. He got his first guitar at age twelve and started appearing in local talent contests, singing the current country hits. In 1954, he heard Elvis Presley and gave up trying to sing like Lefty Frizzell and Hank Williams. He was an Elvis man now.

A main figure in the rockabilly revival of the 1970s, Curtis started his recording career as a high-school kid. He recorded sixteen songs for King in four sessions during 1956 and 1957. Although the records weren't big hits, they are highly prized by collectors who hail Curtis as one of the founding fathers of Texas rockabilly.

"The first session," said Curtis, "took place [in April 1956] with Ralph Bass and Bernie Pearlman at the Jim Beck studios in Dallas. Every record label was looking for an Elvis Presley. I walked up into the control booth [at the studio] as they were doing some playbacks, and Bernie Pearlman had a copy of Presley's first album. He would play a little bit of it and compare it with what we were doing to see if we were getting close to the sound."[13]

Curtis's first two singles, "If I Had Me a Woman," "Just So You Call Me," "Half Hearted Love," and the prime "Grandaddy's Rockin'," are, in the words of writer Bill Millar, "perfect examples of Texan rockabilly. Light and airy but unarguably powerful, they lift you up and bite your ankles at the same time."[14]

A second four-song session was held in July; "That Ain't Nothin' but Right" and "You Ain't Treatin' Me Right" are the stand-outs. The singles gained enough attention that Curtis was asked to perform on Alan Freed's "Christmas Shower of Stars" program in New York. Perhaps that experience or a subsequent tour with Little Richard distracted Curtis, as his third King session, in February 1957, was a complete change of pace.

Three of the cuts suggest that someone saw Curtis as a romantic pop balladeer. Just like Elvis. "Say So," "I'll Be Gentle," and "Blue Jean Heart" *do* sound a bit like Elvis, but the latter two are pretty lame. A rocking but unreleased cover of Charlie Feathers's "Goosebumps" was all that redeemed the session.

Curtis enlisted in the Army nine months later. His last session for King was in 1957, while he was home on Christmas leave. These four songs returned Curtis to comfortable territory—uptempo, upbeat rock and roll and rockabilly—and ended his King days on a high note. "Little Miss Linda" and "What You Want" are fine rockers, and "You Are My Very Special Baby" and "Missy Ann" aren't far behind.

Louis Innis wore many hats at King over the years: session musician, songwriter, recording artist, and, for a few years in the mid-1950s, A&R director for "folk and western" music. Born in Indiana, Innis (1919–82) worked as a radio musician in Chattanooga and Atlanta before moving to WLW in Cincinnati in the early 1940s. Innis played bass or guitar as a sideman on a number of early King records.

After recording for Sterling and Mercury, Innis returned to King in 1953 as a singer. He cut more than twenty songs for King and DeLuxe over the next three years. Before moving into the A&R field, Innis made his mark more as a songwriter than a singer; "Good Morning Judge" (a huge R&B hit for Wynonie Harris) and "I Ain't Got a Pot (to Peel Potatoes In)" are among his better-known songs.

As a producer, Innis was a sucker for novelty songs. "Rock 'n' Roll Nursery Rhyme" by Dave Dudley (a few years before his truck-driver hits), "You Tell Her, I Stutter" by Jimmy Lee Prow, "Top Ten Rock" by Fuller Todd, and "No Good, Robin Hood" by Delbert Barker are just a few of Innis's production efforts in this vein.

Nathan expected his A&R men to search constantly for new talent to record. Innis frequently visited Memphis for that purpose, holding auditions at the King branch office at 1092 Union Avenue, just a few blocks down the street from Sun

Records (at 706 Union). Innis found it a convenient location to connect with local talent rejected or ignored by Sun, including such artists as Charlie Feathers and Fuller Todd.

Innis made quite an impression on some of the starry-eyed young musicians. Todd remembered his audition well. "When I went there, there were about six or seven others besides me," he recalled. "So Louis Innis had me do my thing while he walked around the room listening. He came right up close, putting his ear against my mouth, just checking out my voice. I was the only one signed that day."[15]

Louis Innis spent most of the 1960s in Nashville working in music publishing. He returned to King in 1969 and worked coordinating album releases. Innis died in 1982.

• • •

The 1950s in America was a time of overreaction, to everything from communism to long sideburns. The radio payola "scandal" is an example that has come to stand for the era. Payola—essentially paying someone at a radio station to play a record—was suddenly a major national crisis.

The crusade to root it out involved the Federal Communications Commission (FCC), the Federal Trade Commission (FTC), the Internal Revenue Service, a Congressional subcommittee, and local grand juries. Framed as a matter of restoring integrity to the American airwaves, the agenda was actually a concerted effort to crush rock and roll, defang the emerging youth culture, and restore corporate control of the music and radio industries.

Many independent record companies were among the targets. In November 1959, King, Coral, Kapp, Roulette, Dot, Imperial, Cadence, Liberty, and Gone were subpoenaed by Frank Hogan, New York District Attorney.[16] The same day the subpoena was announced, Nathan said in the Cincinnati Post that King "has paid off disc jockeys all over the country and that he has the checks to prove it."[17] One can only imagine the panic this statement caused among compromised disc jockeys, many of whom had vehemently denied taking payola.

In the Post article, Nathan complained that payola "is a dirty rotten mess and it has been getting worse in the last five years."[18] He said King made regular monthly payments to disc jockeys in 1957 and 1958, in the amount of "$1,800 a month," but that the company had largely abandoned the practice because "our statistics showed that we didn't get our records played any more whether we paid or not."[19]

"There are more than 10,000 disc jockeys in the country and less than 200 demanded payola," Nathan said. "That small number couldn't make or break a record. So we cut it out."[20] He said that most of the pressure to pay came from disc jockeys in Philadelphia and New York. As for paying with checks, Nathan asked, "How else could we account for the money unless it was on our books for what it was? We told the disc jockeys that if they didn't want to declare it on their incomes, it was their business, but if they were going to get paid [by King], it would be by check."[21]

Payola took many forms, the most common of which was a record company or distributor compensating a disc jockey to play a particular record. Cash was preferred, but gifts ranging from liquor to hi-fi sets to visits from prostitutes were also accepted. A more insidious practice (in that it cheated songwriters and music publishers who had no say in the matter) was to "cut in" radio people on the publishing royalties by listing them as co-writers of a song.

Because 1960 was an election year, ambitious politicians jumped on payola with the gusto of a dog on a bone. On February 8, the House of Representatives Special Subcommittee on Legislative Oversight opened hearings on radio payola. DJs from Cleveland and Boston were the first to testify.

That same day, the FCC and the FTC entered the fray. The FCC concentrated on radio and took a twofold approach. Its first move was to transfer legal liability from individual disc jockeys to the station licensee, meaning that station management couldn't avoid sanctions by claiming ignorance of employee behavior. Because FCC broadcasting licenses were valuable commodities, the threat of losing them was significant. The FCC also began drafting legislation that would outlaw payola, making it illegal for the first time. (Yes, you read that correctly.)

The Federal Trade Commission, for its part, went after record companies and distributors. The chairman of the FTC opined in *Variety* that an "exceedingly high percentage" of record labels and distributors employed payola as "a standard commercial procedure."[22] On March 4, the FTC formally accused King Records of making payments to DJs. That should have been an easy case to make because Syd Nathan had admitted it in print several months earlier.

At the end of March, Representative Emmanuel Celler of New York introduced two anti-payola bills in Congress, saying that payola was responsible for "the cacophonous music called rock & roll" and that without payola, rock and roll would never have become popular, "especially among teenagers."[23] His bills proposed a $1,000 fine and one year in jail for either giving or receiving payola. And to think that *Newsweek* called Allen Freed a cynic for noting, "What they call payola in the disc-jockey business, they call lobbying in Washington."[24]

The matter was essentially resolved for King in October 1960 when the label agreed to an FTC "consent order" prohibiting the payment of payola. King Records and Nathan came through the whole ordeal relatively unscathed. The primary consequence for King—and it was a major one—was the loss of Henry Glover, who left in 1959 because he felt that Nathan had betrayed him during the investigations.

• • •

Rockabilly hits often come with a story, but few tales can top that of "Jungle Rock," the signature song of Hank Mizell and a minor classic of the rockabilly era. A churning, bottom-heavy novelty similar in concept to Warren Smith's "Ubangi Stomp," it's a relentless rocker, as simple as first-grade arithmetic.

Living in Chicago in the mid-1950s, Hank Mizell formed a band with guitarist Jim Bobo and started playing in seedy dives, most notably the Napoleon Lounge. In the fall of 1958, Mizell and Bobo recorded "Jungle Rock" (and at least one other song, "When I'm in Your Arms") for a tiny local label called Eko. Their single received a positive review in *Billboard*, though sales were likely in the low three figures. Then Eko folded.

Six months later, someone from King's Chicago office walked into the Napoleon Lounge and heard "Jungle Rock" on the jukebox. Sensing a hit, he purchased the master and the publishing rights for King, cutting the owner of the club in as co-writer for his help. King rushed "Jungle Rock" onto the market and . . . nothing happened. It stiffed.

Mizell and Bobo had a subsequent session for King, in November 1960. Of the six songs recorded, two country-oriented songs were released on a single and another song ended up on a various-artists Christmas album; the others were not released. Mizell worked outside music for the next fifteen years.

In 1976, rockabilly fanatics in Europe discovered "Jungle Rock." The ensuing buzz elevated Hank Mizell and his long-forgotten record to cult status. Then "Jungle Rock" crossed over from the rockabilly crowd to the English disco scene, where it was such a hit in the dance clubs that a re-release of "Jungle Rock" made it into the Top Ten of the UK pop chart. Mizell was reportedly bemused by this turn of events (one would hope so), but he made the most of the unexpected attention with an English tour and a few new recordings.

The Johnny Otis story is one of the most fascinating in American music. Born in 1921 to Greek immigrant parents in Vallejo, California, John Veliotes got his first taste of the music business drumming in swing bands in nearby Oakland. From that point on, Otis led a new life. He described it in a 1953 article in *Our World* magazine titled "I Pass for Negro."[25]

Otis was a session drummer in Los Angeles by 1945, working with Wynonie Harris, Charles Mingus, Lester Young, and others. He formed the Johnny Otis Orchestra and began recording. Otis had several huge R&B hits on Savoy, including chart-toppers "Double Crossin' Blues," "Mistrustin' Blues," and "Cupid Boogie," all of which showcased Otis protégés Little Esther, Mel Walker, and the Robins. He also worked with Charles Brown, Johnny Ace, Etta James, and Big Mama Thornton.

By the time Otis finally got around to recording for King, he had been involved with the label for almost a dozen years in a variety of capacities, mostly as talent scout and record producer. In four sessions in 1961 and 1962, Otis recorded fifteen sides, most of which stand up very well today. Otis was a good singer and surrounded himself with good musicians. The band on these sessions included organist Robert Gross, drummer Gaynel Hodge, and guitarists Johnny Rogers, Charles Norris, and Johnny "Guitar" Watson.

The band dished up a wide variety of west coast rock and roll and R&B—upbeat rockers ("Bye, Bye Baby," "Somebody Call the Station"), early soul music ("She's All Right," which sounds like a lost hit by the Impressions), remakes of Otis's big hit "Willie and the Hand Jive" ("Hand Jive One More Time" and "Queen of the Twist"), a pair of vocal group releases by the Interludes, and such superb instrumentals as "Let's Rock" (aka "Let's Surf Awhile"), "Oh, My Soul," "Yes," and "Early in the Morning Blues."

After his sojourn on King, Otis moved on to other labels and interests. He was active in California politics and also became an ordained minister. Otis started painting and sculpting and took up organic farming. This incredible renaissance man of R&B, the white man who was once known as "the Duke Ellington of Watts," was fittingly inducted into the Rock & Roll Hall of Fame in 1994.

Johnny "Guitar" Watson was one of Otis's many associates. Born in Houston, Watson (1935–96) was a singer, songwriter, showman, pianist, and trailblazing electric guitarist. He didn't make much headway at the time, but Watson was a rock and roll original who recorded, in two separate stints on King, some of the wildest guitar ever. It's easy to hear why Frank Zappa cited him as an influence.

Watson was living in Los Angeles in 1950, sitting in on piano with area bands. After a few local records, Watson signed with Federal, where he made his proper solo debut, billed as Young John Watson. His first Federal session, in January 1953, produced four songs that showed him to be a solid pianist with deep blues roots and a decent singer with an effective declamatory style. While certainly respectable for a seventeen-year-old, the singles were not especially distinctive and contained no hint of future greatness.

His second session, in May 1953, was more energetic, thanks to a few extra horns in the band. Watson was less tentative and his original material was more original. "I Got Eyes," "What's Going On," and "Thinking" are the keepers. By his third and final session for Federal in February 1954, Watson was confident enough (or assertive enough) to forsake the piano and take over the lead guitar work.

The transformation was startling. A competent pianist, Watson was an extraordinary guitarist, one or maybe two generations ahead of his time. With jagged bursts of notes, a highly amplified tone, and quirky improvisational ideas, Watson stepped out fully formed as a major stylist. The instrumental "Space Guitar" sounds futuristic even now, and his playing on "Getting Drunk" cuts like a razor.

Watson left Texas in his early teens, but not before thoroughly absorbing the state's electric guitar aesthetic, in which great playing is only the beginning. T-Bone Walker is usually credited as the first great electric guitarist in blues, but he was also among the first to establish the electric guitarist as flamboyant showman and center of attention. Walker set the bar high. A blues guitarist from Texas who hoped to stand out from the pack was expected to play great, look better, and put on one hell of a show.

When Watson returned to King in 1961 after a few years on other labels, he was Johnny "Guitar" Watson, guitar-slinger. "I used to do some fantastic things," Watson said, "like playing the guitar while standing on my hands. I used to have a 150-foot guitar cord and I could get on top of the auditorium, come in from the walls. Those things Jimi Hendrix was doing—I started that shit, but you would have been down in the earth to know."[26]

For those not "down in the earth," there were Watson's King singles. In four sessions between July 1961 and May 1963, Watson cut fifteen songs. The material ranged from a cover of Hank Williams's "Cold, Cold Heart" to a Sam Cooke-ish "Cuttin' In," Watson's only R&B hit on King. Although some of the material misses the mark ("Posin'," for example), the bulk of Watson's work on King is pretty cool stuff.

Some of Watson's best records from this period ("You Better Love Me," "Cold, Cold Heart") feature a female vocal group similar to Ray Charles' Raelettes. The others include slow burners ("I Just Wants Me Some Love," "That's the Chance You've Got to Take," and "In the Evening"), early 1960s rock and roll ("I Say I Love You," "Sweet Lovin' Mama," "Those Lonely, Lonely Nights") and what would become Watson's signature song, "Gangster of Love."

After leaving King in 1963, Watson recorded for Chess and Okeh and then, in the 1970s, emerged reinvented as a deeply soulful funk musician. This second career produced several successful recordings on DJM and Fantasy as well as guest appearances on two Frank Zappa albums. Watson had another unexpected revival in the mid-1990s, spurred by the R&B hits "Bow Wow" and "Hook Me Up." His career ended in Japan in 1996 when Watson collapsed and died on stage in Yokohama. It was a sad but fitting curtain call for the Gangster of Love, an exit even T-Bone Walker might have admired.

THE HARDEST-WORKING MAN
IN SHOW BUSINESS

Mr. James Brown

• • •

JAMES BROWN is a concept, a vibration,
a dance. It's not me, the man. JAMES BROWN
is a freedom I created for humanity.

—James Brown

James Brown was the most important musician to record for King Records—
the most important, most influential, most innovative, and most misunderstood.
Brown was a musical revolutionary who changed the world. The influence of
James Brown's music is universal at the beginning of the twenty-first century.
One hears it in American hip hop, funk, and rock, the Afro-pop of Nigeria, Mali,
and other countries, Jamaican reggae, and in the playing of musicians from Japan
to Sweden. Among American musicians of the twentieth century, probably only
Louis Armstrong and Elvis Presley had a comparable impact.

James Brown was King's biggest seller. Indeed, for the last several years of King's
existence, Brown's hits kept the company afloat. Among those hits were "Please,
Please, Please" and "Try Me" in the early days, and such later ground-shaking
singles as "Papa's Got a Brand New Bag," "I Got You (I Feel Good)," and "Cold
Sweat."

Brown's recording career was monumental. From 1956 through 1988, Brown
had ninety-eight records on the Top 40 R&B singles chart in *Billboard*, a record
unsurpassed by any other artist. He had seventeen Number One R&B singles,
a total topped only by Louis Jordan and Stevie Wonder and equaled by Aretha
Franklin.[1]

The impact of James Brown was obscured somewhat at the time by the British
Invasion and Motown soul music, but perspective has shown that Brown's records

of the 1960s were the blueprint for the future. Brown not only birthed funk and soul music, he also made them popular. Appearing on such television programs as the *Ed Sullivan Show, Shindig,* the *Tonight Show, Where the Action Is,* and the *Mike Douglas Show,* Brown took the heavy funk into America's living rooms.

At a time when other black artists were cleaning up their music for white consumption, Brown took his music in the opposite direction, back to its black church roots. His mighty buzz saw of a voice, among the roughest and rawest in R&B, was patterned after two of his gospel music idols, Julius Cheeks of the Sensational Nightingales and Reuben Willingham of the Swanee Quintet. Brown's fans, black *and* white, reacted to his music with a fervor rarely seen outside church.

Brown ruled the R&B charts during his time on King. He recorded the first million-selling R&B album, *Live at the Apollo,* one of the greatest concert recordings of all time. He upstaged Mick Jagger in a film called *The T.A.M.I. Show* and shook up Frankie Avalon in *Ski Party.* He helped calm America in the fiery days after the murder of Dr. Martin Luther King Jr. For all of that, perhaps the surest sign of his greatness was that when James Brown proclaimed himself "Soul Brother Number One," nobody argued.

James Brown had it rough from the start. He was born dead. Stillborn on May 3, 1933, the tiny body was set aside in the one-room shack a few miles outside Barnwell, South Carolina. An older relative, Aunt Minnie, refused to give up. Finally, after several minutes of her attention, the baby let out a loud cry. He was alive after all. The boy was named after his father Joe, but for some reason "James" was thrown in, too, so the name went into the books as James Joe Brown Jr.

Brown's parents split up when he was four, and after a short time with his father, James was shipped off to live with an aunt who ran a brothel in Augusta, Georgia. At seven, James was buck-dancing in the street for nickels and dimes. He was about twelve when he drifted into petty crime. Arrested at fifteen for breaking and entering, he was sentenced to eight to sixteen years in prison. He served three years, mostly in the small Georgia town of Toccoa.

Brown turned to music after his release in 1952. He joined a group in Toccoa that sang both gospel and the R&B hits of the day. The group, which would develop into the Famous Flames, worked local gigs, gradually earning a solid reputation. Brown had largely taken over the lead singing duties by the time the group worked up a demo in 1955 of "Please, Please, Please," a fervent remake of the Orioles' hit "Baby Please Don't Go." This crude little recording was the demo on which Ralph Bass bet his career.

The group that went to Cincinnati with Brown for that first session included singers Bobby Byrd, Johnny Terry, Sylvester Keels, Nash Knox, and guitarist Nafloyd Scott. Assuming that they would soon be famous, they changed the group name to the Famous Flames, a move that reportedly cracked up Little Richard, who kidded Brown, "Y'all are the onliest people who made yourselves famous before you *were* famous."[2]

Syd Nathan hated "Please, Please, Please" but released the single anyway, mainly to humiliate Ralph Bass when it failed. The first sign of the record's potential came when *Billboard* gave it a positive review, noting astutely that "A dynamic, religious fervor runs through the pleading solo here. Brown and the Famous Flames group let off plenty of steam."[3]

The record received a major boost when Bill "Hoss" Allen, a disc jockey on WLAC in Nashville, began playing it. Allen found the single in a box of rejects at the station. "We had a big box of records that were discards in our little music room," Allen said. "I just happened to pull this out. James Brown and the Famous Flames. It didn't mean anything to me. I put it on, and it came to 'please, please,' you know, and I said, 'Oh, my lord. This has got to be a hit.' I started playing it that night. Within two weeks, it was a hit."[4]

"Please, Please, Please" was a big R&B hit, particularly in the south, but Brown's next nine singles flopped. Nathan continued to have doubts about Brown's commercial viability, particularly his ability to appeal to white record buyers. For what it's worth, Nathan wasn't wrong about that—none of Brown's first sixteen singles made the Top 40 of the pop charts. Nathan was ready to drop Brown from the label, but a plaintive ballad called "Try Me" saved Brown's career.

Before presenting "Try Me" to Nathan, Brown had thoroughly road-tested his original song and knew that it caused pandemonium at his shows. Nathan rejected it out of hand. "I'm not spending my money on that garbage," he told Brown,[5] who offered to pay for the session himself. Brown booked the studio time and musicians and cut the song. Nathan still hated it, said it didn't "make sense," and he didn't want it for his company.[6] So Brown took the tape with him when he left.

Brown then had a few copies of the record pressed and took them around to the disc jockeys he knew. When WLAC started playing it, the orders flooded into King—for a record that didn't exist. Nathan held firm until the orders represented more than 20,000 records. He then called Brown and said, "Well, James, I've decided to give the song a try."[7] Brown thanked him, but insisted on re-recording the song. On Nathan's dime this time.

Re-recorded in November 1958, "Try Me" was Brown's first number one R&B hit. The success allowed Brown to hire a high-powered booking agent (and later manager), Ben Bart of Universal Attractions. Even better, it allowed Brown to begin working with his own band. These were huge steps in the trip from James Brown to JAMES BROWN.

Under the direction of bandleaders Lucas "Fats" Gonder, Pee Wee Ellis, and Fred Wesley, the James Brown Band (aka the JBs) grew into a mighty force, becoming by the mid-1960s probably the hottest performing band on the planet. Players came and went, but some made indelible marks, including Clyde Stubblefield, Melvin Parker, John "Jabo" Starks (drums); Jimmy Nolen, "Country" Kellum, Phelps "Catfish" Collins (guitar); Maceo Parker, St. Clair Pinckney (saxophones); Bernard Odum, William "Bootsy" Collins (bass); and Waymon Reed (trumpet).

As Alan Leeds, former tour director for Brown, pointed out, "Prior to the mid-1970s, artists didn't 'tour'—they worked. Big stars like James Brown had the 'luxury' of working often."[8] Thanks to a string of R&B hits from 1959 through 1961 that included "I'll Go Crazy," "Think," "You've Got the Power," "I Don't Mind," "Bewildered," "Baby You're Right," and "Lost Someone," Brown worked constantly. He had become "The Hardest Working Man in Show Business."

"Arenas, theatres, stadiums, night clubs," Leeds says, "the James Brown Show played them all, fifty-one weeks of the year . . . We carried a single truck for uniforms, musical instruments, a modest audio system, and a lone strobe light. The only microphones were for vocals and horns . . . Yet night after night, we tore the roof off whatever venue we were in."[9]

"We crisscrossed the country year round," wrote Fred Wesley, "making stops in most cities twice a year. We only slowed down long enough to record or play theaters. Most theaters were on the East Coast: the Royal in Baltimore, the Howard in Washington, the Regal in Chicago, the Uptown in Philadelphia, and the Apollo in New York City. Theater stints were three-to-five day stops. All other gigs were one-nighters. The only other time the bus stopped was to record."[10]

In 1962, Brown got the idea to record one of his concerts and release it on a full-length album. Predictably, Nathan hit the ceiling, explaining in a loud and profane manner why the idea was crazy: King was a singles-oriented company; Brown was a singles-oriented artist who had cracked the pop Top 40 only once; black people didn't buy albums; white people who bought albums had never heard of James Brown; radio stations would have a hard time fitting an album into their playlists; and there wouldn't be any hit singles.

But Brown held firm, for he had his reasons, too. He knew there was a disparity between his record sales and the hysteria his show caused night after night in city after city. The show really did blow the roof off most nights. People had never seen anything like it—trumpet players doing flips, the whole band doing intricate, choreographed routines, the Famous Flames singing and dancing, Brown doing the camel walk across the stage while screaming out his latest hit. There had to be a better way to capture the excitement of the James Brown Show than a three-minute single.

After a few more heated arguments on the subject, Nathan finally told Brown that if he wanted to do a "live" album so much, he should pay for it himself. To Brown's eternal credit, he again put his money where his mouth was and financed the project himself.

• • •

"For moments he seemed motionless at center stage. Then Brown was *moving.* He cruised across the Apollo stage on a cushion of air, his black shoes skating rapidly. When he fell to his knees, microphone cradled in his hands, I was frightened. Was he sick? Did he have a headache? I turned to ask my mother what was bothering James Brown, but she was too busy smiling and bopping to the music to notice me."[11]

—Nelson George, from "'Right on!' to 'Word Up!'" *Star Time*

The Apollo Theatre, on 125th Street in Harlem, was black America's most important music venue in the 1950s and 1960s. The Apollo was the ultimate peak, the pinnacle for an R&B performer. Careers and reputations were made and lost on its stage. Apollo audiences were legendarily tough judges of talent, ready to be impressed but merciless to those who failed the test. It was a perfect place for Brown's grand experiment. If he could pull this off, he would without question be Soul Brother Number One.

Brown rented the Apollo Theatre for six days of performances in October 1962. He planned to record the shows on the last day, Wednesday the 24th. The band had caught Brown's enthusiasm for the project. "He had a sincere, deep belief that a live album could happen," says St. Clair Pinckney. "That's what drove him, made him gamble on the whole ball of wax."[12]

When Nathan realized that Brown was actually going ahead with the idea at his own expense, he committed King to the project. Hal Neely, the company vice president who had joined King in 1958, supervised the actual recording. King engineer Chuck Seitz flew in from Cincinnati to oversee the technical aspects of recording the performances.

By show time, fifteen hundred devotees were more than ready to give it up. After a florid introduction from Fats Gonder, Brown and the band cut loose. They pounded out some of the most exciting R&B ever recorded, from the first guitar chords on "I'll Go Crazy" through a frenetic bebop-tinged workout on "Night Train." It's a thrilling roller-coaster ride of music—wild singing, precise playing, blaring horns, screaming audience, and Brown outdoing his own bad self.

The show contains seven songs, connected by instrumental vamps that serve as a kind of theme. A razor-sharp version of "I'll Go Crazy" starts the show on a high note. "Try Me" demonstrates how effective Brown could have been as a gospel singer. "Think," the old 5 Royales hit, comes next; Brown spits the lyrics out at hyper speed, more beats than actual words. He uses his voice here as a rhythm instrument—not as a means to communicate verbally. It was a revolutionary idea that Brown perfected by the end of the decade.

Ethnomusicologist Portia Maultsby says "listening to James Brown is listening to a black preacher."[13] On "Try Me" and "I Don't Mind," James and the Flames— Bobby Byrd, Bobby Bennett, and Lloyd Stallworth—come together like a great gospel quartet, carrying the audience from peak to peak. The ten-minute version of "Lost Someone" is pure church—agony, ecstasy, sin, and redemption all rolled into one song. It is among Brown's finest performances.

The climax is a six-minute medley (sort of) that blends bits and pieces of songs, mostly recent Brown hits, into a new song. It begins and ends with torrid chunks of "Please, Please, Please" and, in between, quotes from songs ranging from Bull Moose Jackson's "I Love You (Yes I Do)" to "Bewildered." It's a strangely effective mélange.

In Brown's autobiography, he remembers that the shows on the 24th got better as the day wore on. "By the end of the last [show]," he wrote, "we had four reels of tape. Mr. Neely was so excited he brought the master up to the dressing rooms and passed around the headphones for us to listen. None of us had ever heard ourselves live like that. It sounded fantastic. We knew we really had something."[14]

Brown and company had reason to be proud. They had done the nearly impossible, capturing, brilliantly and accurately, the visceral intensity and emotional heights of a great concert performance. They had recorded a masterpiece, an album that would be hailed as a classic for decades to come.

Nathan trusted Neely's judgment. Neely was raving about the tape, so Nathan wanted in. Once again, Brown pointed out that because he had financed the recording, he owned the tape. Once again, they argued. Once again, Nathan was over a barrel. As Brown wryly noted, "He hadn't even heard the tape and here he was already squabbling about it."[15]

Released in January 1963 as *The James Brown Show Live at the Apollo*, the album was a hit of unprecedented magnitude. It sold more than a million copies, reportedly the first R&B album to do so. It was Brown's first hit album and the best-selling album in King's history. The album made the *Billboard* pop album chart, where it spent an unbelievable sixty-six weeks. It peaked at number two.

Radio *did* have a problem with the record—there weren't enough hours in the day to play the album as often as listeners demanded. As for the supposedly fatal lack of hit singles, radio stations solved that by playing the album in its entirety, treating the album as two fifteen-minute-long hit singles. Rocky G., a disc jockey at New York's WWRL at the time, says, "In the evening, we had to play the whole thing through. People were always calling in."[16]

Live at the Apollo made truckloads of money for King Records. The album is today recognized as a classic, with many critics calling it the greatest "live" album ever recorded. It's one of the very few albums from 1963 that still sounds fresh and exciting. Snubbed at that year's Grammy Awards, the album has since been buried in time capsules, shot into space, and played at millions of parties. It is essential listening for anyone interested in American music.

Not even a hot album could make for a peaceable Kingdom on Brewster Avenue. By the end of 1963, Brown was ready to leave. According to Hal Neely, "James had just had enough of Syd. Syd at the time was growing more ill, with the heart attack and all. He still came into work but what little patience he ever had was gone. Syd spent half the year at a condo in Miami but when he would come back into town, all hell would break loose. It just came to a point where there was simply no reasoning between the two."[17]

Brown was frustrated not only with Nathan personally, but also with King's distribution system, once an innovative and effective operation but showing its age by the early 1960s. Brown felt that for as much as he worked (roughly 300 days a year) and as much as his audiences loved his music, his record sales were simply not keeping pace with his growing stardom. It's hard to disagree with him.

Though he was contractually bound to King, Brown and Ben Bart formed an independent production company in 1963, pointedly named Fair Deal Productions. At first, Fair Deal was a vehicle through which Brown's production efforts with other artists were placed with Smash, a subsidiary of Mercury. By April 1964, Brown himself was recording for Smash. As expected, Nathan sued.

Smash released several singles by Brown, including early versions of "I Got You" and "It's a Man's World," before Nathan's suit forced Smash to halt all James Brown releases. When the dust finally settled, it was a legal decision worthy of Solomon: only King could release vocal records by Brown, whereas Smash could release only instrumentals and James Brown's productions of other artists.

Nathan demanded that Brown honor his contract. Brown demanded that the contract be renegotiated. Once again, Nathan was over the barrel; in the absence of new recordings by Brown, King had sunk to re-releasing "Please, Please, Please" with fake applause and crowd noise added. Nathan simply couldn't afford to lose his best-selling artist.

When Brown returned to King, he had a new deal worthy of one of America's major musical forces, a creatively structured ten-year personal services contract that guaranteed him a weekly payment of $1,500 and one of the highest royalty rates in the industry. The publishing contracts were also restructured, a key point in that Brown wrote or co-wrote most of his material.

Most important, Brown, and not King Records, now owned his recordings, which gave Brown complete control over his recording career, something very few artists had at the time. Offices were created at the King complex for Brown's various business ventures, which included Try Me, a record label, and a publishing firm, Jim Jam Music.

"James Brown Productions was housed in a modest suite of offices adjacent to the King Records plant," remembered Alan Leeds. "Working there proved to be just short of joining a cult. Nonperformers were expected to dress in conservative business suits and ties. Brown insisted that we all refer to each other by surname . . . We were liable to be fined for the smallest of 'infractions.'"[18]

So were the members of Brown's band. There were fines for unpolished shoes, bad haircuts, missed cues on-stage, and, the ultimate, not being able to recite the current set list, song by song, within a mandated time. If a gaffe happened on stage, punishment was immediate and delivered by Brown himself: "I'd mash potatoes [one of his signature dance steps] over to where the person who'd messed up could see me and I'd flash my open hand once for each $5 fine—five times for a $25 fine, and so on. I did it right on the beat of the music so it looked like part of the act."[19]

The bus carrying the James Brown Band made few unscheduled stops. It stopped only to record, which is why the band was at Arthur "Guitar Boogie" Smith's studio in Charlotte, North Carolina, one February night in 1965. The band was on its way to a gig somewhere and Brown wanted to get his newest idea down on tape. They played for just under an hour and then got back on the bus and rolled down the road. The new song was called "Papa's Got a Brand New Bag."

It was to be Brown's first new single for King in over a year, but what Brown submitted was an unedited seven-minute take, a relaxed and extended vamp with *two* solos by sax player Maceo Parker, one on tenor and one on baritone. Ron Lenhoff, the chief engineer at King who worked extensively with Brown, remembers it well: "The original tape was so bad—muffled—that when Syd Nathan heard it, he exclaimed, 'My God, I can't put that out.' I had to edit it and [equalize] it section by section. It took two days."[20]

Despite Brown's confident "This is a hit" at the beginning of the song, the original version of "Papa's Got a Brand New Bag" would never have been a hit single in 1965. Finally released in 1991, the cut is both brilliant and radical—but it needed major postproduction surgery to become a hit. Lenhoff cut out both sax solos, speeded the tape up, added echo and reverb, turned up Bernard Odum's great bass line, cut the seven-minute take down to two minutes of pure funk, and produced an instant classic that lived up to its boastful title.

"Papa's Got a Brand New Bag" was Brown's first R&B Number One since 1958 and his first single to make the pop Top Ten. It earned his first Grammy Award, for "Best Rhythm & Blues Recording" of 1965.

After "Brand New Bag" returned Brown to the top of the R&B charts, he followed with a string of hits that changed the sound of popular music. The first was "I Got You (I Feel Good)," a revamping of "I Found You." Brown felt that the earlier record had been "too sharp." As he explained to bandleader Nat Jones, "This song is too hip. We're taking some of the funk out of it and making it too jazz."[21] With the funk restored, the record hit number one on the R&B chart and, amazingly, number three on the pop singles chart.

"It's a Man's Man's Man's World," recorded in March 1966, was a dramatic change of pace. Lushly orchestrated, the record was a remake of a single Brown cut for Smash. The song was written by Betty Newsome, who said she "wrote the lyrics from the Bible . . . I don't believe in equal rights for women. I believe a woman has a place, a man has a place. And I was saying that whatever happens, whether he has the first word or the last word, he's nothing without a woman."[22]

The record was pretty bizarre, even for 1966. Not only were the lyrics a bit strange, the feel of the song was more Las Vegas than Apollo Theatre. It sure didn't come from papa's brand new bag, but the single topped the R&B chart and entered the pop Top Ten.

Brown's next R&B chart-topper was "Cold Sweat (Part 1)," co-written with bandleader Pee Wee Ellis. Brown was angry when he wrote the song. He felt that, with their current hit singles of "Funky Broadway," Wilson Pickett and the group Dyke and the Blazers were trying "to get into my thing."[23] And that made Soul Brother Number One break out in, well, a cold sweat.

According to Ellis, "Cold Sweat" was born when "James called me into his dressing room after a gig. He grunted the rhythm, the bass line, to me. I wrote the rhythm down on a piece of paper. There were no notes; I had to translate it. I made some sort of graphic of where the notes should be."[24] Ellis worked up an arrangement from his notes and taught the new song to the band. "Cold Sweat" was recorded in May 1967 in two takes at the King studio in Cincinnati.

Engineer Ron Lenhoff recalls the session as being quick, even by Brown's standards. "For 'Cold Sweat,'" says Lenhoff, "we made a record right then and there:

set up, got it down, mixed it to mono, mastered it, got it ready for the street."[25] The seven-minute song, issued that summer on the album *Cold Sweat*, may be Brown's most monumental creation, the purest dose of James Brown's new bag ever recorded. It's perfect, especially the screams.

"Cold Sweat (Part 1)," a three-minute distillation of the seven-minute groove, was a huge hit. As unusual as it was—where were the melody and the chord changes?—the record crossed over in a big way, peaking at number eight on the pop chart. It was a major presence on the radio that summer.

"'Cold Sweat' deeply affected the musicians I knew," says Jerry Wexler, the legendary producer at Atlantic who worked with Aretha Franklin, Wilson Pickett, and Ray Charles. "It just freaked them out. For a time, no one could get a handle on what to do next."[26]

It wasn't a matter of just copying. As drummer Jabo Starks says, "So many things that were done weren't written, because you just couldn't. You couldn't write that *feel*. Many, many times we'd just play off each other, until James would say, 'That's it!'"[27]

The big hits continued for Brown in 1968 and 1969. "I Got the Feelin'," "Say It Loud—I'm Black and I'm Proud," "Give It Up or Turnit a Loose," "Mother Popcorn," and "Super Bad" all topped the R&B charts.

James Brown possessed a singular musical genius, but the realization of his vision required collaboration. Brown knew (more or less) what he wanted, but as he ventured farther away from conventional musical forms and structures, he lacked the knowledge of music theory to articulate his complex ideas. As Fred Wesley, Brown's bandleader in the early 1970s, explains, "It would have been impossible for James Brown to put his show together without the assistance of someone like Pee Wee [Ellis], who understood chord changes, time signatures, scales, notes, and basic music theory.

"The show depended on having someone with musical knowledge remember the show, the individual parts, and the individual song, then relay these verbally or in print to the other musicians. Brown could not do it himself. He needed musicians to translate [his ideas] into music and actual songs in order to create an actual show."[28]

Records were done the same way. Wesley would go to Brown's dressing room after a show and Brown "would hum stuff to me to put together for the next session. He would hum, sing, or beat out bass lines or drum licks or horn parts, and I would write this stuff down and translate it to the band the next day at rehearsal or on the bus as we traveled."[29]

Wesley described a typical session in *Hit Me, Fred*: "We set up and Pee Wee [Ellis] proceeded to put together a song—with no written music. He started by

giving Clyde [Stubblefield] a simple drumbeat. Clyde started the beat and held it
steady while Pee Wee hummed a bass line to Charles Sherrell . . . When the bass
line had become clear to Charles and locked with the drumbeat, Pee Wee moved
to Country [Kellum], the rhythm guitar player, and began to choose a chord that
would fit with the bass notes.

"A B-flat 9 was finally settled on and a chunky rhythm was matched up with
the bass line and the drumbeat . . . Jimmy Nolen was allowed to find his own thing
to fit the developing groove. With the rhythm section solidly in place, Pee Wee
proceeded to hum out horn parts. We were given some strategic hits with carefully voiced chords and a melodic line that happened whenever it was signaled[30]
. . . The music of James Brown is very simple, musically. The main thing is to play
the simple parts with enthusiasm and to have the endurance to hold those parts
in a groove for long periods of time."[31]

If Brown's working methods in the studio appeared strange, it was partly because he was working by a new set of rules. He had a brand new bag, remember,
and melodies and lyrics were no longer the foundations of a song. It was now the
groove, and only the groove. And that started with the beat, and the beat started
in Brown's head.

As Brown said in *Godfather of Soul*, "You can hear the band and me start to
move in a whole other direction rhythmically. The horns, the guitar, the vocals,
everything was starting to be used to establish all kinds of rhythm at once. You
can hear my voice alternate with the horns to create various rhythmic accents. I
was trying to get every aspect of the production to contribute to the rhythmic
patterns.[32]

"I had discovered that my strength was in the rhythm. I was hearing everything,
even the guitars, like they were drums. I had found out how to make it happen.
On playbacks [in the studio], when I saw the speakers jumping, vibrating a certain
way, I knew that was it: deliverance. I could tell from looking at the speakers that
the rhythm was right."[33]

Guitarist Jimmy Nolen, the man who introduced "chank" to the musical vocabulary, is a relatively unsung architect of James Brown's musical sound—and
therefore the music of much of the modern world. A veteran blues guitarist,
Nolen (1934–83) joined the James Brown Show in 1965. His impact was felt immediately.

Nolen joined the band just in time to record "Papa's Got a Brand New Bag."
His guitar work subsequently played a crucial role on such seminal funk records
as "I Got You (I Feel Good)," "Cold Sweat," "I Got The Feelin'," "Say It Loud—I'm
Black and I'm Proud," "Funky Drummer," "The Popcorn," "Mother Popcorn," and
"Let a Man Come in and Do the Popcorn (Part One)."

The English magazine *Mojo*, in its survey of "The 100 Greatest Guitarists of All Time," ranks Jimmy Nolen number twelve. Among American guitarists, he trails only B.B. King, T-Bone Walker, Chuck Berry, Steve Cropper, and Jimi Hendrix. In describing Nolen's style, Alan Paul wrote that "Nolen practically invented funk guitar.'Papa's Got a Brand New Bag,' with its chinga-chinga-ching break, made the vamp a central part of Brown's music, a development as central to the definition of funk as the rhythmic first beat stress—'the one.'"[34]

Brown certainly appreciated Nolen's playing."You can hear Jimmy Nolen [on "Papa's Got A Brand New Bag"]," wrote Brown, "starting to play scratch guitar where you squeeze the strings tight and quick against the frets, so the sound is hard and fast without any sustain. He was what we called a chanker; instead of playing the whole chord and using all the strings, he hit his chords on just three strings."[35]

A native of Oklahoma, Nolen had recorded as a solo artist for King in the mid-1950s. Between November 1955 and May 1956, Nolen cut twelve songs, all issued on Federal singles. His version of "After Hours" appeared on a King compilation album later in the decade. But it is Nolen's work during sixteen years with James Brown that earned him universal acclaim. Funk music wouldn't be funky without Nolen.

For a rhythm guitarist who rarely played a solo, Nolen has been inordinately influential upon other guitarists. The keys to Nolen's widely imitated "chank" are fast sixteenth-note strumming on the guitar's treble strings and extensive use of 7th and 9th chords during extended vamps. Nolen began developing the style during his days with Johnny Otis, primarily to cover for deficient drummers. Nolen told writers Lee Hildebrand and Henry Kaiser that some of the drummers he worked with "were just lazy. I used to try to play and keep my rhythm going as much like a drum as I possibly could. So many times I had to just play guitar and drums all at the same time."[36]

Jimmy Nolen died of a heart attack in 1983, before he really received the credit due him. But his music lives on, and in some surprising places. It's there in albums by the Red Hot Chili Peppers, Talking Heads, U2, the Meters, Parliament/Funkadelic, the Rolling Stones, Tower of Power, and Earth, Wind and Fire. Nolen's style permeates modern African music. His percussive approach touched such guitar masters as Jimi Hendrix, Jeff Beck, and Roy Buchanan, as well as every funk guitarist who ever lived.

James Brown's post-King career had its ups and downs. The triumphs include a 1974 appearance at a massive music festival in Zaire; a movie-stealing appearance as a preacher in *The Blues Brothers* in 1980; an appearance in *Rocky IV* in 1986 singing his big pop single, "Living in America"; Lifetime Achievement Awards at the 1992 Grammy Awards and from the Rhythm and Blues Foundation in 1993; and induction as a charter member into the Rock & Roll Hall of Fame in 1986.

The lows have been pretty low. The worst was Brown's 1988 arrest for drug, assault, and vehicular charges after leading police on a wild car chase through two states while high on the mind-bending drug PCP. The Hardest-Working Man in Show Business was taken off the road in December 1988, sentenced to six years in prison. He was paroled in February 1991. Brown's post-prison life was dogged by problems but also had occasional bright spots.

In August 2003, James Brown received one of five Kennedy Center Honors, an annual arts award presented by the Kennedy Center for the Performing Arts in Washington, D.C., to honor those who have made "unique and extremely valuable contributions . . . to the cultural life of our nation." He richly deserved the honor.

James Brown died on December 25, 2006, in Atlanta at the age of 73. The cause of death was congestive heart failure. Brown's burial was delayed by an ugly and very public squabble between Brown's domestic partner (she and Brown were not legally married) and the singer's grown children. Brown's body was finally buried March 10, 2007, in a temporary tomb at the home of one of his children until the legal matters are resolved. May he eventually rest in peace.

Eighteen

BROTHER CLAUDE ELY AND
EDDIE "LOCKJAW" DAVIS

The Rest of the Catalog

• • •

I'm not a genius and I don't have any geniuses
working for me. We work at it as if it was the
coffin business, the machinery business, or any
other business. It has to pay for itself.

—Sydney Nathan

If Syd Nathan thought a record would sell, he would release it. He even released records he didn't think would sell (by James Brown, for example) in case he was wrong. Musical merit was not his primary concern when evaluating a record. He cared about sales. His tireless quest for sales led Nathan and King down many a path that other record companies never even noticed.

Brother Claude Ely (1922–78), a singing, guitar-playing itinerant preacher known as the "Gospel Ranger," was unique on the King roster. His records are among the most fascinating of the label's releases. They sound like field recordings from a remote past, which they are, in a sense, but the records were commercially released and sold reasonably well. Ely's material was issued on several singles and two albums, *At Home and at Church* and *Gospel Ranger*.

Ely was born in southwestern Virginia, and after a youthful bout with tuberculosis, he became a coal miner. He returned to the mines after military service in World War II, but in 1949 he was "born again" and launched a career as a traveling evangelist. Over the next two decades, Ely preached at churches and revival services throughout Virginia, Kentucky, and Tennessee. He later settled in Florence, Kentucky, where he pastored the Charity Tabernacle in nearby Newport.

The first "session" Ely did for King was recorded at a church service in Cumberland, Kentucky, in October 1953. Ely's powerhouse, church-rocking voice is showcased on some of his best songs, including "There Ain't No Grave Gonna

Hold My Body Down" and "There's a Leak in This Old Building." The accompaniment is minimal, mostly just Ely's thrashing rhythm guitar and occasional whoops and screams from the congregation. This is among the most primal music King ever recorded.

Based on the records, Ely's theology was somewhat vague. His preaching was spirited though not particularly gifted, his favorite rhetorical device a "Thank the lord" repeated at every opportunity. When he gets going, Ely sounds as if he might start speaking in tongues at any moment. At one point, he borrows from the Pentecostal preaching tradition, ending most words and phrases with the syllable "uh" (like-uh this-uh). But preaching wasn't Ely's claim to fame, singing was, and the Gospel Ranger could sing up a storm.

Another service was recorded eight months after the Cumberland recordings. Eight songs were recorded, of which "Little David Play on Your Harp" is the most well known. This material is a bit more subdued than the earlier material, but still pretty spirited. Ely is backed by the Cumberland Five, a group of young women singers who helped pump up the excitement and fervor. Two singles resulted from this service.

Ely continued evangelizing into the early 1960s. He went into the King studio in 1962 and cut fourteen songs in a single session. This material, straightforward country gospel songs that made no attempt to recreate a revival service, was released on *Gospel Ranger*. Ely's final King session took place in 1968. He recorded six songs, of which five were released on *At Home and at Church*. Ely died in 1978 after a heart attack during a revival service at the Charity Tabernacle.

Syd Nathan professed to like all kinds of music, with one exception. He said on more than one occasion that he disliked jazz, by which he specifically meant the jazz being made from the late 1940s into the 1960s. He said he didn't understand it. "I still can't get this bop and I've really tried," Nathan complained. "They go around talking about flatted fifths, and sometimes it seems it's just people with inferiority complexes trying to bolster their egos."[1]

Nathan was a perfect example of a type of listener Duke Ellington astutely described in a 1960 essay. "Jazz has developed into one of those intellectual art forms that scare people away," wrote Ellington. "People will not come into places where jazz enthusiasts congregate if they are going to be made to feel ignorant . . . [if] the man next to them might look down his nose at them, so to speak, with a flatted fifth. Nothing can be worse than to have somebody look down his nose with a flatted fifth, believe me."[2]

Nathan may have disliked jazz, but he released it from the earliest days, on Queen Records in 1944 and 1945. The Chubby Jackson Sextet, in fact, had the second release on Queen, "I Gotcha Covered." That band, which included Flip

Phillips on tenor sax, Neil Hefti on trumpet, and Jackson on bass, recorded four songs for Queen in 1944. Also on Queen was hipster Slim Gaillard, an unusual character who sang and played piano, guitar, vibes, and the harpsichord (actually a "doctored" piano). Gaillard cut fourteen songs for Queen in 1945, six with a big band including such stellar players as Howard McGhee, Lucky Thompson, and Teddy Edwards.

King also recorded two of the most important women jazz musicians of the late 1940s and early 1950s. Pianist Mary Lou Williams, best known for her work with Andy Kirk's band, recorded eight tunes in 1949 and 1950, working with a septet at the first session and a quartet at the latter. "(In the Land of) Oo-Bla-Dee," a "bop fairy tale"[3] recorded at the first session, was a fairly big hit. Marian McPartland, another highly esteemed pianist, cut four tunes for Ralph Bass in 1951 with a rather unconventional quintet including both harp and cello. The tunes were released on Federal singles.

Pianist Cecil Young recorded extensively with a quartet for King in the early 1950s. He had several singles released on King, including a version of "Yes Sir, That's My Baby," praised by *Billboard* as a "very progressive arrangement of the standard." The review noted, however, that the release was "for cool characters only" and "jazz jox."[4] Young's singles were released on an early King album, *A Concert of Cool Jazz*, as well as an Audio Lab album, *Jazz on the Rocks*.

Eddie "Lockjaw" Davis, a superb and highly regarded tenor sax player from New York, was the most prolific jazz artist on King. In several sessions between 1949 and 1958, Davis cut more than sixty sides for King. Davis usually fronted a sax-organ-drums trio on his records, with organist Doc Bagby in the early days and Shirley Scott after 1955. King released numerous singles by Davis, and he was featured on one of the first King LPs, *Modern Jazz Expressions*. His other King albums included *Jazz with a Horn* (reissued as *This and That*), *Jazz with a Beat*, and *Uptown*.

A few other jazz notables also recorded for King. Pianist Earl "Fatha" Hines cut eight sides in 1953, two featuring vocals by the great Johnny Hartman and two sung by boxing champ Sugar Ray Robinson. Multi-instrumentalist Roland Kirk did a quartet session in 1956 on tenor sax that was released on the album *Triple Threat*; another tenor man, Charlie Ventura, recorded twelve tunes with his quintet in 1957, released on *Adventure With Charlie*.

The real name of Babs Gonzales, one of the first bebop vocalists, was Lee Brown, but he also performed as Ricardo Gonzalez and (wearing a turban) Ram Singh, apparently in an attempt to pass for something other than a black man from New Jersey. Gonzales made several hip records for King in the mid-1950s, including "Still Wailin'" and "Bebop Santa Claus," a jive retelling of "The Night Before Christmas," in which Santa, "a cat all covered in red . . . from the cool North Pole," invites the listener to "cast thy peepers into my righteous bag and see/what insane object I shall lay on thee."

King also leased and purchased master tapes from other companies. The jazz artists who came to King in this way, and the labels from which they came, include Errol Garner (Recorded In Hollywood), Russell Jacquet and his All-Stars (which included Sonny Stitt, Sir Charles Thompson, and J. J. Johnson), and Milt Jackson (from Sensation).

In 1958, Nathan acquired a half interest in Bethlehem Records in exchange for "distribution and other services," probably including manufacturing. The New York–based label had been started in 1953 by Gus Wildi. Initially a pop label, Bethlehem switched to jazz after the company's first several releases flopped. Known for giving its artists complete artistic control, the label attracted an impressive roster of musicians and singers that included Duke Ellington, Charles Mingus, Mel Torme, Art Blakey, Dexter Gordon, Carmen MacRae, and Nina Simone. In 1962, Wildi sold his share of the company to Nathan, who phased out the label within a couple of years.

During King's involvement with Bethlehem, King tried to broaden the audience for Bethlehem's artists by releasing a series of multiple-artist compilation LPs with such cornball titles as *Nothing Cheesy about This Jazz*, *We Cut This Album for Bread*, *Jazz Music for People Who Don't Care about Money*, *A Lot of Yarn but a Well Knitted Jazz Album*, and *No Sour Grapes, Just Pure Jazz*.

Kent Records, a subsidiary of the great English reissue label Ace, has several CDs devoted to King's "Northern Soul" artists of the 1960s. With the exception of James Brown's protégé Marva Whitney, these artists are unknown to all but the most knowledgeable soul scholars. The King Pins, also known as the Kelly Brothers, was the most successful of these acts; the group's only hit, "It Won't Be This Way Always," peaked at number eighty-nine on the *Billboard* pop chart.

Many of these soul singers had the talent to be successful. It doesn't take much imagination to listen to cuts by such artists as Junior McCants, Thomas Bailey, Charles Spurling, Dan Brantley, or Cody Black and hear them as hits. Same thing with records by Shirley Wahls, Connie Austin, Mary Johnson, or Christine Kittrell.

Pop quiz: What two things do the following recording artists have in common: Dick Brown, the Johnny Long Orchestra, Mary Small, George Wright, the Larry Fotine Orchestra, Tommy Prisco, the Leslie Brothers, Liza Morrow, Danny Sutton, the Holidays, and Paul Bruno?

The first is obscurity—the preceding artists are all but unknown. The second is that these artists comprised King Records' pop music roster. "Pop" is, of course, short for popular, but, sadly, none of these acts were. Success with pop music—as opposed to rock or R&B—remained an elusive dream for King. As Colin Escott writes, "The pop market, accounting for 50 percent of overall sales [for the industry], loomed like a mirage just outside Nathan's myopic field of vision, tantalizing him but never letting him get close."[5]

In his pursuit of pop success, Nathan hired Dewey Bergman, a former arranger for Guy Lombardo's orchestra, in 1948. When that failed to get results, Nathan hired legendary record man Eli Oberstein in 1951. Oberstein was an industry pioneer who had worked with countless country, blues, jazz, and swing artists at Bluebird in the 1930s, but not even Oberstein could scare up a hit for King. Pop music was the province of the major labels, and King simply couldn't compete.

Though King's pop efforts failed for a number of reasons, a 1952 *Billboard* review tells part of the story. In a review of "Poinciana," the debut recording of future star Steve Lawrence, then a sixteen-year-old King discovery, *Billboard* wrote, "If King goes after this one, something could happen."[6] Well, King did go after it, and something *did* happen—Lawrence was wooed away by Coral Records, a subsidiary of Decca, a much larger label with much deeper pockets.

The one bright note on the pop front for King in the 1950s also points out the futility of the label's efforts to be a force in pop music. Not counting the R&B or blues singles that crossed over to the pop market, the only King "pop" record to chart in *Billboard* was "Nuttin' for Christmas," which reached number twenty in 1955. The record was by Joe Ward, an eight-year-old from New York who was a regular on NBC-TV's *Juvenile Jury*, and the record was a double novelty in that it was not only a Christmas song but also one by a little kid. This was truly the margins of pop music, but it was all that was attainable by King and companies like it.

With everything that has already been discussed, what more could be left for Nathan and King to record? You'd be surprised. There were albums by the University of Cincinnati Bearcat Band and the Miami University Symphonic Band. There were a half-dozen or more licensed albums by French singers Yves Montand, Gilbert Becaud, and George Jouvin. There was Borrah Minevitch and His Harmonica Rascals.

For folks whose tastes ran to polka, there were albums by Romy Gosz and Louie Bashell. Square dancers were served by albums (some with dance calls) by Doc Journell, Charlie Linville, and Red Herron. There was Hawaiian music by Paul Blunt and the Islanders, and Latin music by Pepe Villa and Pepe Jaramillo.

There were comedy albums by Kermit Schaefer, "King of the Bloopers," and adult "party albums" by Redd Foxx and Ruth Wallis.

There were Big Ben's Banjo Band and the Tokyo Happy Coats. There were plenty of organists: George Wright (aka Sister Slocum), Hank Marr, Doc Bagby, Luis Rivera, Paul Renard, and Milt Buckner. And, finally, there was marimba player Jimmy Namaro, who earns a mention for his so-bad-it's-good album title, *Mallets of Four Thoughts.*

Nineteen

LIFE AFTER DEATH

King Records, 1968–2009

• • •

The day will come when I pass on and
maybe King will be better for it. But I'm
gonna wait around, because I don't
have a contract with God.

—Sydney Nathan

King Records threw a gala party in 1967 to celebrate the company's twenty-fifth anniversary. The party was at Nathan's house in the Bond Hill section of Cincinnati, and the seventy-five guests included Max Frank, who had hired Nathan to work in his radio store so many years before, Hal Neely, and several current and past King employees. Nathan was in a good mood because King had shipped 100,000 copies of "Cold Sweat" that day. Crowned the "King of King," he was presented with a cardboard and velvet crown. Only one thing was strange about the party: it was a year early.

Nathan had been in failing health for several years, and the celebration was likely moved forward in fear that he wouldn't make it to the real anniversary. After a couple of serious heart attacks, Nathan seemed resigned to his fate. "I have a very serious illness," he wrote in a 1965 letter to Little Willie John. "It could take me in twenty seconds, twenty minutes, twenty days, twenty months, or twenty years. I sit on a keg of dynamite all the time."[1]

The end came on March 5, 1968, in Miami Beach, Florida. The official cause of death was heart disease complicated by pneumonia; Nathan was sixty-four when he died. After funeral services at the Weil Funeral Home in Cincinnati, Nathan was buried on March 7 at Judah Torah Cemetery. He was survived by his widow, Zella; a son, Nathaniel; a daughter, Beverly Cook; and his siblings, Dorothy Halper and David Nathan.[2]

The *Billboard* article announcing Nathan's death noted that "many prospective buyers have tried to purchase King . . . and it is known that bidders are still anxious for the property."[3] That isn't as ghoulish as it seems. With Nathan's health declining and no "heir apparent" to take over the reins, several overtures had been made about buying the company, as it seemed likely the family might want to sell. According to the article, however, "the Nathan family intends to keep King functioning."[4]

The plan had changed by October, when it was announced that King Records would be sold to Starday Records, the Nashville-based country label. Starday president Don Pierce had been a friend of Nathan's since the early 1950s, as well as a customer—Starday's LPs were pressed, warehoused, and shipped by King.

Pierce thought highly of Nathan. "He was brilliant, at times," said Pierce. "He helped me a lot in my career. If Syd liked you, there was nothing he wouldn't do to help you. He was a heck of a good record man."[5]

Pierce was in the process of selling Starday when he bought King. "I had agreed to sell Starday to the LIN Broadcasting Company [a Nashville company that owned radio and television stations]," said Pierce. "We were negotiating the price when Syd passed away.[6]

"Hal Neely, who had been a vice president at King, was now working for Starday. Hal was very familiar with the King operations and he knew James Brown. So the subject came up with Fred Gregg, the president of LIN, and he said, 'As long as we're making this acquisition, and since James Brown is the hottest thing in the country, might King also be available?' Neely said 'I think I could get it.'

"Jack Pearl was the lawyer who handled the estate, so Hal went up and negotiated a deal. They needed to have some earnest money, so I went to the bank and got $100,000 and signed a memorandum agreement. That enabled us to combine the King company with the Starday company in a package for resale to LIN Broadcasting."

Operating in Nashville as King-Starday, King releases continued to roll out through 1971. The records by James Brown were all that sold, but he kept up a torrid pace, with three R&B number one hits during this period, "Give It Up or Turnit a Loose," "Mother Popcorn," and "Super Bad," as well as such important records as "Brother Rapp" and "Funky Drummer."

Brown was dissatisfied with the situation at King by 1971 and wanted out. That was possible to do because his contract was highly unusual for the time; instead of a standard recording contract with King Records, which would not have relished losing Brown to a competitor, Brown had a personal-services contract with Hal Neely, who got paid either way. After months of negotiations, the contract was sold to Polydor, a European company that had entered the American market a year or two earlier.

The deal was a whopper. Polydor ended up with not only James Brown but also Brown's entire catalog on Federal and King dating back to 1956. Polydor also received the songwriting and publishing copyrights on all Brown's original material.

Brown received a new long-term contract, a hefty cash advance, the promise of complete artistic freedom, a production company, and office space. He also received ten percent of the sale price of the masters to Polydor, thanks to a promise from Nathan, fulfilled by Hal Neely. Brown hated to leave—"King Records had been my family for fifteen years"[7]—but there was no reason to stay. It was over.

Though he stayed with Polydor for years, Brown noticed a big difference between the labels. "Whatever King had been about, Polydor was the opposite," he wrote. "Every King act was individual; Polydor tried to make all their acts the same. King wanted to be an independent company with individual artists; Polydor wanted to be a conglomerate. King wanted to be a little company with big acts; Polydor wanted to be a big company with little acts."[8]

Shortly after Brown's contract and catalog had been sold to Polydor, LIN Broadcasting sold King-Starday in 1971 to Tennessee Recording and Publishing, a company formed by Jerry Leiber and Mike Stoller (the premier songwriters of early rock), former King and Starday vice president Hal Neely, and music publisher Freddy Bienstock, an industry force with Hill and Range Songs.

In 1975, Tennessee Recording and Publishing divided its King-Starday assets into two parcels. The first consisted of thousands of master records and tapes—everything (in theory) that had ever been recorded for King and Starday and their respective subsidiary labels—along with the legal rights to exploit (the industry term) those recordings. Also included were all the record covers, photographs, promotional materials, contracts, and other ephemera that had accumulated during thirty years of running the companies.

The second parcel was potentially much more lucrative—the publishing rights to thousands of songs that had appeared on King and Starday. Many of those songs, including some of the biggest hits of the era, had been published by in-house companies. In King's case, this included the music publishing companies Lois, J & C, Armo, Lonat, Mar-Kay, Arnel, and several others, and such valuable copyrights as "Fever," "Blues Stay Away from Me," "Dedicated to the One I Love," "Please, Please, Please," "Think," "I'll Sail My Ship Alone," "Please Come Home for Christmas," and "Work with Me, Annie."

Because Leiber, Stoller, and Bienstock had publishing backgrounds, it was not surprising when Tennessee Recording and Publishing put the master recordings up for sale. They were purchased in 1975 by GML, Inc., a Nashville company owned by Moe Lytle. He bought the masters primarily to get the Starday material and viewed the King catalog as something of an "add-on."

• • •

One thing about owning a bunch of great master tapes: they generate income only when used—that is, released on recordings and sold to the public. It's a good investment only if one also has a record company to properly exploit the masters, or some alternative means of reaching the audience.

Since Nathan's death in 1968, the subsequent owners of King have all faced this challenge, with varying degrees of finesse and success. Deprived of King's biggest-selling artist, James Brown, the post-Nathan owners of the label have tended to view it as a budget-oriented label. That's been the path of least resistance through the years, but also the path of least imagination.

Under the ownership of LIN Broadcasting and Tennessee Recording and Publishing, the material in the King archives was made available in a variety of ways. Key albums by a core group of artists—including Freddie King, Bill Doggett, the Stanley Brothers, Hank Ballard, Reno & Smiley, and Earl Bostic—were kept in print and have been more or less continuously available in the original format and packaging.

There were also new multiple-artist compilations, many of which blended the King and Starday catalogs. New albums were released during this period on Federal, DeLuxe, King, and King-Starday. The most notable were ten multiple-artist collections dubbed "Old King Gold," the first productions to systematically present the treasures of the King vaults.

Moe Lytle bought the King and Starday companies in 1975 and has now owned King Records for longer than Nathan did. Four significant developments during his ownership have had a major positive impact upon the availability of the music recorded for King.

The first was the launch in 1978 of Gusto Records, a budget label that released LPs, cassettes, and 8-track tapes. A boon for fans and collectors, Gusto albums were affordable, plentiful, and easy to find. Because the company was generous with promotional records for radio, many country, bluegrass, R&B, blues, and "oldies" DJs gave them plenty of airplay—in turn introducing the music to a new generation.

The highlights on Gusto included dozens of single-artist albums; several thematic multiple-artist compilations; an eleven-volume series of albums by Reno and Smiley released as "1983 Collector's Edition"; a similar series by the Stanley Brothers; and a series titled variously *Original Hits* or *Greatest Hits* that presented most of the major R&B and blues artists who recorded for King.

The second significant development was the introduction of digital compact discs. When CDs first appeared in the U.S. in the early 1980s, the industry opinion was that the expensive new recording format would be reserved for rock and pop albums that sell millions. It seemed unlikely that CDs would have much of an impact in the world of blues, bluegrass, and other "roots" styles of music. That assumption could not have been more wrong.

The introduction of a new recording format provided the financial incentive for record companies to reissue their back catalogs, the idea being that people would replace their favorite LPs with CD versions of them. While that did happen, the labels were surprised to find that a demand also existed for all kinds of older music, even stuff that had not sold particularly well when first released.

Lytle's company reacted to the new recording format in various ways. At first, existing titles on Gusto were simply issued on CD. This made International Marketing Group, Inc. (the company established to manufacture and market the master recordings owned by GML, Inc.) perhaps the only record company in America that was releasing *both* CDs and eight-track tapes in the early 1990s.

Fans and collectors were happy when IMG began issuing exact reproductions of original King albums. Available on CD, LP, and cassette tape, most of the releases were from the big names—Little Willie John, Hank Ballard & the Midnighters, Bill Doggett, Earl Bostic, Moon Mullican, Billy Ward & the Dominoes, Reno & Smiley, the Stanley Brothers, Freddie King, and the 5 Royales.

This group of reissues contained some nice surprises—albums by Tiny Bradshaw, Lula Reed, and Mainer's Mountaineers, and a pair of cool Audio Lab albums, one by Bull Moose Jackson and one pairing John Lee Hooker and Stick McGhee—and some truly odd-ball choices: three albums by jazz singer Lorez Alexandria, one by Bubber Johnson, and one that paired organists Doc Bagby and Luis Rivera.

The drawback to these album reproductions was that they didn't measure up to similar efforts being issued by other labels. Many of the albums contained only one or two hits and a bunch of filler (as was the custom when these albums were originally released), the running time was short, the albums had no session or discographical information or liner notes, and the sound was not always as good as it could have been. Just like the original King albums.

Fans were much better served by CD box sets the company began issuing in the early 1990s that included the annotation, historical context, and informed selection that modern collectors expect. Three of the sets, each containing four CDs, were produced by bluegrass researcher-producer Gary B. Reid. The first two, released in 1993, presented recordings by the Stanley Brothers and by Reno and Smiley. After a delay of several years, a second Stanley Brothers set was issued. Reid also produced *Rockin' on the Waves: Complete King Recordings 1946–1952*, an essential two-CD set by the Brown's Ferry Four released in 1997.

The King R&B Box Set, a four-CD set annotated by Colin Escott, was released in 1995. At the top of many collectors'"wish lists," this set covers most of the blues and R&B high points from the late 1940s into the 1960s (minus James Brown, of course, though "Papa's Got a Brand New Bag" *is* here for a taste). The fourth CD is a bit of a waste, as it contains only seven songs; the remainder is devoted to excerpts from three speeches by Nathan; although interesting to, say, someone researching a book on King Records, it's hard to imagine many people listening to these segments more than once.

IMG also began allowing other record companies access to the King vaults. Access was limited and not easily gained, but for those companies able to forge a business relationship with IMG, the rewards were significant. In part because IMG had not mined the catalog very deeply, there was significant interest in the King material.

Time-Life and Rhino, companies dedicated to the specialist market, were among the first labels to license King recordings from IMG, usually the R&B classics. These generally appeared on multiple-artist compilations, though Rhino also issued several single-artist "greatest hits" albums.

Other licensing requests were refused; some record companies came up empty-handed every time they tried to license King material. Two American labels that were successful in the quest were County, which released an album of King sides by the Delmore Brothers, and Modern Blues Recordings, which licensed three albums' worth of great blues by Freddie King and Albert King.

Some of the best historical reissues have come from Europe. The precedent was set in the 1980s by the German label Bear Family, which released superb albums by the Delmore Brothers, Bob Newman, and other King country artists. The standard for CD reissues was set in the early 1990s by the English labels Ace and Charly, both of which have long been active and articulate in their championing of American roots music and the labels that recorded it.

Ace released several great CDs of King country and blues material in the early and mid-1990s, including *Freight Train Boogie* by the Delmore Brothers, *Satan Get Back!* by Brother Claude Ely, *Going Back to Kay Cee* by Little Willie Littlefield, and *Stick McGhee and His Spo-Dee-O-Dee Buddies* by McGhee, Ralph Willis, and Big Tom Collins.

Charly first attracted attention in America with its exemplary presentation of the Sun Records catalog. Turning its attention to King in 1990, Charly hired Neil Slaven, a veteran British record producer, writer, discographer, and researcher, to oversee the most comprehensive CD reissue series devoted to King Records produced by any label.

Slaven made two trips to Nashville, spending several weeks during the summer of 1991, followed by a shorter stay the next year. Slaven had temporary working quarters at IMG, the cooperation of management, and unlimited access to the King "vault," the huge basement room containing hundreds of shelves of aging master tapes. Although he was unable to find some of the tapes he wanted because they no longer existed or had been misfiled, he found enough to fill dozens of CDs.

Several CDs in the series covered the expected big names—Bill Doggett, Earl Bostic, Little Willie John, Hank Ballard, Billy Ward & the Dominoes, Wynonie Harris, and so on. There is the obligatory compilation of "dirty songs," *Ride, Daddy, Ride.* John Lee Hooker, Lonnie Johnson, Freddie King, and Roy Brown all rate full CDs, as do Ike Turner, Johnnie Otis, Lucky Millinder, Jimmy Witherspoon, Big Jay McNeely, Little Esther, Johnny "Guitar" Watson, and Tiny Bradshaw.

King's rock and roll efforts are represented by CDs of Boyd Bennett and Mac Curtis. The series includes some nice combo platters by jazz and blues artists who didn't record enough for King to fill a CD, such as Lynn Hope, Clifford Scott, Cal Green, Slim Gaillard, Jimmy Nolen, Pete "Guitar" Lewis, and Roy "Professor Longhair" Byrd.

Just when the Charly CDs were becoming difficult to find in the late 1990s, they began reappearing, with one difference: the Charly logo had been replaced by one saying King Masters. Everything else was the same—song selection, sequence, design, liner notes, and photos. The discs are marked "Made in UK," and an English address appears on the packaging, but the CDs were now being marketed by IMG.

This was more good news for collectors because the King Masters CDs are less expensive and easier to find than the Charly CDs. Presumably all the CDs Slaven produced for Charly will be reissued in this series. Nearly two dozen CDs have already been released.

Other labels continue to mine the catalog and produce outstanding CDs, many of which are making material available that hasn't been heard in fifty years. Ace Records is still hard at work; among the label's releases are CDs by Wynonie Harris, Little Willie John, Roy Brown, Wayne Raney, and Smokey Smothers, and a series of marvelous multiple-artist compilations, including *Hillbilly Bop n' Boogie: King/Federal Roots of Rockabilly 1944–56, Honky Tonk!: The King & Federal R&B Instrumentals, The Best of King Gospel, King Rockabilly, Queens of King,* and *Chicago Blues from Federal Records.*

Ace subsidiary Kent Records has issued several CDs of soul music for serious collectors, including *King New Breed Rhythm & Blues, King Northern Soul, Too Much Pain: King's Serious Soul,* and *Counting the Teardrops: King's Serious Soul, Vol. 2.*

Another British label, Westside, a subsidiary of Demon Music, has done some of the nicest, most carefully produced King reissues. The CDs on the country artists are especially valuable and illuminating because this material has been only sporadically released over the years. The best of Westside's country CDs include *Copasetic* by Cowboy Copas, *I'm a Rattlesnakin' Daddy* by Hawkshaw Hawkins, *Hillbilly Be-Bop* by Hank Penny, *I'm Not Broke But I'm Badly Bent* by Lattie Moore, a multiple-artists compilation *Shuffle Town: Western Swing on King, 1956–50*, and two must-have albums by Moon Mullican, *Showboy Special: The Early King Sides* and *Moon's Tunes: The Chronological King Recordings, vol. 2, 1947–1950.*

Westside has also been active with King's blues, R&B, and rock masters, producing excellent CDs by Tiny Bradshaw (*Walk That Mess!*) and Gatemouth Moore (*Hey Mr. Gatemouth*) and a pair of jumping compilations, *Roc-KING Up a Storm* and *Mule Milk 'n' Firewater.*

Back in the U.S., Rhino has long since outgrown its early niche as a novelty label and now stands as a major force in American music, chronicling the past sixty-five years of music with an expansiveness Nathan would have admired. Among the hundreds of Rhino releases are several essential CDs in the "King Master Series": *Sexy Ways* by Hank Ballard & the Midnighters, *Good Rocking Tonight* by Roy Brown, *Bloodshot Eyes* by Wynonie Harris, *Fever* by Little Willie John, *60 Minute Men* by Billy Ward & the Dominoes, and *Hide Away* by Freddie King.

The oldies reissue label Collectables is also exploring the King catalog with a series that currently includes almost forty CDs of blues and R&B. The most significant releases are three that present the complete Federal and King recordings of blues giant Freddie King: *The Very Best of Freddy King*, volumes 1, 2, and 3. With all the recent activity, it's hard to keep up with the CDs coming from the King archives. One thing is certain: there has never been a better time than right now to be a fan, collector, or student of King Records.

• • •

The only real legacy of a record company is its catalog—the body of recordings the label produced and released. There is nothing intrinsically exciting or interesting about the offices and physical facilities of a record company or anything that might attract tourists. The King plant on Brewster Avenue was never much to look at anyway, just a drab, dark-brown brick building hard by Interstate 71.

Still, the lack of formal recognition of King Records by the city of Cincinnati (or the state of Ohio) seems wrong. History *did* happen there. Records made there changed the world. King Records was a big deal, once the sixth largest record company in the country. In a city that renamed one of its streets to honor baseball player Pete Rose, some sort of tribute to King should be possible.

The last remnants of King left the Brewster Avenue plant—the old icehouse—in 1970. For most of the years since, the building was leased by United Dairy Farmers, a chain of convenience stores that used the building as a warehouse. A giant plastic cow stood in the parking lot. The sole reminder of the glory days was a photo of James Brown that some UDF employees had put up.

That's not enough for people who feel that King Records was an artistic and commercial success story of which Cincinnati should be proud. For more than thirty years, almost since King left town, a diverse, loose-knit coalition of people in Cincinnati has been arguing the case with the local powers-that-be, pushing for some sort of official historical acknowledgment of King Records.

Producer James Austin of Rhino ranks King "with Chess, Sun, and Specialty as the four most important independent record labels in American music."[9] He was speaking for many when he told Cliff Radel of the *Cincinnati Enquirer*, "I can't believe the lack of respect people have given King. This is the long-lost treasure of R&B and rock 'n' roll history and they totally ignore it. You guys in Cincinnati have a lot to be proud of, what came out of King Records . . . The music that came out of King is a national treasure."[10]

Numerous proposals have been made over the years concerning the Brewster Avenue complex. Some envision a museum on the site. Others floated the idea of a recording studio for the use of neighborhood kids. The president of the Evanston Community Council was hopeful that whatever happened might be a tourist attraction.[11] Everyone seems to agree that at the very least, an official plaque should be installed.

According to Jack Johnson of United Dairy Farmers, any of those plans are feasible because the building is still structurally sound. "You could build in it if you wanted," Johnson told Randy McNutt of the *Enquirer*. "We know where the old studio used to be in there."[12]

But Cincinnati City Councilman Dwight Tillery was thinking big. "We could get a plaque put up," he said, "but a plaque means nothing. What if somebody tears down the building? If somehow we could commemorate King's history, and at the same time give the kids a way to express themselves [the recording studio], we could possibly do something."[13] The King Records Museum Project Committee, which included Tillery, was established to explore the options.

Tillery had recently been mayor of Cincinnati. While mayor, he said putting up a plaque "wouldn't be difficult to achieve,"[14] but it didn't get achieved during his single term. Tillery wasn't reelected as mayor, but he was elected to City Council, where he chaired the Finance Committee. "The plaque could still happen," he told Radel. "As chairman of the finance committee, I could have some fun with it. We could get the big companies in town involved."[15]

Several weeks later, he spoke with Radel of his plan to "bring the King Records building back to life. To make a museum would not be enough. [There] has to be a museum to recognize the impact King Records and Cincinnati had on the recording industry. It also has to be a community training center—with a working recording and video studio—to educate the youth in the area about the recording business."[16]

Tillery headed a movement to get the Brewster Avenue building listed on the National Register of Historic Places, maintained by the National Parks Service within the Department of the Interior. To qualify for such status, a building must meet four criteria; it must be (1) the site of a historic event; (2) associated with historically significant people; (3) architecturally significant; and (4) archeologically significant.

Because the King headquarters score low on the last two counts, making the Register will be difficult. The record business is barely represented on the list. "There is only one site associated with the modern recording industry listed on the National Register," explained Register historian Patrick Andress. "That's the WFIL studios in Philadelphia where Dick Clark started his *American Bandstand* show."[17]

Formal recognition for King Records is a back-burner issue for all but a few people in Cincinnati. The subject surfaces from time to time, usually in the pages of the city's newspapers. In October 1996, for example, Radel wrote in the *Enquirer* that Cincinnati's Historic Conservation Board voted to investigate 1540 Brewster and its history to see whether it qualifies for historic landmark status and protection.[18]

Six months later, Radel's successor at the *Enquirer*, Larry Nager, was blunt. "In Cincinnati," Nager wrote, "it's as if King and Mr. Nathan never existed. There's no museum and even a proposed historical marker remains controversial. Many say it's because Mr. Nathan's crudely direct style and the rawness of King's music don't fit Cincinnati's refined, blue-chip self-image."[19]

Unfortunately, that is in many ways true. Dorothy Halper, Nathan's sister and original partner, said the Cincinnati establishment cared little about King during its existence and even less afterwards. Howard Kessel, another original partner, expressed doubt that anything would ever happen to commemorate the label.

"I'll be surprised if the city recognizes the building," he told Radel in 1996. "They never wanted anything to do with us. To them, we were just making records for hillbillies and black people."[20]

Popular interest in King Records increases whenever the label is in the spotlight for something. There was a flurry of media interest in 1997 when Syd Nathan was inducted into the Rock and Roll Hall of Fame, and another in 2002 with the release of *Hidden Treasures: Cincinnati's Tribute to King Records Legacy*, a heartfelt and all-over-the-map collection of King classics performed by an eclectic group of Cincinnati musicians.

A fundraiser for the Inclusion Network (a Cincinnati advocacy group for the disabled), *Hidden Treasures* presents seventeen performances that range, like King Records itself, from bluegrass to blues to funk to rock to all of them mixed together. The CD is an intriguing blend of Cincinnati rock bands such as the Ass Ponys, Over the Rhine, and Blessid Union of Souls, country singers Katie Laur and Ed Cunningham, King session drummer Phillip Paul, intergalactic funk pioneer Bootsy Collins, and 1970s rock megastar Peter Frampton.

The album has several outstanding cuts that honor the original versions but stretch them a bit, too. The initial production run of 10,000 copies sold out within six months of its debut, and the album was picked up for national release by Ryko Distributing in 2003. It won the Cammy Award for "Recording of the Year" from the *Cincinnati Enquirer* in 2003.[21]

Once again, the King "movement" had a bit of traction with local politicians. According to *Enquirer* columnist Jim Knippenberg, City Council members John Cranley and Alicia Reece had been "talking up a King museum. Or at least a memorial." They wanted "to make sure the nation knows of Cincinnati's and King Records' grand contributions to rock 'n' roll, R&B, country, and our history of blacks and whites making music together." Cranley called King "one of Cincinnati's greatest exports."[22]

As of 2009, the King Records complex has not made it onto the National Register of Historic Places, which doesn't guarantee one of those historic plaques anyway. The National Parks Service cut that out years ago when it became too expensive (there are 45,000 "historic places" in Ohio alone). "If you want a plaque for a building, you're on your own," says the Register's Andress. "The Interior Department will lend its seal and supply a list of approved monument makers. But that's it."[23]

It was estimated in 1994 that it would cost about $800 to make and install a two-foot-by-two-foot plaque. It's too bad that Nathan isn't around to take care of it, because he *would* get it done. He'd find some unused corner of the property, build a foundry, learn how to cast and engrave metal monuments, design and write the text for the plaque, manufacture the memorial, and take the damn thing outside and screw it on the wall himself, with screws he'd made earlier that morning from scrap metal. And then he'd go eat lunch.

"WE BROKE THE SHIT DOWN"

The Meaning of King Records

• • •

We do not have the resources of the
major companies. So we've got to get there
in a Ford while they're trying to get there in
a Cadillac. It don't ride quite as nice but it's
sure easier to park.

—Sydney Nathan

If Syd Nathan said it once, he said it a thousand times: King made records for "the little man." Nathan also said that as a Jew, he identified with those on the margins of society, those viewed with disdain and condescension by the social elite. This was not just image building on Nathan's part or empty rhetoric. He *was* an outsider. Even after he was wealthy and well established, Nathan never forgot his early struggles or humble roots.

King Records was a successful company that sold millions of records and made millions of dollars, but King was important for reasons beyond artistic and commercial success. By doing things his own way and blazing his own path through the record industry wilderness, Nathan gave his peers and followers a new way of looking at the world, the music in it, and the people who make and consume that music.

The policies and practices of King Records might not pass muster at a business school, but in the real-world environment, they worked well enough to make King a leading independent record company for a quarter of a century. King was a quirky operation, and if the day-to-day operations appeared random, there were in fact a few underlying tenets that guided King Records from its start. They can be called the lessons of King Records.

The primary lesson was that there is more than one way to run a record company. King was the first of the great postwar independent record companies in America.

It was also the most influential independent label of the 1940s and 1950s, providing a blueprint for success that many new companies followed. King showed that in the new American world after the war, anything was possible. By demonstrating what could be done, King inspired many a label to go out and do it.

What the new labels learned from King's example varied from case to case, but there was plenty to absorb: follow your instincts *and* your dreams; don't hesitate to try new approaches to old problems; there is rarely just one solution to a particular problem; ignore conventional wisdom if it seems wrong; what works for one label may not work for another; when in doubt, do it yourself; learn from your mistakes; money beats prestige almost every time; hire quality people and let them do their jobs; and, perhaps most important, don't be afraid to make it up as you go along.

Nathan made his share of mistakes early in his career, but at his peak, he was an astute, creative executive. As Grandpa Jones, who was with Nathan at the beginning, said, "Syd was a businessman, all right. He was pretty shrewd. When it came to money he was pretty stubborn. Syd didn't care about prestige. He just made money, that's all."[1]

The most important formative influence upon King Records was the time Nathan spent operating a used record shop in Cincinnati. As the store's only employee, Nathan did it all, and gained an invaluable education in the process. Nathan bought his stock directly from record distributors and jukebox operators, giving him insight into those sectors of the record business and allowing him to forge relationships within the industry that would serve him well in later years.

More significant was Nathan's work in the front of the store waiting on his customers. Most of them were displaced blacks from the Deep South and white mountaineers from Kentucky and Tennessee, people who especially appreciated Nathan's welcoming and respectful attitude. Nathan was gregarious and curious by nature, so as he sold records, he quizzed his customers about their likes and dislikes.

He asked why they preferred one record over another, why some groups were popular and some weren't, and, in an early form of market research, where they had heard a given record—on what radio station or jukebox. Nathan became friends with many of the store's regulars, including a group of country musicians from WLW including Merle Travis, Grandpa Jones, and Alton and Rabon Delmore. It's impossible to overstate the importance of this connection to King Records.

Nathan's record store experience was the perfect training ground for King. It is hard to imagine some of his industry peers following this path, but it worked for Nathan. It gave him an introduction into many segments of the industry, sharpened his instincts for recognizing a hit, and introduced him to several of his first recording artists.

Finally, working in the store gave Nathan an understanding of the audience that would support independent record companies in the 1940s and 1950s. Nathan had firsthand knowledge of these record buyers that few of his contemporaries shared. With the possible exception of Sam Phillips at Sun, Nathan was more closely attuned to his artists *and* his customers than any other record company executive of the time.

Because Nathan believed that all one needed to start a record company was a desk, a telephone, and a lawyer, King Records could have happened anywhere. It happened in Cincinnati because that was Nathan's hometown. In an earlier era, Nathan might have gone to New York to seek his fortune in the record business, but by the mid-1940s, such a move was unnecessary. King's success sent a message to other would-be entrepreneurs that business could indeed be done in the hinterlands.

Within a few years, independent record companies dotted the map, in small cities such as Johnson City, Tennessee, and Jackson, Mississippi, and in such larger cities as Memphis, Detroit, Houston, New Orleans, Nashville, and Chicago. This decentralization of the recording industry was something of a reversal of the earlier business model, in which roving talent scouts and producers traveled the country looking for talent to record. Locating record companies in areas of intense musical activity was both logical and efficient.

Nathan's core philosophy was that success for an independent record label was rooted in the company's independence. To Nathan, that meant controlling as much of the recording and manufacturing processes as he could. The corporate infrastructure that he eventually built at King—the studio, pressing plant, mastering lab, printing shop, and the rest—was unmatched in the industry. It was expensive, but it gave Nathan the control he wanted.

Such an extensive operation was well beyond the reach of most companies, but several labels emulated at least part of the King approach. The most copied of Nathan's innovations was the in-house recording studio. Nathan was forced into building a studio after his abrasive personality got him banned from Cincinnati's only commercial studio, so he saw it as a last resort. But after the King studio was operational, Nathan immediately grasped what a huge asset it was.

In a commercial recording studio, time is money. Studios are rented by the hour; the longer a project takes to record, the more it costs. As a consequence, even the well-heeled keep one eye on the clock, and all involved are painfully aware of the passing of time. Such an atmosphere rewards efficiency but discourages the kind of tinkering and experimentation that might make a good record great. The studio is not the cheapest place to brainstorm new ideas.

Now imagine a studio that was essentially free for the producers and artists using it. The pressure is reduced, and people are free to be creative, no matter how long it takes. New arrangements can be worked out, harmonies refined, and riffs turned into songs. It's an ideal arrangement for younger musicians new to working in the studio and those still searching for a sound and an identity.

Coupled with a "house band" of red-hot musicians, an in-house studio could become a veritable hit factory that paid for itself many times over. This idea brought riches to many labels besides King, especially Stax in Memphis and Motown in Detroit.

Nathan doesn't get enough credit for what he accomplished at King. He had some extraordinarily talented people working for him—Henry Glover, Ralph Bass, Hal Neely, and many others—but the only constant at King was Nathan. It was his vision that drove King.

As Colin Escott points out, "There aren't many dogs in the King catalog, and that can't be attributed to one A&R man or another, because it's a recurrent theme through the country recordings, the R&B recordings, and the gospel recordings cut over a twenty-five year period. The only person there all that time was Nathan himself."[2]

Howard Kramer, assistant curator at the Rock & Roll Hall of Fame, shares that assessment. "There are few label operators in history who can spot talent and have the business acumen to exploit it," he says. "Syd is on the short list of those. There were other important independents at the time, but they were narrowly defined. In Chicago, Chess focused on blues. At Atlantic, they focused on R&B. But King was all over the map, [from] the Delmore Brothers [to] James Brown."[3]

Nathan was a dreamer, but he was also a realist. He said he wanted his label to be "King of them all," but he knew that King Records could never really match a company like Decca. He could live with that. Addressing a company sales meeting in 1952, Nathan sounded like a man who had found his niche in life. "We realize we're not a Victor, a Decca, a Columbia, a Capitol, or even a Mercury," he said. "But we're happy, boys. Give me six million records a year and you've got the happiest little fat man you ever saw in your life."[4]

American music of the first half of the twentieth century came in every conceivable variety, but most of it can be shoehorned into two categories. The first might be called "top-down" music—that sanctioned and created by the cultural establishment and consumed by the cultural elites and those with aspirations toward that status. Examples of this category include classical music, vaudeville and stage songs created by the professional songwriters of Tin Pan Alley in New York, formal religious music, and martial music for brass bands.

The second category, what might be termed "bottom-up" music, was that made by ordinary Americans for their own amusement and maybe, if skill and opportunity allowed, that of their family and neighbors. This was "homemade" rather than "store-bought" music. Scholars call this kind of music—blues, country, bluegrass, folk, jazz, "ethnic" music and gospel—"vernacular" music. Nathan called it "the music of the little people."

At first listen, one hears primarily the differences between, say, bluegrass and blues, or Cajun music and western swing. Put enough time and effort into listening, though, and one begins hearing patterns, themes, and similarities. Listen some more, connect some dots, and think about how things fit together, and an astonishing but undeniable truth emerges: It's all the same thing.

Not precisely the same thing, of course, but close enough. The distance between Hank Williams and Howlin' Wolf—or Bill Monroe and Muddy Waters—is minimal. Two hundred years from now, they'll be seen as two sides of the same coin.

Blues isn't really a matter of race. It's more a matter of poverty, hard luck, and bad times. Nor has country music ever been the exclusive province of white people. Thousands of listeners of both races thought that Uncle Dave Macon was black and Mississippi John Hurt was white, but the fact that the reverse was true didn't matter. If people liked a record, they bought it, and the race of the performer was mostly irrelevant.

Nathan probably came to this realization while he was running Syd's Record Shop. He had both black and white customers at the store and saw with his own eyes that white people sometimes bought blues records and black people sometimes bought country records. As Nathan talked to his customers, whatever preconceptions he had about race and musical preference were replaced by a more realistic perspective shaped by direct research.

Nathan wasn't the first to recognize that black and white musical traditions sprang from the same source or that black and white musicians fished from the same ponds, both literally and figuratively. But he was among the first in the record industry to see what that meant. He shut down Queen Records and began issuing blues, R&B, and black gospel recordings alongside the country releases on King.

It seems strange how little recognition Nathan gets for this. It's one thing to make unconventional assumptions about American culture. It's another thing altogether to bet your own money that those assumptions are correct. Nathan was a natural-born gambler, but betting that his vision of American society was an accurate one was a tremendous risk, the biggest of his life. It was a bold venture for a man to whom a dollar had never come easily.

Nathan's gamble bought a certain kind of freedom for his company, employees, and artists. It was the freedom to use an R&B drummer on a country record, jazz players on an R&B record, or country guitar players on a rock and roll record. It was the freedom to have the Stanley Brothers record a Hank Ballard song and Hank Ballard record a Reno & Smiley hit. It was having Henry Glover produce everyone from Moon Mullican and the Delmore Brothers to Bull Moose Jackson and Little Willie John. It was the freedom to make music without rules.

King artists and producers were encouraged to think expansively, particularly about repertoire. No idea was too outlandish to at least consider: Nathan once proposed pairing Bull Moose Jackson and Grandpa Jones on a record. Songs that had already been a hit in another style for another artist on King were seen as an especially good source of material. On one level, this was simple economics. Because King's in-house publishing companies owned many of the songs recorded on the King labels, the more times a song was recorded, the more money it made in publishing. Nathan's record companies paying royalties to his publishing companies was about as good as it got in Nathan's mind.

This "recycling" of songs in different styles also reflected Nathan's belief that it was the song that drove a hit record—not the artist or the beat or the arrangement or anything else. People bought the song. To Nathan it seemed logical that if country fans found a song appealing, R&B fans would like it, too. "Syd always said that if it was a good song, it could be done in any style," remembered King veteran Louis Innis.[5]

Because King and its associated labels recorded country, blues, R&B, bluegrass, gospel, jazz, and everything else, the company had to develop more comprehensive marketing and sales strategies than did more specialized labels. Instead of trying to reach one discrete target audience, King was trying, essentially, to reach everybody. How the company achieved this had far-reaching implications for the industry, for American music, and for American culture.

Nathan was way ahead of the curve when it came to racial matters. He always said he hired ability, not race, and that approach served him well over the years. Nathan integrated King Records in 1946 when he hired Henry Glover. The process expanded the following year when Nathan folded Queen Records into King. (For local context, the Cincinnati Reds baseball team added its first black player in 1954.)

Glover's career at King was keenly watched by many observers, and his success undoubtedly encouraged many black men and women to seek their own places within the industry. Prior to Henry Glover at King, Mayo Williams was the only prominent black executive in the record business. Nathan and Henry Glover changed that.

Along with the dozens of other important independent record companies that flourished between 1945 and 1965, King Records helped create a new kind of music fan and consumer for whom race was fairly unimportant. It's not that race didn't matter to these fans, because it sometimes did. But race was no longer a barrier when it came to the enjoyment of music.

Young black people in the south had always listened to country music on the radio. In most places, they had no choice; it was that or nothing. The converse— white kids listening to black music—was becoming increasingly common by the late 1940s and early 1950s. The portal, as often as not, was late-night radio programming, from blues and R&B powerhouses such as WLAC in Nashville and the crazy-quilt stations operating just across the Mexican border. These young white listeners, in Peter Guralnick's memorable phrase, saw the music as "the key to a mystery they were pledged never to reveal."[6]

Rufus Thomas, a black musician and DJ at WDIA in Memphis (the station known as "the Mother Station of the Negroes"), witnessed this phenomenon firsthand. "When I was a disc jockey some time ago on WDIA," Thomas recalled, "there were white college kids that always wanted to come on my show at night. I came on at midnight and they'd come in with me and sit down till three, sometimes six in the morning when the other disc jockey came. Their parents still did not want them to listen to the blues, so they learned it on their own."[7]

This cultural phenomenon flew under the mainstream radar for several years. The black press, however, had observed it as early as 1950. In January, a somewhat incredulous writer noted in *Ebony* that Bull Moose Jackson—not an *Ebony* favorite by any stretch—was attracting significant numbers of young white people to his shows: "Soon [Jackson] was packing them in at one-nighters in the Deep South, where he confounded the experts by showing a surprising box-office appeal for white audiences. In Knoxville, Tenn., last year he played a 'colored' one-nighter in a Negro dance hall. Over 700 whites jammed the upper balcony, reserved for them according to the state's segregation law, and demanded the right to go onto the floor, mingle with the Negroes, and get a better look at 'the Moose.'"[8]

Racism is based on fear, ignorance, and hatred, and music can be a potent antidote for those poisons. It's almost impossible to be a racist and love black music at the same time; it's hard to be a fan of someone you consider inferior. And when one's musical heroes include such titanic artists as Muddy Waters, Howlin' Wolf, James Brown, and Little Willie John, the idea of black inferiority is laid bare as not only a baseless fiction but a pretty preposterous one as well.

Musical acceptance has paved the way in many cases for human acceptance. The road to social consciousness can start at many points, and music was a crucial first step for millions of young people. Although we are not yet "one nation under a groove" (to quote George Clinton of Funkadelic), music has done much to move us closer to the ideal of a truly color-blind society.

The United States went through a tremendous change in racial attitudes and customs in the 1940s, 1950s, and 1960s. It is difficult (perhaps impossible) to accurately assess the role of popular music in those cultural changes, but music was obviously a social lubricant that helped make such change possible.

Change on a major level is always preceded by change on an individual level. The racial integration of this country was no different. A kind of critical mass had to be attained—in the hearts and minds of the American people—before the victories of the civil rights movement could be realized.

In a 1952 survey, students at the University of Mississippi named Gene Nobles of WLAC their favorite radio disc jockey.[9] As were his WLAC colleagues Bill "Hoss" Allen and John Richbourg (aka John R), Nobles was a jive-talking white DJ whom most people thought was black. The WLAC jocks played a steady stream of blues, R&B, and gospel recordings by black artists, interspersed with ads selling everything from mail-order baby chickens to, reportedly, autographed photos of Jesus. According to William Ferris, Mississippi native and former chairman of the National Endowment for the Humanities, "Every Southerner, white and black, heard that music."[10]

That shared experience had to have some impact upon racial attitudes. It also seems likely that without music breaking down at least some of the barriers between people, the story of this era would have a different and far less positive ending.

The tale of King Records is ultimately one of a partnership between the races. Writing about soul music (though it also applies to R&B), Guralnick has noted of this relationship that "it did bear out the promise of integration, and one participant after another—black *and* white—has credited the partnership as evidence that the American dream can work, has laid the success of soul music to 'blacks and whites working as a team.'"[11]

Discussing "meaning" in connection with a record company might strike some as absurd, even pretentious. But King Records merits an exemption because the company really did mean something—in that it stood for a principle—in both musical and historical contexts. The company sometimes fell short of its goals and ideals, but even in its failures, King advocated a progressive philosophy that placed it in the social vanguard among American record companies.

• • •

"I'll tell you the major contribution of King Records," Ralph Bass answered without a moment's hesitation when asked the question in 1983.[12] "I think we did as much [as any record company] to bring blacks and whites together—even though that wasn't the intent of the company—with music. Without getting up on a soapbox, without having marches, we brought blacks and whites together with music.

"I remember in Atlanta, Georgia, when 'The Twist' came out so big, the white bands weren't playing 'twist music' yet. And Hank Ballard was the headline act at this big club, and the whites were lined up—blacks and whites together—were lined up all down Auburn Avenue to try to get in to this club. Now the law was that whites couldn't go into black clubs except on one night a week. They called it 'white night,' and no blacks were allowed to attend.

"The police came, saw the line, and said, 'We'll have a riot. Let 'em alone. Let 'em go.' So here, whites and blacks together, we gave them a common denominator, a common love of music. We appealed to something that the law couldn't do a damn thing about. We gave them something to share. That was King's big contribution: to break the shit down, especially in the Deep South. Break it down. That was our major contribution to American culture. We broke the shit down."

NOTES

...

CHAPTER 1: SYD STARTS A RECORD COMPANY

The epigraph is from Jim Wilson interview.

1. This account of James Brown's first recording session is a composite drawn from two sources: interview with Ralph Bass, and Brown, *James Brown: The Godfather of Soul*.

2. Walt Trott, "AFM," *The Encyclopedia of Country Music*, 6–7.

3. Russell, *The Blues from Robert Johnson to Robert Cray*, 21.

4. Malone, *Country Music U.S.A.*, 94.

5. "Sydney Nathan, a Pioneer Record Exec, Dead at 64," *Billboard*; Jon Hartley Fox, "Sydney Nathan," *The Encyclopedia of Country Music*, 372.

6. Tracy, *Going to Cincinnati*, 116.

7. Wilson interview.

8. McNutt, "Ohioans: Syd Nathan," 15.

9. Jethro Burns interview.

10. Tape of King sales meeting, circa 1952, in author's collection.

11. Gordon, *Saga*, 63.

12. "Shooting Gallery Head Held on False Pretense Charge," *Cincinnati Enquirer*.

13. "New Warrant Names Sidney [sic] Nathan," *Cincinnati Post*.

14. "Two Charges Dismissed," *Cincinnati Enquirer*.

15. Ramey, "Juke-Box Operator," *Cincinnati Enquirer*.

16. Ibid.

17. Ibid.

18. Ibid.

19. Gordon, *Saga*, 64.

20. Ibid.

21. Merle Travis interview.

22. Grandpa Jones interview.

23. Travis interview.
24. Jones interview.
25. Jones, *Everybody's Grandpa*, 97.
26. Travis interview.
27. Jones interview.
28. Jones, *Everybody's Grandpa*, 98.
29. Ruppli, *The King Labels*, 1.
30. Travis interview.
31. Jones, *Everybody's Grandpa*, 98.
32. Travis interview.

CHAPTER 2: THE HILLBILLY BOOGIE

The epigraph is from Grandpa Jones interview.

1. Jim Stanton interview.
2. Jones, *Everybody's Grandpa*, 100–101.
3. Jones interview.
4. Jones, *Everybody's Grandpa*, 112.
5. Ibid., 113.
6. Perry, *Not Just a Sound*, 14.
7. Ibid., 58.
8. Ibid., 45–48.
9. Jethro Burns interview.
10. Malone, *Country Music U.S.A.*, 226.
11. Burns interview.
12. Delmore, *Truth Is Stranger Than Publicity*, 173.
13. Russell, liner notes, *Freight Train Boogie*, 2–3.
14. Jones interview.
15. Delmore, *Truth Is Stranger Than Publicity*, 172.
16. Ibid.
17. Russell, liner notes, *Freight Train Boogie*, 2.
18. Wolfe, liner notes, *Sand Mountain Blues*, 2.

CHAPTER 3: THE KING GETS A QUEEN

The epigraph is from Gordon, *Saga*, 65.

1. Tracy, "King of the Blues, part 1," 4–5.
2. Grendysa, "Musin' with the Moose," 16.
3. Ibid.
4. Daniels, "Queen Records," 10.
5. Ibid.
6. Coffey, liner notes, *Shuffle Town*, 3.
7. Ibid., 4.

CHAPTER 4: HENRY GLOVER

The epigraph is from Dr. John, *Under a Hoodoo Moon*, 227–8.

1. Rumble, "Roots of Rock & Roll," 30.
2. Ibid., p. 31
3. Tracy, "King of the Blues, part 1," 4.
4. Ibid., 5–6.
5. Ibid., 5.
6. Rumble, "Roots of Rock & Roll," 30.
7. Ibid.
8. Ibid., 38.
9. Ibid., 40.
10. Tracy, "King of the Blues, part 2," 9.
11. Shaw, *Honkers & Shouters*, 278–9.
12. Rumble, "Roots of Rock & Roll," 40.
13. Ibid., 33.
14. Ibid., 39.
15. Tracy, "King of the Blues, part 3," 9.
16. Rumble, "Roots of Rock & Roll," 39–40.

CHAPTER 5: GOOD ROCKIN' TONIGHT

The epigraph is from Penny, liner notes, *Good Rocking Tonight*.

1. Bull Moose Jackson obituary, *Billboard*, August 19, 1989.
2. Grendysa, "Musin' with the Moose," 16.
3. Bernholm, liner notes, *Moose on the Loose*.
4. Ibid.
5. Hildebrand, *Stars of Soul and Rhythm & Blues*, 91.
6. *Billboard*, April 26, 1952.
7. Penny, liner notes, *Good Rocking Tonight*.
8. Ibid.
9. Hildebrand, *Stars of Soul and Rhythm & Blues*, 28.
10. Penny, liner notes, *Blues DeLuxe*.
11. Hildebrand, *Stars of Soul and Rhythm & Blues*, 28.
12. Ibid., 29.
13. Berry, Foose, and Jones, *Up from the Cradle of Jazz*, 66.
14. Brown and Weine, liner notes, *Good Rockin' Tonight*.
15. Tracy, "King of the Blues, part 1," 8.
16. White and Weinger, liner notes, *Messing with the Blues*.
17. Tracy, "King of the Blues, part 2," 8.
18. Tracy, *Going to Cincinnati*, 131.
19. Pavlow, *The R&B Book*, 23.
20. Ibid.

21. Ibid., 24.
22. Ibid., 30.
23. Ibid., 33–50.

CHAPTER 6: WHERE THE HELL'S THE MELODY?

The epigraph is from Gordon, *Saga*, 65.

1. Jethro Burns interview.
2. Grandpa Jones interview.
3. Burns interview.
4. Charles Wolfe interview.
5. Kienzle, "Hank Penny," 9.
6. Ibid.
7. Burns interview.
8. Ibid.
9. Ibid.

CHAPTER 7: BUSINESS AS USUAL WAS PRETTY UNUSUAL

The epigraph is from Escott, *Tattooed on Their Tongues*, 63.

1. Escott, *Tattooed on Their Tongues*, 63.
2. "Syd Nathan Addresses an A&R Meeting," *The King R&B Box Set*.
3. Ibid.
4. Tracy, *Going to Cincinnati*, 118.
5. Ibid.
6. Gordon, *Saga*, 64.
7. Tracy, *Going To Cincinnati*, 114–5.
8. McNutt, "King Records," 92.
9. Earl Herzog interview.
10. Ibid.
11. Ibid.
12. Gordon, *Saga*, 64.
13. "Syd Nathan and Eli Oberstein Address a Sales Meeting," *The King R&B Box Set*.
14. Gordon, *Saga*, 64.
15. Ibid., 63.
16. Ibid., 64.
17. Tracy, *Going to Cincinnati*, 119.
18. Gordon, *Saga*, 64.
19. Charles Wolfe interview.
20. Jim Wilson interview.
21. Ibid.
22. Gordon, *Saga*, 65.

23. Ransohoff, "Record Firm Here Smashes Jim Crow," 6.

24. Kennedy, "King Records Rocks into History," *Cincinnati Magazine*, 79.

25. Escott, liner notes, *The King R&B Box Set*, 3.

26. Don Pierce interview.

27. Escott, *Tattooed on Their Tongues*, 65.

28. Wilson interview.

29. McNutt, "King Records," 92.

30. "Syd Nathan Addresses an A&R Meeting," *The King R&B Box Set*.

31. Wilson interview.

32. Nager, "Seymour Stein learned the ropes at King," 4.

33. Wilson interview.

34. Nager, "Seymour Stein learned the ropes at King," 4.

35. Ibid.

36. Ibid.

CHAPTER 8: MASTERS OF THE GROOVE

The epigraph is from Penny, liner notes, *Your Daddy's Dogging Around*.

1. Penny, liner notes, *Blows a Fuse*.

2. Tracy, *Going to Cincinnati*, 132.

3. Ron Wynn and Michael Erlewine, "Earl Bostic," *All Music Guide*, 57.

4. Penny, liner notes, *Blows a Fuse*.

5. Feather, *The Encyclopedia of Jazz*, 396.

6. *Billboard*, October 18, 1952.

7. Dawson, "Big Jay McNeely: An Original Rock 'n' Roll Honker," 14.

8. Bill Millar, liner notes, *The Best of Big Jay McNeely*.

9. Dawson, "Big Jay McNeely," 16.

10. Ibid.

11. Almost Slim, "Bill Doggett," 20.

12. Ibid.

13. Ibid.

14. Ibid.

15. Ibid.

16. Ibid., 18.

CHAPTER 9: I'LL SAIL MY SHIP ALONE

The epigraph is from Jethro Burns interview.

1. Coffey, liner notes, *Showboy Special*.

2. Escott, *Hank Williams*, 196.

3. Janet Bird, "Hawkshaw Hawkins," *Definitive Country*, 377.

4. Rumble, "Roots of Rock & Roll," 37.

5. Ibid.

6. Coffey, liner notes, *Shuffle Town.*

7. *Billboard,* April 5, 1952.

8. *Billboard,* January 31, 1953.

9. "Women in the News," *Cowboy Songs,* 27.

10. *Billboard,* March 28, 1953.

11. Whitburn, *The Billboard Book of Top 40 Country Hits.*

12. Jethro Burns interview.

CHAPTER 10: RECORD MAN

The epigraph is from Ralph Bass interview.

1. Ralph Bass interview.

2. Ibid.

3. Ibid.

4. Hildebrand, *Stars of Soul and Rhythm & Blues,* 244.

5. Bass interview.

6. Ibid.

7. Ibid.

CHAPTER 11: THE SIXTY-MINUTE MEN

The epigraph is from Bill "Hoss" Allen interview.

1. Gillett, *Sound of the City,* 166.

2. Hildebrand, *Stars of Soul and Rhythm & Blues,* 188.

3. Gillett, *Sound of the City,* 167.

4. Hildebrand, *Stars of Soul and Rhythm & Blues,* 151.

5. Hirshey, *Nowhere to Run,* 37.

6. Goldberg, "Marv Goldberg's R&B Notebooks: The Dominoes—Part 1."

7. Ralph Bass interview.

8. Goldberg, "Marv Goldberg's R&B Notebooks: The Royals."

9. Ibid.

10. Coleman, "Hank Ballard and the Midnighters," 33.

11. White, liner notes, *What You Get When the Gettin' Gets Good.*

12. Shannon and Javna, *Behind the Hits,* 99.

13. Bernholm, liner notes, *The Real Thing.*

14. Guralnick, *Sweet Soul Music,* 116.

15. Brown, *James Brown,* 120.

16. Goldberg, "Marv Goldberg's R&B Notebooks: The Dominoes—Part 1."

CHAPTER 12: YOU GIVE ME FEVER

The epigraph is from Hirshey, *Nowhere to Run*, 102.

1. Tracy, "King of the Blues, part 2," 7.
2. Ibid.
3. Hirshey, *Nowhere to Run*, 59.
4. Tracy, "King of the Blues, part 2," 8
5. Blackman, "Blast from the Past," 15.
6. Field, "Little Willie John's Fever and Fate," 20.
7. Ibid., 22.
8. Hirshey, *Nowhere to Run*, 59.
9. "Annisteen Allen," online biography, http://music.lycos.
10. Vera, liner notes, *I'll Drown in My Tears*.
11. Ibid.
12. Tracy, "King of the Blues, part 2," 9.

CHAPTER 13: EVERY TIME I FEEL THE SPIRIT

The epigraph is from "The Swan Silvertones," online, http://www.eyeneer.com/America/Genre/Gospel/Profiles/silvertones.html.

1. Heilbut, *The Gospel Sound*, 117.
2. Heilbut, liner notes, *Yesterday and Today*.
3. Leblanc, "Claude A. Jeter," online, http://www.island.net/~blues/cjeter.htm.
4. Heilbut, *The Gospel Sound*, 118.
5. Heilbut, liner notes, *Yesterday and Today*.
6. Heilbut, *The Gospel Sound*, 118.
7. Leblanc, "Claude A. Jeter."
8. Heilbut, *The Gospel Sound*, 118.
9. Ibid., 47.
10. Ibid., 46.
11. Ibid.
12. Allen, liner notes, The Spirit of Memphis Quartet, *Original Greatest Hits*.
13. Lornell, "*Happy in the Service of the Lord*," 108.
14. Ibid., 109.
15. Stone, *Living Blues*, 38.
16. Ward, *Dark Midnight When I Rise*.
17. "Wings Over Jordan Choir," online, *Encyclopedia of Cleveland History*.
18. Ibid.
19. Boyer, *The Golden Age of Gospel*, 182–83.
20. Ibid., 183.
21. "Etta James," online, www.prettyugly.com.
22. Boyer, *The Golden Age of Gospel*, 222.

23. *Billboard*, March 14, 1953.

24. Funk, liner notes, *Preachin' the Gospel: Holy Blues*.

CHAPTER 14: HOW MOUNTAIN GIRLS CAN LOVE

The epigraph is from Jethro Burns interview.

1. Reid and Vernon, liner notes, *1951–1959*.
2. Liner notes, *Folk Concert*.
3. Ralph Stanley interview.
4. Ibid.
5. Ibid.
6. Reid, liner notes, *The Early Starday and King Years, 1958–1961*.
7. Stanley interview.
8. Wright, *Traveling the High Way Home*, 60.
9. Ibid., 61.
10. Tribe, "Johnnie & Jack," *Definitive Country*, 423.
11. Tribe, "Wade Mainer," *The Encyclopedia of Country Music*, 323.
12. Stanley interview.
13. Young, liner notes, *The Golden Guitar of Don Reno*.
14. Reid and Vernon, liner notes, *1951–1959*.
15. Wright, *Traveling the High Way Home*, 91–92.

CHAPTER 15: LET'S HAVE A NATURAL BALL

The epigraph is from Trynka, "The 100 Greatest Guitarists of All Time," *Mojo*.

1. King's first name is variously spelled as "Freddie" or "Freddy." Except in the case of album titles or citations, I have opted for the former.
2. Bill "Hoss" Allen interview.
3. Gilmore, liner notes, *Don't You Remember Me*.
4. Dahl, liner notes, *Blues Masters: The Very Best of Albert King*.
5. Ibid.
6. Jacoubovitch, liner notes, *Let's Have a Natural Ball*.
7. Shuster, "Guitarist Albert King dies," *Los Angeles Times*.
8. Russell, *The Blues from Robert Johnson to Robert Cray*, 179.
9. Penny, liner notes, *Jay's Blues: The Complete Federal Sessions*.
10. O'Neal and Van Singel, *The Voice of the Blues*, 366.
11. Booth and Escott, "Freddie King," 6.
12. O'Neal and Van Singel, *The Voice of the Blues*, 366.
13. Ibid., 369.
14. Ibid., 367.
15. Ibid., 362.
16. Rubin, *Inside the Blues, 1942–1982*, 99.
17. Ibid., 100.

18. Escott, liner notes, *The King R&B Box Set*, 24.

19. Trynka, "The 100 Greatest Guitarists of All Time," 99.

20. Tefteller, Sax, and Dahl, liner notes, *Smokey Smothers Sings the Backporch Blues*.

21. O'Neal and Van Singel, *The Voice of the Blues*, 369.

22. Coleman, "Charles Brown's New Orleans Blues," 30.

23. Hildebrand, *Stars of Soul and Rhythm & Blues*, 26.

24. Slaven, liner notes, *Hey Mr. Gatemouth*.

25. Ibid.

CHAPTER 16: THAT AIN'T NOTHIN' BUT RIGHT

The epigraph is from Guralnick, liner notes, *Get With It*.

1. Dahl, liner notes, *Here and Now*.

2. Trynka, "The 100 Greatest Guitarists of All Time," 68.

3. Guralnick, liner notes, *Get With It*.

4. Ibid.

5. Ibid.

6. Finnis, liner notes, *King Rockabilly*.

7. Guralnick, liner notes, *Get With It*.

8. Ibid.

9. Guralnick, *Lost Highway*, 107.

10. Komorowski, liner notes, *Tennessee Rock 'n' Roll*.

11. Ibid.

12. Ibid.

13. Millar, liner notes, *Blue Jean Heart*.

14. Ibid.

15. Finnis, liner notes, *King Rockabilly*.

16. "Cincinnati Firm Called in on Disc Jockey Payoffs," *Cincinnati Enquirer*.

17. "Local Firm to Give Data to Probers," *Cincinnati Post*.

18. Ibid.

19. Ibid.

20. "Local Recorder Tells of Payoffs to Disk Jockeys," *Cincinnati Enquirer*.

21. Ibid.

22. "FCC and FTC Would Outlaw Payola Via Broadcaster, Diskery, DJ Clamps," *Variety*.

23. *Rolling Stone Rock Almanac*, 53.

24. "Jockeys on a Rough Ride," *Newsweek*.

25. Escott, liner notes, *Loud, Fast & Out of Control*, 63.

26. Penny, liner notes, *Gangster of Love*.

CHAPTER 17: THE HARDEST-WORKING MAN IN SHOW BUSINESS

The epigraph is from White and Weinger, liner notes, *Star Time*, 15.

1. Hildebrand, *Stars of Soul and Rhythm & Blues*, 26.

2. Brown, *James Brown*, ix.

3. *Rolling Stone Rock Almanac*, 20.

4. Bill "Hoss" Allen interview.

5. Brown, *James Brown*, 91.

6. Ibid.

7. Ibid., 92.

8. Leeds, liner notes, *Star Time*, 11.

9. Ibid.

10. Wesley, *Hit Me, Fred*, 110.

11. George, liner notes, *Star Time*, 5.

12. Weinger, liner notes, *The Apollo Theatre Presents, In Person, The James Brown Show*.

13. Portia Maultsby interview.

14. Brown, *James Brown*, 136.

15. Ibid., 137.

16. Weinger, liner notes, *The Apollo Theatre Presents, In Person, the James Brown Show*.

17. Blase, "The Man Who Was King."

18. Leeds, liner notes, *Star Time*, 9.

19. Brown, *James Brown*, 157.

20. White and Bronson, *The Billboard Book of Number One Rhythm & Blues Hits*, 10.

21. Ibid., 12.

22. Ibid., 17.

23. Ibid., 35.

24. Ibid.

25. Ibid.

26. White and Weinger, liner notes, *Star Time*, 31.

27. Ibid.

28. Wesley, *Hit Me, Fred*, 97.

29. Ibid., 146.

30. Ibid., 106.

31. Ibid., 143.

32. Brown, *James Brown*, 149.

33. Ibid., 158.

34. Trynka, "The 100 Greatest Guitarists Of All Time," 95.

35. Brown, *James Brown*, 158.

36. Hildebrand, "Jimmy Nolen," 41.

CHAPTER 18: BROTHER CLAUDE ELY AND EDDIE "LOCKJAW" DAVIS

The epigraph is from Escott, *Tattooed on Their Tongues*, 67.

1. Gordon, *Saga*, 65.

2. Feather, *Encyclopedia of Jazz*, 13.

3. Ibid., 464.

4. *Billboard*, March 21, 1953, 45.

5. Escott, *Tattooed on Their Tongues*, 66.

6. *Billboard*, May 24, 1952, 38.

CHAPTER 19: LIFE AFTER DEATH

The epigraph is from Escott, *Tattooed on Their Tongues*, 67.

1. Escott, *Tattooed on Their Tongues*, 67.

2. "Country Music King Dies of Heart Ailment," *Cincinnati Enquirer*.

3. "Sydney Nathan, a Pioneer Record Exec, Dead at 64," *Billboard*.

4. Ibid.

5. Don Pierce interview.

6. Ibid.

7. Brown, *James Brown*, 226.

8. Ibid., 240.

9. Radel, "With reissue series, King Records finally gets its due," *Cincinnati Enquirer*.

10. Ibid.

11. McNutt, "Music fans seek to save history," *Cincinnati Enquirer*.

12. Ibid.

13. Ibid.

14. Radel, "Tribute to King remains overdue," *Cincinnati Enquirer*.

15. Ibid.

16. Radel, "King-Sized Dreams," *Cincinnati Enquirer*.

17. Ibid.

18. Radel, "King Records plant touches souls in city," *Cincinnati Enquirer*.

19. Nager, "For The Record, Nathan Was King," *Cincinnati Enquirer*.

20. Radel, "King Records plant touches souls in city," *Cincinnati Enquirer*.

21. Nager, "King tribute goes national," *Cincinnati Enquirer*.

22. Knippenberg, *Cincinnati Enquirer*.

23. Radel, "It's been on the charts; is the Register next?" *Cincinnati Enquirer*.

CHAPTER 20: "WE BROKE THE SHIT DOWN"

The epigraph is from "Syd Nathan Addresses An A&R Meeting, December 11, 1954," *The King R&B Box Set*.

1. Grandpa Jones interview.

2. Escott, *Tattooed on Their Tongues*, 68.

3. Bird, "Rock Hails a King," *Cincinnati Post*.

4. Escott, *Tattooed on Their Tongues*, 66.

5. Kienzle, "The King Records Story," *Pickin*,' 10.

6. Guralnick, *Sweet Soul Music*, 2.

7. David McGee, "Roots Music Begats Rock & Roll," *American Roots Music*, 213.

8. Bernholm, liner notes, *Moose on The Loose*.

9. Lord, "What made Elvis wiggle," 60.

10. Ibid.

11. Guralnick, *Sweet Soul Music*, 10.

12. Ralph Bass interview.

BIBLIOGRAPHY

•••

INTERVIEWS

All interviews conducted in person and recorded by the author unless otherwise indicated.

Allen, Bill "Hoss," Nashville, Tenn., June 27, 1984.

Ballard, Hank, unrecorded telephone interview, June 17, 1990.

Bass, Ralph, Chicago, Ill., April 19, 1984.

Burns, Jethro, Evanston, Ill., April 20, 1984.

Deak, Jim, Cincinnati, Ohio, July 16, 1984.

Edwards, Ben, Nashville, Tenn., June 28, 1984.

Fitzgerald, Bill, Nashville, Tenn., June 28, 1984.

Jones, Grandpa, Nashville, Tenn., June 29, 1984.

Grendysa, Peter, Caledonia, Wisc., July 1984. (Self-interview with questions supplied by author.)

Herzog, Earl, Cincinnati, Ohio, July 16, 1984.

Mathias, Frank, Dayton, Ohio, September 4, 1984.

Maultsby, Portia, Bloomington, Ind., April 30, 1984.

Pierce, Don, Hendersonville, Tenn., June 27, 1984.

Pinson, Bob, Nashville, Tenn., June 26, 1984.

O'Neal, Jim, Chicago, Ill., April 19, 1984.

Stanley, Ralph, Warsaw, Ky., June 3, 1984.

Stanton, Jim, Nashville, Tenn., January 26, 1984.

Travis, Merle, interviewed by William Lightfoot, Chicago, Ill., September 15, 1979.

Wilson, Jim, Nashville, Tenn., January 26, 1984.

Wolfe, Charles, Murfreesboro, Tenn., June 29, 1984.

BOOKS

Artis, Bob. *Bluegrass* (New York: Hawthorn Books, Inc., 1975).

Berry, Jason, Jonathan Foose, and Tad Jones. *Up from the Cradle of Jazz: New Orleans Music Since World War II* (Athens: The University of Georgia Press, 1986).

Boyer, Horace Clarence, text, and Lloyd Yearwood, photography. *The Golden Age of Gospel* (Urbana: University of Illinois Press, 2000).

Brown, James, with Bruce Tucker. *James Brown: The Godfather of Soul* (New York: Macmillan, 1986).

Bruce, Chris, editor. *Crossroads: The Experience Music Project Collection* (Seattle: Experience Music Project, 2000).

Bufwack, Mary A., and Robert K. Oermann. *Finding Her Voice: The Illustrated History of Women in Country Music* (New York: Henry Holt and Company, 1993).

Cantwell, Robert. *Bluegrass Breakdown: The Making of the Old Southern Sound* (Urbana: University of Illinois Press, 1984).

Carson, Phil. *Roy Buchanan: American Axe* (San Francisco: Backbeat Books, 2001).

Charles, Ray, and David Ritz. *Brother Ray: Ray Charles' Own Story* (New York: Da Capo Press, 1978, 1992 revised edition).

Cohodas, Nadine. *Spinning Blues into Gold: The Chess Brothers and the Legendary Chess Records* (New York: St. Martin's Press, 2000).

Delmore, Alton. *Truth Is Stranger Than Publicity: Alton Delmore's Autobiography* (Nashville: Country Music Foundation Press, 1977).

Dickerson, James. *Goin' Back to Memphis: A Century of Blues, Rock 'n' Roll, and Glorious Soul* (New York: Schirmer Books, 1996).

Dr. John (Mac Rebennack), with Jack Rummel. *Under a Hoodoo Moon: The Life of the Night Tripper* (New York: St. Martin's Press, 1994).

Erlewine, Michael, Vladimir Bogdanov, Chris Woodstra, Stephen Thomas Erlewine, editors. *All Music Guide: The Expert's Guide to the Best CDs, Albums and Tapes* (San Francisco: Miller Freeman Books, 1997).

Escott, Colin. *Tattooed on Their Tongues: A Journey Through the Backrooms of American Music* (New York: Schirmer Books, 1996).

Escott, Colin, with George Merritt and William MacEwen. *Hank Williams: The Biography* (Boston: Little, Brown and Company, 1994).

Feather, Leonard. *The Encyclopedia of Jazz* (New York: Horizon Press, 1960).

Fowler, Gene, and Bill Crawford. *Border Radio* (Austin: Texas Monthly Press, 1987).

Gillett, Charlie. *The Sound of the City: The Rise of Rock 'n' Roll* (New York: Dell Publishing Co., 1972).

Ginell, Cary. *Milton Brown and the Founding of Western Swing* (Urbana: University of Illinois Press, 1994).

Graff, Gary, Josh Freedom du Lac, and Jim McFarlin. *MusicHound R&B: The Essential Album Guide* (Detroit: Visible Ink, 1998).

The Grammy Winners Book (Burbank, Cal.: National Academy of Recordings Arts and Science, Inc, 1988).

Grand Ole Opry: WSM Picture—History Book (Nashville: Opryland, 1984).

Guralnick, Peter. *Sweet Soul Music: Rhythm and Blues and the Southern Dream of Freedom* (New York: Harper & Row, 1986).

———. *Feel Like Going Home: Portraits in Blues and Rock 'n' Roll* (Boston: Back Bay Books, 1999).

———. *Lost Highway: Journeys and Arrivals of American Musicians* (Boston: Back Bay Books, 1999).

Hagan, Chet. *Grand Ole Opry* (New York: Henry Holt and Company, 1989).

Heilbut, Anthony. *The Gospel Sound: Good News and Bad Times* (New York: Limelight Editions, 1989).

Hildebrand, Lee. *Stars of Soul and Rhythm & Blues* (New York: Billboard Books, 1994).

Hirshey, Gerri. *Nowhere to Run: The Story of Soul Music* (New York: Penguin Books, 1985).

Jones, Grandpa, with Charles K. Wolfe. *Everybody's Grandpa: Fifty Years Behind the Mike* (Knoxville: University of Tennessee Press, 1984).

Kennedy, Rick, and Randy McNutt. *Little Labels—Big Sound: Small Record Companies and the Rise of American Music* (Bloomington: Indiana University Press, 1999).

Kingsbury, Paul, editor. *The Encyclopedia of Country Music* (New York: Oxford University Press, 1998).

Logan, Horace, with Bill Sloan. *Elvis, Hank, and Me: Making Musical History on the Louisiana Hayride* (New York: St. Martin's Press, 1998).

Lornell, Kip. *"Happy in the Service of the Lord": Afro-American Gospel Quartets in Memphis* (Urbana: University of Illinois Press, 1988).

Malone, Bill. *Southern Music/American Music* (Lexington: University Press of Kentucky, 1979).

———. *Country Music U.S.A.* (Austin: University of Texas Press, 1985, revised edition).

———. *Don't Get Above Your Raisin': Country Music and the Southern Working Class* (Urbana: University of Illinois Press, 2002).

McCloud, Barry, and contributing writers. *Definitive Country: The Ultimate Encyclopedia of Country Music and Its Performers* (New York: Perigee Books, 1995).

Miller, James. *Flowers in the Dustbin: The Rise of Rock and Roll, 1947–1977* (New York: Simon & Schuster, 1999).

Miller, Jim. editor. *The Rolling Stone Illustrated History of Rock & Roll* (New York: Random House/Rolling Stone Press, 1976).

Morthland, John. *The Best of Country Music* (Garden City, N.Y.: Doubleday & Company, Inc, 1984).

Murrells, Joseph. *The Book of Golden Discs: The Records That Sold a Million* (London: Barrie & Jenkins, 1974).

Nicolas, Alain. *From Hillbilly Blues to Hillbilly Boogie with the Delmore Brothers: Sessionography & Discography* (Quincy sous Senart, France: Ara Graphic, 2001).

O'Neal, Jim, and Amy Van Singel, editors. *The Voice of the Blues: Classic Interviews from "Living Blues" Magazine* (New York: Routledge, 2002).

Pavlow, Big Al. *The R&B Book: A Disc-History of Rhythm & Blues* (Providence, R.I.: Music House Publishing, 1983).

Perry, Dick. *Not Just a Sound: The Story of WLW* (Englewood Cliffs, N.J.: Prentice-Hall, Inc., 1971).

Reid, Gary B. *Stanley Brothers: A Preliminary Discography* (Roanoke, Virg.: Copper Creek Publications, 1984).

Rolling Stone Rock Almanac: The Chronicles of Rock and Roll (New York: Rolling Stone Press/ Collier Books, 1983).

Rosenberg, Neil. *Bluegrass: A History* (Urbana: University of Illinois Press, 1985).

Rubin, Dave. *Inside The Blues, 1942–1982: Four Decades of the Greatest Electric Blues Guitarists* (Milwaukee: Hal Leonard Corporation, 1995).

Rucker, Leland, editor. *MusicHound Blues: The Essential Album Guide* (New York: Schirmer Books, 1998).

Ruppli, Michel. *The King Labels: A Discography, vols. 1–2* (Westport, Conn: Greenwood Press, 1985).

Russell, Tony. *The Blues from Robert Johnson to Robert Cray* (New York: Schirmer Books, 1997).

Sanjek, Russell, and David Sanjek. *American Popular Music Business in the 20th Century* (New York: Oxford University Press, 1991).

Santelli, Robert, Holly George-Warren, Jim Brown, editors. *American Roots Music* (New York: Abrams/Rolling Stone Press, 2001).

Shannon, Bob, and John Javna. *Behind the Hits: Inside Stories of Classic Pop and Rock and Roll* (New York: Warner Books, Inc., 1986).

Shaw, Arnold. *The World of Soul* (New York: Cowles Book Company, 1970).

———. *Honkers & Shouters* (New York: Macmillan Publishing Co., Inc, 1978).

Tracy, Steve. *Going to Cincinnati: A History of the Blues in the Queen City* (Urbana: University of Illinois Press, 1993).

Tribe, Ivan M. *Mountaineer Jamboree: Country Music in West Virginia* (Lexington: University Press of Kentucky, 1984).

Ward, Andrew. *Dark Midnight when I Rise: The Story of the Jubilee Singers Who Introduced the World to the Music of Black America* (New York: Farrar, Straus and Giroux, 2000).

Wesley, Fred, Jr., *Hit Me, Fred: Recollections of a Sideman* (Durham: Duke University Press, 2002).

Wexler, Jerry, and David Ritz. *Rhythm and the Blues* (New York: Alfred A. Knopf, 1993).

Whitburn, Joel. *Top Rhythm & Blues Records, 1949–1971* (Menomonee Falls, Wisc.: Record Research, 1973).

———. *The Billboard Book of Top 40 Hits* (New York: Billboard Books, 1996).

———. *The Billboard Book of Top 40 Country Hits* (New York: Billboard Books, 1996).

———. *Top R&B Singles, 1942–1999* (Menomonee Falls, Wisc.: Record Research, 2000).

Whitcomb, Ian. *After the Ball: Pop Music from Rag to Rock* (Baltimore: Penguin Books Inc., 1972).

White, Adam, and Fred Bronson. *The Billboard Book of Number One Rhythm & Blues Hits* (New York: Billboard Books, 1993).

Wolfe, Charles K. *Tennessee Strings: The Story of Country Music in Tennessee* (Knoxville: University of Tennessee Press, 1977).

———. *The Grand Ole Opry: The Early Years, 1925–35* (London: Old Time Music, 1975).

———. *Kentucky Country: Folk and Country Music of Kentucky* (Lexington: University Press of Kentucky, 1982).

———. *A Good-Natured Riot: The Birth of the Grand Ole Opry* (Nashville: Country Music Foundation Press and Vanderbilt University Press, 1999).

The World Book Encyclopedia (Chicago: World Book, Inc., 2001).

Wright, John. *Ralph Stanley & the Clinch Mountain Boys: A Discography* (Evanston, Ill.: Self-published, 1983).

———, editor. *It's The Hardest Music in the World to Play: The Ralph Stanley Story in His Own Words* (Evanston, Ill.: Self-published, 1987).

———. *Traveling the High Way Home: Ralph Stanley and the World of Traditional Bluegrass Music* (Urbana: University of Illinois Press, 1993).

MAGAZINE ARTICLES

"Ackerman Statement to Payola Probers," *Billboard*, May 9, 1960, 8, 18.

"Annual Music—Record Programming Guide: Country & Western Recording Artists," *Billboard*, February 28, 1953, 103–105.

Blackman, JoAnn. "Blast from the Past," *Jam Sessions*, March 1990, 15.

Blase, Darren. "The Man Who Was King," *Cincinnati Citybeat*, March 27–April 2, 1997, 13.

Bonner, Brett J. "The Next Generation of Blues: Little Jimmy King," *Living Blues*, March/April 1995, 56–59.

Booth, Dave "Daddy Cool," and Colin Escott. "Freddie King: A Profile," *Goldmine*, June 22, 1984, 6, 8, 10, 14.

Bundy, June. "House-FCC Payola Probe Threat Stirs Aircasters," *Billboard*, November 16, 1959, 2, 11.

———. "Payola Probe Keys Widespread Effect," *Billboard*, November 30, 1959, 1–2.

Burns, Jethro, obituary, *Billboard*, February 18, 1989, 39.

Buskin, Richard. "The Hardest Working Man in the Studio: Ron Lenhoff, James Brown's Main Man," *Music and Sound Output*, July 1988, 98–99, 102–103.

Calas, Terrington. "Hank Ballard, Stylist," *New Orleans Art Review*, November/December 1988, 28–29.

"Clark's Interest—Tune Plays Get New Analysis," *Billboard*, May 9, 1960, 8.

Coleman, Rick. "Hank Ballard and the Midnighters: Hank Takes Annie to the Jazz Fest," *Wavelength*, May 1988, 33–34.

———. "Charles Brown's New Orleans Blues," *Wavelength*, May 1988, 30–32.

"Congressional Payola Probe Puts Cleve, Boston Jockeys on Hot Seat; Finan Says He Took, Others Deny It," *Variety*, February 10, 1960, 55–56.

Considine, J. D. "'Star Time' Burns Bright," *Rolling Stone*, May 30, 1991, 72.

Curry, Andrew. "Men in Blackface," *U.S. News and World Report*, July 8/July 15, 2002, 24–26.

Daniels, Bill. "Queen Records," *Whiskey, Women, and . . .*, 10, November 1982, 10–14.

Dawson, Jim. "Big Jay McNeely: An Original Rock 'n' Roll Honker," *Goldmine*, December 6, 1985, 14–16, 30.

———. "Hank Ballard: Work with Me, Annie," *RIP Magazine*, June 1987, 27–28.

"Distrib Payola Sampling Bared by Committee," *Billboard*, May 9, 1960, 8.

"Editorial: Lame, Halt and Blind," *Billboard*, November 30, 1959, 2.

"FCC and FTC Would Outlaw Payola Via Broadcaster, Diskery, DJ Clamps," *Variety*, February 10, 1960, 55, 60.

"FTC Cites Eight More Disk Firms," *Billboard*, March 28, 1960, 3, 48.

Funk, Ray. "Historical Gospel: Wings over Jordan," *Rejoice*, Spring 1988, 10.

Garrett, Amos. "Amos Garrett on Jimmy Nolen" *Guitar Player*, April 1984, 39.

"Gimme, Gimme, Gimme on the Old Payola," *Life*, November 23, 1959, 45.

Glover, Henry, obituary, *Rolling Stone*, May 16, 1991, 20.

Goldberg, Michael. "James Brown addicted to PCP," *Rolling Stone*, November 17, 1988, 42.

———. "Wrestling with the Devil: The Struggle for the Soul of James Brown," *Rolling Stone*, April 6, 1989, 36–37, 39–41, 44, 91–92.

Gordon, Richard L. "The Man Who Is King," *Saga*, January 1951, 63–65.

Grendysa, Peter. "Musin' with the Moose: Bull Moose Jackson," *Goldmine*, November 1979, 16–18.

———. "Moose Captures Pittsburgh," *Goldmine*, November 23, 1984, 56, 62, 64, 66.

———. "The Royals: Ballard Blows Away the Ballads," *Goldmine*, August 12, 1988, 29, 77.

Hall, Mildred. "Exhaustive Probe for Whole Music Industry on Way," *Billboard*, December 21, 1959, 1, 26.

Hannusch, Jeff (Almost Slim), "Bill Doggett: Mr. Honky Tonk," *Goldmine*, May 10, 1985, 18, 20, 22.

Hawkins, Martin, with additional research by Colin Escott. "The History of the King Label," part 1, *Country Music People*, September 1973, 18–19.

———. "The History of the King Label," part 2, *Country Music People*, October 1973, 18–19.

———. "The History of the King Label," part 3, *Country Music People*, November 1973, 28–29.

Hildebrand, Lee, with Henry Kaiser. "Jimmy Nolen: A Rare Interview with James Brown's Longtime Sideman—The Father of Funk Guitar," *Guitar Player*, April 1984, 34, 36, 38, 39, 41, 42, 44, 45.

Hirshey, Gerri. "Presenting the One and Only Mr. Dynamite, Mr. Sex Machine, Soul Brother Number One (Part 1)," *Rolling Stone*, August 23, 1990, 98, 101–2.

———. "I Feel Good! The Reeducation and Umpteenth Resurrection of James Brown," *Rolling Stone*, June 27, 1991, 60–62, 64, 86.

Holmes, Emory, II, "Hank Ballard & Midnighters: R&B's 'Answer' Men," *The R&B Report*, March 31–April 10, 1988, 26–27.

"In Memoriam," *BMI: The Many Worlds of Music*, May 1968, 9.

Jackson, Bull Moose, obituary, *Billboard*, August 19, 1989, 71.

"Jockeys on a Rough Ride," *Newsweek*, December 7, 1959, 98.

Kennedy, Rick. "King Records Rocks into History," *Cincinnati Magazine*, January 1997, 78–80.

Kienzle, Rich. "Hank Penny," *Old Time Music*, Spring 1978, 7–10.

———. "Hank Penny Discography," *Old Time Music*, Spring 1978, 12–14.

———. "The King Records Story," *Pickin',* October 1979, 9–11.

Light, Alan. "'Star Time' James Brown on CD," *Rolling Stone*, April 18, 1991, 19.

———. "Brown Released on Parole," *Rolling Stone*, April 18, 1991, 19.

Lord, Lewis. "What Made Elvis Wiggle," *U.S. News & World Report*, July 8/July 15, 2002, 59–60.

Mazor, Barry. "The Label That Would Be King," *No Depression*, January–February 2003, 84.

McKenzie, Ed. "A Deejay's Expose—and Views of the Trade," *Life*, November 23, 1959, 46–47.

McNutt, Randy. "Ohiona: A Lament for Ohio's Singing Cowboy," *Ohio Magazine*, October 1988, 13–14, 16, 34.

———. "King Records: The Country Side of a Rhythm 'n' Blues Label," *Goldmine*, February 9, 1990, 90–92.

———. "Ohioans: Syd Nathan," *Ohio Magazine*, September 1990, 15–21.

———. "Pickin' and Grinnin,'" *Ohio Magazine;* May 1998, 66–69.

Mieses, Stanley. "The Hardest-Working Emcee in Showbiz," *Rolling Stone*, September 27, 1984, 76, 81.

Milward, John. "James Brown: He Feels Good," *TV Guide*, June 8, 1991, 16.

Moen, Debi. "Hank Ballard and the Midnighters: Creator of 'The Twist' Celebrates the Sensation's 30th Anniversary," *Performance*, 17:50, April 29, 1988, 12–14.

Moody, Clyde, obituary, *Billboard*, April 22, 1989, 73.

Thurston Moore and Ed Kahn, "King 500 Series Numerical, parts 1–8," *JEMF Quarterly*, 4:10 (June 1968), 66–71; 4:11 (September 1968), 115–20; 4:12 (December 1968), 156–62; 5:13 (Spring 1969), 34–40; 5:14 (Summer 1969), 75–80; 5:15 (Autumn 1969), 111–16; 5:16 (Winter 1969), 151–56; 6:17 (Spring 1970), 45–46.

Morthland, John. "I, James Brown," *High Fidelity*, November 1984, 92.

"National Barn Dance Favorites," *Hillbilly and Western Hoedown*, April 1954, 16–21.

Neely, Kim. "James Brown in Work Release," *Rolling Stone*, May 31, 1990, 27.

Newman, Melinda. "James Brown Faces Charges in 2 States," *Billboard*, January 14, 1989, 75.

"'Now Don't Cry,'" *Time*, December 7, 1959, 47.

"Record Maker Describes Payoff," *Life*, November 23, 1959, 48.

Rosenberg, Neil. "The Osborne Brothers," *Bluegrass Unlimited*, September 1971, 5–10.

———. "Thirty Years Ago This Month," *Bluegrass Unlimited*, September 1980, and most subsequent issues through September 1996.

Roth, Arlen. "Arlen Roth on Jimmy Nolen," *Guitar Player*, April 1984, 38.

Rumble, John W. "Roots of Rock and Roll: Henry Glover at King Records," *Journal of Country Music*, 14:2 (1992), 30–42.

Santoro, Gene. "Maceo, Blow Your Horn!" *Pulse*, November 1990, 47, 138.

Satchell, Michael. "Birth of the Cool," *U.S. News and World Report*, July 8/July 15, 2002, 56–59.

Schmidt, Ted. "Hank Ballard: A Rock and Roll Legend," *Catholic New Times*, July 9, 1989, 12.

Schuller, Mit., with Bruce Iglauer, "Freddie King, 1934–1976," *Living Blues*, March/April 1977, 7–11.

Sklaroff, Sara. "One Nation under a Groove," *U.S. News & World Report*, July 8/July 15, 2002, 20–21.

Slaven, Neil. "The King Tapes," *B&R*, No. 59, March/April 1991, 10–11.

———. "The King Tapes Revisited," *B&R*, No. 68, April 1992, 14–15.

Stiernberg, Don. "Jethro Burns," *Frets Magazine*, April 1989, 34–41.

Stone, Robert. "Sacred Steel Guitar: From Little Willie and His Talking Guitar to the Campbell Brothers and Beyond," *Living Blues*, September/October 1998, 36–43.

"Sydney Nathan, a Pioneer Record Exec, Dead at 64," *Billboard*, March 16, 1968; 3, 10.

Topping, Ray, Daddy Cool, Colin Escott, and Bill Daniels, "Freddie King Discography," *Goldmine*, June 22, 1984, 6.

Tracy, Steve. "King of the Blues: The Story of a Record Label, part 1," *Blues Unlimited*, #87, December 1971, 4–8.

———. "King of the Blues: The Story of a Record Label, part 2," *Blues Unlimited*, #88, January 1972, 7–10.

———. "King of the Blues: The Story of a Record Label, part 3," *Blues Unlimited*, #89, February–March 1972, 8–10.

Trynka, Paul, with Jim Irvin, editors. "The 100 Greatest Guitarists of All Time," *Mojo*, June 1996, 54–105.

"The Virginia Barn Dance," *Hillbilly and Western Hoedown*, February 1954, 18–21.

"The Wages of Spin," *Time*, December 7, 1959, 47.

Wolfe, Charles. "The Brown's Ferry Four: Country's First All-Star Quartet," *Precious Memories*, November/December 1988, 6–12.

———, "The Delmore Brothers," *Journal of Country Music*, 6:1 (1975), 2–11.

"Women in the News," *Cowboy Songs*, September 1953, 27.

Zhito, Lee. "FCC Free Record Bomb Hits Coast," *Billboard*, March 28, 1960, 3, 20.

NEWSPAPER ARTICLES

Bird, Rick. "Rock Hails a King," *Cincinnati Post*, May 2, 1997, 1B, 7B.

Boucher, Geoff. "Obituary: Hank Ballard Originally Sang Hit song 'The Twist,'" *Sacramento Bee (Los Angeles Times)*, March 7, 2003, B7.

"Cincinnati Firm Called in on Disc Jockey Payoffs," *Cincinnati Enquirer*, November 20, 1959, 1.

Cornell, Si. "King of King's 25th Year," *Cincinnati Post*, July 21, 1967, 17.

"Country Music King Dies of Heart Ailment," *Cincinnati Enquirer*, March 6, 1968, 9.

Field, Kim. "The Strange Story of Little Willie John: Fever and Fate," *Village Voice Rock and Roll Quarterly*, 3:1 (Spring 1990), 20–27.

Goldsmith, Thomas. "James Brown to Serve Time as Deejay?" *Nashville Tennessean*, February 14, 1990, 1F, 6F.

———. "James Brown Gets a Job," *Nashville Tennessean*, April 4, 1990, 2F.

Heckman, Don. "The Blessings of Bethlehem," *Los Angeles Times*, March 24, 1996, CAL78.

"Johnny Bailes, Country Singer/Songwriter, Dies," *Nashville Tennessean*, December 23, 1989, 3D.

Knippenberg, Jim. "Knip's Eye View: Politicians Push King Records Tribute," *Cincinnati Enquirer*, April 10, 2003, E1.

"Local Firm to Give Data to Probers," *Cincinnati Post*, November 20, 1959, 1.

"Local Recorder Tells of Payoffs to Disk Jockeys," *Cincinnati Enquirer*, November 21, 1959, 1.

McNutt, Randy. "Music Fans Seek to Save History," *Cincinnati Enquirer*, April 28, 1994, 1, 3.

Nager, Larry. "H-Bomb Ferguson Doesn't Just Sing," *Cincinnati Post*, August 28, 1984, 11C.

———. "King Remembered; Cincinnati's Major Chapter in Rock History," *Cincinnati Post*, January 17, 1990, 1C-4C.

———. "Ballard Owes Career to Nathan," *Cincinnati Post*, January 17, 1990, 1C-4C.

———. "Seymour Stein Learned the Ropes at King," *Cincinnati Post*, January 17, 1990, 4C.

———. "King Records to Crown Rock Hall," *Cincinnati Enquirer*, January 24, 1997, E2.

———. "For The Record, Nathan Was King," *Cincinnati Enquirer*, May 4, 1997, E1, E7.

———. "King Tribute Goes National," *Cincinnati Enquirer*, April 20, 2003, E1.

"And the Newest Kennedy Center Honorees Are . . .," *Sacramento Bee*, August 6, 2003, A2.

"New Warrant Names Sidney [sic] Nathan," *Cincinnati Post*, August 26, 1938, 28.

Radel, Cliff. "With Reissue Series, King Records Finally Gets Its Due," *Cincinnati Enquirer*, April 19, 1994, 1C, 2C.

———. "King-Sized Dreams: Making Former Cincinnati Recording Plant into Museum Would Revive an Era," *Cincinnati Enquirer*, November 6, 1994, G1, G8.

———. "It's Been on the Charts; Is the Register next," *Cincinnati Enquirer*, November 6, 1994; G8.

———. "Tribute to King Remains Overdue," *Cincinnati Enquirer*, December 28, 1993, C5.

———. "King Records Plant Touches Souls in City," *Cincinnati Enquirer*, October 21, 1996, B1.

Ramey, Jack. "Juke-Box Operator," *Cincinnati Enquirer*, February 6, 1949, sect. 3, p. 1.

Ransohoff, Jerry. "Record Firm Here Smashes Jim Crow," *Cincinnati Post*, March 21, 1949, 6.

Ratliff, Ben. "Charlie Feathers, 66, a Rockabilly Original," *New York Times*, August 30, 1998, A25.

"Shooting Gallery Head Held on False Pretense Charge," *Cincinnati Enquirer*, August 21, 1938, 12.

Shuster, Fred. "Guitarist Albert King Dies," *Los Angeles Daily News*, December 23, 1992, 37.

"Two Charges Dismissed," *Cincinnati Enquirer*, September 9, 1938, 3.

ALBUM LINER NOTES

Allen, Bill "Hoss." The Spirit of Memphis Quartet, *Original Greatest Hits*, Gusto K-5020X, 1978.

———. Swan's Silvertone Singers, *Greatest Hits*, Gusto K-5022X, 1978.

———. Various Artists, *Original Greatest Gospel Hits*, Gusto K-5023X, 1978.

Barrow, Steve. Bill Doggett, *Leaps and Bounds*, Charly Records CD 281, 1991.

Bartolucci, Ron, Bob Schroder, and Andrea Maria Folterbauer. Johnny Otis, *Johnny Otis Show Live in Los Angeles 1970*, Wolf 120.612 CD, ca. 1995.

Bernholm, Jonas. The Five Royales, *The Real Thing*, Dr. Horse H-802, 1984.

———. Bull Moose Jackson, *Moose on the Loose*, Saxophonograph BP 506, 1985.

———. Lucky Millinder and His Orchestra, *Shorty's Got to Go*, Jukebox Lil JB 609, 1985.

———. Lucky Millinder and His Orchestra, *Let It Roll Again*, Jukebox Lil JB 613, 1985.

Briggs, Keith. Lonnie Johnson, *Me and My Crazy Self*, Charly Records CD 266, 1991.

———. Various Artists, *Ride, Daddy, Ride*, Charly Records CD 272, 1991.

Broven, John. Roy Brown, *Mighty, Mighty Man!*, Ace Records CDCHD 459, 1993.

———. Various Artists, *Honky Tonk!: The King and Federal R&B Instrumentals*, Ace Records CDCHD 761, 2000.

Brown, James, Nelson George, Alan M. Leeds, Cliff White, and Harry Weinger. James Brown, *Star Time*, Polydor 849–109/110/111/112–2, 1991.

Brown, Roy, and Bengt Weine. Roy Brown, *Good Rockin' Tonight, 1947–1954*, Route 66 KIX-6, 1978.

Carr, Roy. Lynn Hope/Clifford Scott, *Juicy!*, Charly Records CD 280, 1991.

Coffey, Kevin. Moon Mullican and the Showboys, *Showboy Special: The Early King Sides*, Westside WESA 800, 2000.

———. Various Artists, *Shuffle Town: Western Swing on King, 1956–50*, Westside WESF 111, 2000.

———. Moon Mullican, *Moon's Tunes: The Chronological King Recordings, vol. 2, 1947–1950*, Westside WESA 911, 2001.

———. Moon Mullican, *Seven Nights to Rock: More King Classics 1950–1956*, Ace CDCHD 997, 2004.

Collins, Tony. Wynonie Harris, *Lovin' Machine*, Ace Records CDCHD 843, 2002.

Collis, John. Ike Turner and the Kings of Rhythm, *Trailblazer*, King Masters KCD 6017, 1998.

Croasdell, Ady. Various Artists, *King Northern Soul*, Kent CDKEND 185, 2000.

Dahl, Bill. Albert King, *Blues Masters: The Very Best of Albert King*, Rhino R2 75703; 1999.

———. Freddie King, *The Best of Freddie King: The Shelter Records Years*, Shelter Records 27245, 2000.

Escott, Colin. Various Artists, *The King R&B Box Set*, King (no catalog number), 1995.

Escott, Colin, Hank Davis, Bez Turner, Martin Hawkins, Rob Bowman, and Neil Slaven. Various Artists, *Sun Records: The Blues Years, 1950–1958*, Charly Records CDSUNBOX 7, 1996.

Fileti, Donn. The 5 Royales, *The 5 Royales Sing The Laundromat Blues*, Relic 8016, 1977.

Finnis, Rob. Various Artists, *King Rockabilly*, Ace CDCHD 777, 2001.

Fitzgerald, Bill, Ray Reeves, and Jim Wilson. Various Artists, *Super Hits Country-1950s*, Gusto Records GT-0007, 1978.

Funk, Ray. The Swan Silvertones, *Get Right with the Swan Silvertones*, Rhino Records RNLP 70081, 1986.

———. Various Artists, *Preachin' the Gospel: Holy Blues*, Columbia/Legacy CK 46779, 1991.

Gilmore, Otis. John Lee Hooker, *Don't You Remember Me*, Charly Records CD 245, 1990.

Harris, Paul. Little Willie Littlefield and Friends, *Going Back to Kay Cee*, Ace CDCHD 503, 1994.

Harrison, Pat. The Delmore Brothers, *The Delmore Brothers, Classic Cuts 1933–1941*, JSP Records JSP7727, 2004.

———. The Delmore Brothers, *The Delmore Brothers, Volume 2*, JSP Records JSP7765, 2007.

Heilbut, Anthony. Reverend Claude Jeter, *Yesterday and Today*, Spirit Feel Records SF 1005, 1988.

Hoskyns, Barney. Little Willie John, *Fever*, Charly Records CD 246, 1990.

———. Little Esther, *Better Beware*, Charly Records CD 248, 1990.

Jacoubovitch, Daniel. Freddie King, *Just Pickin'*, Modern Blues Recordings MBCD 721, 1989.

———. Freddie King, *Freddy King Sings*, Modern Blues Recordings MBCD 722, 1989.

———. Albert King, *Let's Have a Natural Ball*, Modern Blues Recordings MBCD 723, 1989.

Jones, Bobby, Carol Cooper, Opal Louis Nations, and Lin. Woods. Various Artists, *Testify: The Gospel Box*, Rhino Records R2 75734, 1999.

Kienzle, Rich. Bob Newman, *Hangover Boogie*, Bear Family Records BFX 15168, 1984.

———. Hank Penny, *Hillbilly Be-Bop: The King Anthology, 1944–1950*, Westside WESA 914, 2001.

Komorowski, Adam. Johnny Otis, *Let's Live It Up*, King Masters KCD 6015, 1997.

———. Various Artists, *Doughboys, Playboys and Cowboys: The Golden Years of Western Swing*, Proper Records Box 6, 1999.

———. Boyd Bennett, *Tennessee Rock 'n' Roll*, King Masters KCD 6025, 2000.

Lamarr, Mark. Various Artists, *Roc-KING Up a Storm*, Westside WESA 801, 1999.

———. Various Artists, *Mule Milk 'n' Firewater*, Westside WESF 103, 2000.

Laughton, Bob. Various Artists, *1950s Gospel Classics*, Document DOCD-5464, 1996.

Love, Preston, Jonas Bernholm, and Per Notini. Wynonie Harris, *Oh Babe*, Route 66 KIX-20, 1982.

McDermott, John. Eric Clapton, *Blues*, Polydor 314 547 178–2, 1999.

McElya, Roger. James Brown, *Live at the Apollo*, Polydor 8223 001–2, 1987.

Millar, Bill. Bull Moose Jackson, *Big Fat Mamas Are Back in Style Again*, Route 66 KIX-14, 1980.

———. Big Jay McNeely, *The Best of Big Jay McNeely, Vol. 2*, Saxophonograph BP 1300, 1985.

———. Stick McGhee/Big Tom Collins/Ralph Willis, *Stick McGhee & His Spo-Dee-O-Dee Buddies*, Ace Records CDCHD 502, 1994.

———. Mac Curtis, *Blue Jean Heart*, King Masters KCD 6011, 1997.

———. Lattie Moore, *I'm Not Broke but I'm Badly Bent: The Best of the King–Starday Recordings*, Westside WESF 109, 2000.

Morgan, Alun. Slim Gaillard/Babs Gonzales, *Shuckin' and Jivin'*, Charly Records CD 279, 1991.

Neely, Hal. James Brown, *The James Brown Show Live at the Apollo*, King 826, 1963.

Nations, Opal Louis. Various Artists, *The Best of King Gospel*, Ace Records CDCHD 873, 2003.

Notini, Per, and Bengt Weine. Roy Brown, *Laughing but Crying*, Route 66 KIX-2, 1977.

———. Wynonie Harris, *Mr. Blues Is Coming to Town*, Route 66 KIX-3, 1977.

Penny, Dave. Todd Rhodes and His Toddlers, *Your Daddy's Dogging Around*, Jukebox Lil JB 615, 1985.

———. Tiny Bradshaw, *I'm a Hi-Ballin' Daddy*, Jukebox Lil JB 621, 1987.

———. Earl Bostic, *Blows a Fuse*, Charly Records CD 241, 1990.

———. Wynonie Harris, *Good Rocking Tonight*, Charly Records CD 244, 1990.

———. Roy Brown, *Blues Deluxe*, Charly Records CD 289, 1991.

———. Lucky Millinder, *Ram-Bunk-Shush*, Charly Records CD 288, 1991.

———. Johnny "Guitar" Watson, *Gangster of Love*, King Masters KCD 6004, 1997.

———. Jimmy Witherspoon, *Jay's Blues: The Complete Federal Sessions*, King Masters KCD 6008, 1997.

———. Hawkshaw Hawkins, *I'm a Rattlesnakin' Daddy: The King Anthology, 1946–1963*, Westside WESA 822, 1999.

———. Walter Brown/Crown Prince Waterford, *Blues Everywhere: The Queen and King Recordings*, Westside WESF 110, 2000.

Reid, Gary B. The Stanley Brothers, *The Early Starday and King Years, 1958–1961*, King KB-SCD 7000, 1993.

———. The Brown's Ferry Four, *Rockin' on the Waves: Complete King Recordings 1946–1952*, King 3506, 1997.

———. Various Artists, *The Best of King and Starday Bluegrass*, King KG-0952–4, 2004.

Reid, Gary B., and Bill Vernon. Don Reno and Red Smiley and the Tennessee Cut-Ups, *1951–1959*, King KBSCD 7001, 1993.

Rounce, Tony. Grandpa Jones, *Steppin' Out Kind*, Ace Records CDCHD 1098, 2006.

Russell, Tony. The Delmore Brothers, *Freight Train Boogie*, Ace Records CDCH 455, 1993.

———. Brother Claude Ely, *Satan Get Back!*, Ace Records CDCH 456, 1993.

Sax, Dave. Various Artists, *Hillbilly Bop n' Boogie: King/Federal Roots of Rockabilly 1944–56*, Ace Records CDCHD 854, 2002.

———. Wayne Raney, *That Real Hot Boogie Boy (The King Anthology)*, Ace Records CDCHD 857, 2002.

———. Cowboy Copas, *Copasetic: The Cream of the King-Starday Recordings, 1944–60*, Westside WESF 115, 2001.

Skadberg, Gordon. Various Artists, *Queens of King: The King Girl Groups*, Ace Records CD-CHD 830, 2002.

Slaven, Neil. Tiny Bradshaw, *Walk That Mess!*, Westside WESA 824, 1999.

———. Gatemouth Moore, *Hey Mr. Gatemouth*, Westside WESF 100, 2000.

Stanley Brothers, The, *Folk Concert*, King 834, 1963.

Stewart, Gary, Michael Ventura, Billy Vera, and Colin Escott. Various Artists, *Loud, Fast & out of Control: The Wild Sounds of '50s Rock*, Rhino Records R2 75704, 1999.

Stone, Robert, and Sherry S. and Herbert C. DuPree. Various Artists, *Sacred Steel: Traditional Sacred African-American Steel Guitar Music in Florida*, Arhoolie CD 450, 1997.

Stubbs, Eddie. Don Reno and Red Smiley, *On the Air*, Copper Creek CCCD-0128, 1996.

Svensson, Bo. Freddie King, *Mojo Blues*, Collectables Records COL-5523, 1994.

Tefteller, John, Dave Sax, and Bill Dahl. Smokey Smothers, *Smokey Smothers Sings the Backporch Blues*, Ace Records CDCHD 858, 2002.

Tosches, Nick, Peter Guralnick, Jim Dickinson, and Colin Escott. Charlie Feathers, *Get with It: Essential Recordings (1954–69)*, Revenant 209, 1998.

Tottle, Jack. Don Reno and Red Smiley, *On Stage*, Copper Creek CCCD-0127, 1996.

Tribe, Ivan M. Whitey and Hogan (with the Briarhoppers), *Volume II*, Old Homestead OHS 90169, 1984.

Various Artists. *All-time Country and Western Hits*, King 537, ca. 1958.

Various Artists. *Hidden Treasures: Cincinnati's Tribute to King Records' Legacy*, Inclusion Network, 2002.

Vera, Billy. Lula Reed, *I'll Drown in My Tears: The King Anthology 1952–55*, Ace Records CDCHD 984, 2003.

Visser, Joop. Sonny Thompson, *The EP Collection*, See for Miles SEECD 702, 1999.

———. Various Artists, *Hittin' on All Six: A History of the Jazz Guitar*, Proper Records Proper Box 9, 2000.

———. Wynonie Harris, *Rockin' the Blues*, Proper Records Proper Box 20, 2001.

Watson, Tony. Hank Ballard, *Let 'Em Roll*, Charly Records CD 240, 1990.

———. Billy Ward and the Dominoes, *Sixty Minute Man*, Charly Records CD 242, 1990.

———. The Five Keys, *Dream On*, Charly Records CD 265, 1991.

———. The Swallows, *Dearest*, Charly Records CD 287, 1991.

Waxie Maxie. Tiny Bradshaw, *Breakin' The House*, Charly Records CRB 1092, 1985.

Weathersbee, Rockin' Robin. Various Artists, *Jiving Jamboree, Volume 3*, Ace Records CDCHD 848, 2002.

Weinger, Harry. James Brown, *The Apollo Theatre Presents, in Person, the James Brown Show* [aka *James Brown Live at the Apollo, 1962*], Polydor P2-43479, 1990.

White, Cliff. Hank Ballard and the Midnighters, *What You Get When the Gettin' Gets Good*, Charly Records CRB 1090, 1985.

———. James Brown, *Roots of a Revolution*, Polydor 817 304-2, 1989.

White, Cliff, and Harry Weinger. James Brown, *Messing with the Blues*, Polydor S47258-2, 1990.

Wolfe, Charles. The Delmore Brothers and Wayne Raney, *When They Let the Hammer Down*, Bear Family Records BFX 15167, 1984.

———. The Delmore Brothers, *Sand Mountain Blues*, County Records CCS 110, ca. 1986.

Young, Chuck. Don Reno, *The Golden Guitar of Don Reno*, King CD-5115, 1999.

ONLINE RESOURCES

Alpern, Tyler. "Correspondence with Gus Wildi, Founder of Bethlehem Records." http://hometown.aol.com/tyleralpern/myhomepage/tunes.html

"Annisteen Allen." http://music.lycos . . . /bio.asp?QT=A&QW=Annisteen+Allen

"Boyd Bennett." www.boydbennett.com

"Etta James." http://www.prettyugly.com

Goldberg, Marv. "Marv Goldberg's R&B Notebooks: The Ravens — Part 1," 1999. http://home.att.net/~marvy42/Ravens/ravens01.html

———. "Marv Goldberg's R&B Notebooks: The Dominoes — Part 1," 1999. http://home.att.net/~marvy42/Dominoes/dom01.html

———. "Marv Goldberg's R&B Notebooks: The Checkers," 1999. http://home.att.net/~marvy42/Checkers/checkers.html

———. "Marv Goldberg's R&B Notebooks: The Royals," 2000. http://home.att.net/~marvy42/Royals/royals.html

———. "Marv Goldberg's R&B Notebooks: The Swallows," 2001. http://home.att.net/~marvy42/Swallows/swallows.html

Inductee biographies for James Brown, Syd Nathan, Ralph Bass, Hank Ballard, Jackie Wilson, Clyde McPhatter, Bootsy Collins, Little Willie John, et al., Rock and Roll Hall of Fame. http://www.rockhall.com/hof/inductee.asp

Leblanc, Eric. "Claude A. Jeter." http://www.island.net/~blues/cjeter.htm

Marion, J. C. "Annisteen Allen." http://home.earthlink.net/~jaymar41/twofems.html

———. "Wynona Carr." http://home.earthlink.net/~jaymar41/wynona.html

———. "Lula Reed: Staying With It." http://home.earthlink.net/~jaymar41/lula.html

———. "Todd Rhodes—Motor City Music Man," http://home.earthlink.net/~jaymar41/todd.html

"The Swan Silvertones." http://www.eyeneer.com/America/Genre/Gospel/Profiles/silvertones.html

"Syd Nathan's King Records." http://www.history-of-rock.com/king_records.htm

"Wings Over Jordan Choir," *Encyclopedia of Cleveland History*. http://ech.cwru.edu/ech-cgi/article.pl?id=WOJC

"Settle, Rev. Dr. Glenn Thomas," *Encyclopedia of Cleveland History*. http://ech.cwru.edu/ech-cgi/article.pl?id=SRDGT

www.otiswilliamshischarms.bigstep.com

OTHER

The Lois Group, alphabetically listed catalog of music publishing holdings listing song title, composer/author, and publisher; published by King; undated.

"King, Starday, Audio Lab" catalog, International Marketing Group, Nashville, Tenn., 1991.

Ace Records Catalogue, London, 2003.

INDEX

•••

JON HARTLEY FOX writes about music and the arts in Sacramento, California. He wrote, produced, and narrated "King of the Queen City: the Story of King Records," a series of sixty-minute documentaries for National Public Radio in the 1980s.

Music in American Life

Never without a Song: The Years and Songs of Jennie Devlin, 1865–1952 •
　Katharine D. Newman
The Hank Snow Story • Hank Snow, with Jack Ownbey and Bob Burris
Milton Brown and the Founding of Western Swing • Cary Ginell, with special assistance
　from Roy Lee Brown
Santiago de Murcia's "Códice Saldívar No. 4": A Treasury of Secular Guitar Music from
　Baroque Mexico • Craig H. Russell
The Sound of the Dove: Singing in Appalachian Primitive Baptist Churches •
　Beverly Bush Patterson
Heartland Excursions: Ethnomusicological Reflections on Schools of Music • Bruno Nettl
Doowop: The Chicago Scene • Robert Pruter
Blue Rhythms: Six Lives in Rhythm and Blues • Chip Deffaa
Shoshone Ghost Dance Religion: Poetry Songs and Great Basin Context • Judith Vander
Go Cat Go! Rockabilly Music and Its Makers • Craig Morrison
'Twas Only an Irishman's Dream: The Image of Ireland and the Irish in American Popular
　Song Lyrics, 1800–1920 • William H. A. Williams
Democracy at the Opera: Music, Theater, and Culture in New York City, 1815–60 •
　Karen Ahlquist
Fred Waring and the Pennsylvanians • Virginia Waring
Woody, Cisco, and Me: Seamen Three in the Merchant Marine • Jim Longhi
Behind the Burnt Cork Mask: Early Blackface Minstrelsy and Antebellum American
　Popular Culture • William J. Mahar
Going to Cincinnati: A History of the Blues in the Queen City • Steven C. Tracy
Pistol Packin' Mama: Aunt Molly Jackson and the Politics of Folksong • Shelly Romalis
Sixties Rock: Garage, Psychedelic, and Other Satisfactions • Michael Hicks
The Late Great Johnny Ace and the Transition from R&B to Rock 'n' Roll •
　James M. Salem
Tito Puente and the Making of Latin Music • Steven Loza
Juilliard: A History • Andrea Olmstead
Understanding Charles Seeger, Pioneer in American Musicology • Edited by Bell Yung
　and Helen Rees
Mountains of Music: West Virginia Traditional Music from Goldenseal • Edited by
　John Lilly
Alice Tully: An Intimate Portrait • Albert Fuller
A Blues Life • Henry Townsend, as told to Bill Greensmith
Long Steel Rail: The Railroad in American Folksong (2d ed.) • Norm Cohen
The Golden Age of Gospel • Text by Horace Clarence Boyer; photography by Lloyd Yearwood
Aaron Copland: The Life and Work of an Uncommon Man • Howard Pollack
Louis Moreau Gottschalk • S. Frederick Starr
Race, Rock, and Elvis • Michael T. Bertrand
Theremin: Ether Music and Espionage • Albert Glinsky
Poetry and Violence: The Ballad Tradition of Mexico's Costa Chica • John H. McDowell

The University of Illinois Press
is a founding member of the
Association of American University Presses.

───────────────────────────────

Composed in 11/13.5 Adobe Jensen Pro
with Candy, Monoline, and Univers display
by Jim Proefrock
at the University of Illinois Press
Designed by Kelly Gray
Manufactured by Sheridan Books, Inc.

University of Illinois Press
1325 South Oak Street
Champaign, IL 61820-6903
www.press.uillinois.edu